Sylvia Dannett, author, historian, and lecturer, has written eleven books, numerous magazine stories, articles, juvenile and scholarly works. Her mystery play *Undercover Woman* appeared as a motion picture.

She has given a seminar at the University of Puerto Rico; has addressed the Session on History of Medicine at the 1960 Meeting of the Medical Society of the State of New York (her address was reprinted in the *New York State Journal of Medicine*); and has lectured at colleges and Civil War Round Tables throughout the country. During the Civil War Centennial she was a member of the nine-woman Centennial Committee, and in 1963 addressed the National Assembly Celebration of the Commission at Boston. She is a member of the Overseas Press Club, The Authors League, the Woman Pays Club, and historical societies; attends meetings of the Revolutionary War Round Table; is serving her third term as director of the CWRT of New York; and edits its newspaper, *The Dispatch*. She also works on the staff of the *Overseas Press Club Bulletin*.

OTHER BOOKS BY SYLVIA DANNETT

Novels
Defy the Tempest with Edwin I. Bennett
The Door to the Tower

Nonfiction
Noble Women of the North
She Rode with the Generals
Down Memory Lane, A Picture History of Ballroom
    Dancing (with Frank R. Rachel)
A Treasury of Civil War Humor
Our Women of the Sixties (with Katherine Jones)
Profiles of Negro Womanhood, 1619–1965 (2 Vols.)
Low Blood Sugar (Hypoglycemia) Gourmet Cookbook

Young Adults and Juveniles
Confederate Surgeon (with Rosamond Burkart)

The Yankee Doodler

Sylvia G. L. Dannett

South Brunswick and New York: A. S. Barnes and Company
London: Thomas Yoseloff Ltd

© 1973 by A. S. Barnes and Co., Inc.

A. S. Barnes and Co., Inc.
Cranbury, New Jersey 08512

Thomas Yoseloff Ltd
108 New Bond Street
London W1Y OQX, England

Library of Congress Cataloguing in Publication Data

Dannett, Sylvia G. L. 1909–
    The Yankee Doodler.

    Bibliography: p.
        1. United States—Popular culture.   2. United
States—Social life and customs—Colonial period.
I. Title.
E163.D35   309.1′73′02   72-6384
ISBN 0-498-01136-4

PRINTED IN THE UNITED STATES OF AMERICA

For
Joseph Kolker, M.D.
In Gratitude

Contents

Preface

When I conceived the idea of doing a pictorial book on the humor and the arts of the Revolutionary period, I didn't realize what a fascinating educational jaunt into history was in store for me.

For a few weeks I was almost overcome by my own ambition and temerity. The research was challenging, but exhaustive to say the least. I had to visit libraries that specialized in music, or the dance, or the theater. I spent days hunting material in historical societies, museums, and public and commercial archives. Sheet music was found in special collections. Musty films produced old newspapers. Almanacs, packed in boxes laden with dust, left me particularly moved. I fingered their withered and discolored paper gingerly, awed by the realization that they had been handled by men like Franklin and Ames and Isaiah Thomas. Two whole centuries ago. That didn't seem so far back now . . .

My work appeared to be unending, then little by little I began to see results. The prints arrived; the sheet music came for marches, for dances, and for songs; xeroxed copies of ballads and selected prose writings were rising higher on my desk every day.

Reviewing all this material was like going through the looking glass and finding myself in the eighteenth century. I became more and more informed about our American heritage. I recaptured its greatness. The founding fathers, the poets, the playwrights, songwriters and authors of the period came alive. I began to understand their partisan feelings. I shared their music. I could hardly wait to dance their hornpipes and jigs. I sang their songs. I read their newspapers and their literature, their broadsides and diaries and letters, not to judge their merit but to help me understand the Americans of another day.

I learned more about American history during the Revolutionary period and about the daily lives of the men and women who forged the Republic through my research than from the textbooks I read in school and college.

I found myself pushing aside the evils and violence that threaten our society today: the

9

mercenary ideal, the drugs, the disillusioning politicians, the inadequate leaders, and the cries of "Yankee go home." I rediscovered the Declaration of Independence, the Bill of Rights, and our Constitution. I reread the immortal words of Jefferson and Adams and Franklin. I began to understand more clearly what we Americans are all about: what we were meant to be. I feel like the Spirit of '76 (although I hope I don't look it). I have grown to know and admire George Washington, who until now was just a face and a name in a history book. The father of our country. The first President. The general who crossed the Delaware on a freezing night. The boy who couldn't tell a lie. The man who slept in many houses, and had hotels, motels, and streets and towns named after him. I have studied his letters, learned of his interests, mentally attended the theater with him and saw him dancing the minuet. Before doing the book, I hadn't known the father of our country and I had so much in common.

Because of all I have learned I find myself taking greater pride in my country. I hope reading *The Yankee Doodler* will do for my readers what writing this book has done for me.

Sylvia G. L. Dannett

Scarsdale, New York

Acknowledgments

I would like to express my indebtedness to the many authors, composers and publishers whose works have been consulted and quoted in *The Yankee Doodler.*

Written permission has been received from the following:

Harry Dichter: "Dog & Gun"; "On the Road to Boston"; "Rural Felicity"; and the right to include the music from *Early American Music, Its Lure & Its Lore,* published by the R. R. Bowker Co., New York, 1941.

J. B. Lippincott Co: Photographs from A HISTORY OF THE THEATRE IN AMERICA FROM THE BEGINNINGS TO THE PRESENT TIME, Vol. I, by Arthur Hornblow: Thomas Wignell, The Manager op. p. 128; Royall Tyler (1758–1826) op. p. 170; Candle Footlights in the early American theatres, op. p. 170.

The Belknap Press of Harvard University Press: illustrations of old magazine covers from Mott, A HISTORY OF AMERICAN MAGAZINES, Vol. I, Copyright, 1930 by the President and Fellows of Harvard College; 1958 by Frank Luther Mott.

W. W. Norton & Company, Inc. from *Music in America: the Landing of the Pilgrims to the close of the Civil War, 1620–1865.* Compiled and edited by W. Thomas Marrocco and Harold Gleason: "Lamentations over Boston" by William Billings.

The World Publishing Company: illustrations from *Colonial Living* by Edwin Tunis: "The Sir Roger de Coverley," p. 150.

Lincoln Kirstien: "John Durang's Hornpipe" from Paul Magriel (ed.), *Chronicles of the American Dance,* New York, p. 17.

Culver Pictures: from *History of Colonial America* by Chitwood; Henry Holt & Co. 1948.

The John Carter Brown Library, Brown University, Providence: *The Liberty Song* by John Dickinson.

Research Library of the Performing Arts: for the following sheet music: Duport Cotillions–AMI–I; 2pp. "The Waltz Cotillion"; 2pp. "The Signal" and "The Polle."

11

The Library of Congress, *Music from the Days of George Washington:* "The Brandywine Quick Step," "General Burgoyne's March."

The New York Historical Society: "The Able Doctor," p. 150; "The Curious Zebra," 1778, p. 156; "A Picturesque View of the State of the Nation for February 1778"; "The Horse America Throwing His Master," p. 157; *English Political Caricatures to 1792,* Vol. I. "*The Scotch Butchery*", Boston, 1775, *Old-Time New England Magazine,* Vol. 46, April–June 1956, op. p. 93; "*Bunker's Hill*" or *America's Head Dress–1775,* R. T. H. Halsey, "English Sympathy with Boston During the American Revolution", *in Old-Time New England, Bulletin* of the Society For the Preservation of New England Antiquities, Vol. XLVI, No. 4, April–June 1956, No. 164, pp. 93–94; "*Liberty Triumphant, or the Downfall of Oppression*", published in London, 1774. From R. T. H. Halsey "English Sympathy with Boston During the American Revolution", from *Old-Time New England,* Vol. XLVI, #4, April–June 1956, No. 164, p. 87.

John Newsom and Peter Fay, Music Division, Library of Congress.

I also want to thank all the wonderful people who helped to make this book possible: Mrs. Georgia B. Bumgardner, Curator of Maps and Prints, American Antiquarian Society, Worcester, Massachusetts; Mr. Manley Stolzman, The Bettmann Archive, Inc., New York, New York; William A. Hunter, Chief, Division of History, Commonwealth of Pennsylvania, Pennsylvania Historical and Museum Commission, Harrisburg, Pennsylvania; Suzanne Flandreau, Reference Department, Library of the Boston Athenaeum, Boston, Massachusetts; Stuart C. Sherman, Librarian, John Hay Library, Brown University, Providence, Rhode Island; Jeannette D. Black, Acting Librarian, The John Carter Brown Library, Brown University, Providence, Rhode Island; Miss Susan T. Lane, Reference Department, Library of the Boston Athenaeum, Boston, Massachusetts; Robert Scudder, Reference Librarian, Free Library of Philadelphia, Philadelphia, Pennsylvania; Dr. Roy Basler, Chief, Manuscript Division, Library of Congress, Washington, D.C.; Mr. Glenn H. Borders, Supervisor, Rare Book Reading Room, The Library of Congress, Washington, D.C.; Helen D. Willard, Curator, Theatre Collection, Harvard College Library, Cambridge, Massachusetts; Peter J. Parker, Chief of Manuscripts and June Pfeil, Secretary, The Historical Society of Pennsylvania, Philadelphia, Pennsylvania; Richard C. Shultz, Executive Director, The Historical Society of York County, York, Pennsylvania; Suzanne Nicole Currier (Mrs. Richard B. Currier), Manuscript Department, The Houghton Library, Harvard University, Cambridge, Massachusetts; S. E. Dyke, President, and Mrs. Charles W. Lundgren, Lancaster Historical Society, Lancaster, Pennsylvania; Mrs. Lillian Tonkin, Reference Librarian, The Library Company of Philadelphia, Pennsylvania; Mrs. Robert H. Mccauley, Jr., Curator of Graphics, Maryland Historical Society, Baltimore, Maryland; Miss Nada Saporite, Photographics Service, The Metropolitan Museum of Art, New York, New York; Alice G. Smith, The Historical Society of Montgomery County, Norristown, Pennsylvania; James Gregory, Librarian, New-York Historical Society, New York, New York; Miss Sue Gillies, New-York Historical Society Library, New York, New York; Miss Charlotte La Rue, Photo Librarian, Museum of the City of New York, New York; Frank C. Campbell, Chief, Music Division, Library and Museum of the Performing Arts, The New York Public Library at Lincoln Center, New York, New York; Richard Jackson, American Collection, Music Division, Research Library of the Performing Arts, The New York Public Library at Lincoln Center, New York, New York; John P. Baker, Executive Assistant, The Research Libraries, The New York Public Library, New York, New York; Librarians of the Dance, Music and

Theatre Divisions, Research Library of the Performing Arts, The New York Public Library at Lincoln Center, New York, New York; Librarians of the Rare Book Room, and the Photoduplication Department, Library of Congress, Washington, D.C.; Lewis Stark, Chief, and Mrs. Maud Cole, First Assistant, Rare Book Room, New York Public Library, New York, New York; The Librarians of The New-York Historical Society, New York, New York; Rocco Lombardo, Library Technical Assistant IV, Photographic Service, The New York Public Library, New York, New York; Barbara Philpott, Assistant Archivist, Division of Archives and Manuscripts, Commonwealth of Pennsylvania, Pennsylvania Historical and Museum Commission, Harrisburg, Pennsylvania; Mrs. Jane Fulton and other Reference Librarians, Scarsdale Library, Scarsdale, New York; Milton C. Russell, Head, Reference and Circulation Section, General Library Branch, and John W. Dudley, Assistant State Archivist, Virginia State Library, Commonwealth of Virginia, Richmond, Virginia; Clare Waldner, Reference Librarian, The Charles Patterson Van Pelt Library, University of Pennsylvania, Philadelphia, Pennsylvania; Miss Genevieve Oswald, Curator, Isabel Kerr, Henry Wisnesky, and Barbara Palfy, Dance Collection of the New York Public Library, New York, New York; Mrs. Gertrude Weis for tirelessly retyping the manuscript, seven days a week; Mrs. Phyllis Formato, who did some of the difficult typing; Mrs. Sally Loeb and Mrs. Janice Martin for coming in for the final typing pitch. And special thanks to Toni Strassman, my agent, for reading parts of the manuscript and offering helpful suggestions and editorial criticism.

AND PARTICULAR thanks to my friend, Rosamond Burkart, who gave of her time and herself to help me locate material for the cartoon and literature sections, before the book was contracted for.

Lester S. Levy of Maryland for lending me a copy of rare Yankee Doodle verses from the 1784 British musical *Two For One.*

Mr. William Lichtenwanger, Head of Reference, Music Division, The Library of Congress, Washington, D.C., who was tireless in securing for me old sheet music for songs and dances.

And last, but not least to my husband, Emanuel Dannett, for sweating it out with me and going over the material with a legal eye.

The Yankee Doodler

1
Cartoons and Caricatures

Eighteenth-century graphic humorists bequeathed to posterity a wealth of caricatures and cartoons which provide an excellent source of information about the social and political history of the period.

By deriding public events, persons, or conditions of life, caricatures and cartoons convey the very essence of the times and familiarize us with the ideals, philosophical and political, of another era. The political cartoon, in particular, with its tendency to satirize, points up—sometimes ruthlessly—the evils, fallacies, and weaknesses involved in topical political or moral issues, while the prejudices and habits of the people are accentuated by the use of popular symbols and slogans.

No distinction was made between the terms *caricature* and *cartoon* until well into the nineteenth century. Formerly all political cartoons, as well as satirical, grotesque, and humorous drawings, were called caricatures. The word caricature is said to be derived from the Italian *caricare,* "to load." In other words, in caricatures the artists may be said to present "overloaded representation," laying it on too thick. This may be applied to many cartoons that appeared between 1765 and 1783.

Certain periods in history offer a greater opportunity to the satirical artist than others. The years before and during the Revolutionary War were such a period. The situations and the leading personalities were natural subjects for cartoon or caricature; by depicting them the graphic humorist traced the course of events.

In England, in the years leading up to and during the war, the American question was a conversation piece among the people, and the subject of heated debates in Parliament. Indeed, there were more cartoons from England relating to the Revolutionary War than from America.

Nearly 200 satirical engravings, both political and personal, on the government's American policy, were issued in London during the period 1765–1783. They were sold in bookstores and print shops at a nominal cost. The majority of these prints cannot be considered great art; they were merely commercial ventures intended to strike a popular note, and there was little intent to propagandize. They remain vital documents in the history of our national progress, and symbolize the popularity in England of America's resistance to British policy. Even the outbreak of war did not alter the English public's opposition to its government's American policy. Fifteen of the seventeen newspapers published in London at that time boldly espoused the colonists' cause.

The first political caricature to appear in America was published by Benjamin Franklin in his *Pennsylvania Gazette,* May 9, 1754. Symbolically the caricature depicts a snake divided into eight parts, each of which has the initials of one of the colonies. The title, "Join or Die," is what we today call a slogan. It helped to focus the attention of the colonists on the importance of uniting against their common foes, the French and Indians. The caricature later appeared in other newspapers, and was then interpreted as a warning to the colonists to unite against England.

Many of the early American cartoons dealing with transatlantic problems were taken from those originating abroad and reengraved in this country. One of Paul Revere's best-known cartoons, "The Able Doctor; or America Swallowing the Bitter Draught," is said to have been a reengraving.

As the war continued cartoons and caricatures reflected the increasing resentments, the deep prejudices and animosities on both sides. Loyalists condemned Patriots and Patriots reviled Loyalists, while public opinion in England continued to condemn the whole policy of George III and his politicians.

Cartoons of George Washington are difficult to find. The opposition newspapers were uncomplimentary, and it may be that cartoons relating to him were destroyed out of patriotism.

If the caricatures, cartoons, and humorous writings of colonial America seem unfunny to Americans close to the third quarter of the twentieth century, it is not because our ancestors lacked a sense of humor, but because their sense of humor was different from ours. It even differed from the English humor of the same period. The so-called Englishman's sense of humor was too sophisticated for the early settlers struggling for their survival. The native humor of the colonies as it developed became indigenous to the New World and unmistakeably our own. Despite these difficulties, it is hoped that the selections in this book will draw forth a hearty chuckle from the reader.

For humor is by and large indigenous to the country in which it originates, and to the period in which it finds expression. To appreciate it requires taste and a sense of timing.

At the end of the Seven Years' War (known in America as the French and Indian War) George III reigned over a vast and growing empire. The struggle had been costly, however, and the English government led by Prime Minister George Grenville decided to compel the colonies to assume a larger portion of the financial burdens of the empire.

From 1763 to 1765 a series of stringent measures designed to regulate American economic and political affairs and to bring money into the British treasury were executed by the King and his advisors. In 1763, a *Royal Order* gave the King the right to dispose of Western lands beyond a certain line. In 1764 Parliament adopted the *Sugar Act,* which taxed certain imports and was to be a means of raising money for the expenses of "defending, protecting, and securing" British colonies in America; she also imposed duties on silks, certain wines, calicoes, and linens imported into the American colonies. The *Currency Act* followed, forbidding the colonies to issue paper money they sorely needed. The ministry undertook to enforce the *Acts of Trade* which attempted to reduce trade between the colonies and the West Indies and so secure a steady revenue from America. A tax of three pence per gallon was placed on molasses imported from those islands. The colonists raised their voices against these and other measures. For generations they had been moving toward home rule, and resented curbs on their commerce. They were strongly opposed to having British authority in the colonies revived or strengthened, and they considered many of the Acts sponsored by Grenville to be violations of colonial charters. England turned a deaf ear to their protests.

The passage of the *Stamp Act* in 1765, which was to provide money for the British treasury "towards defraying the expenses of defending, protecting and securing the British colonies and plantations in America, through a tax on numerous articles and transactions in America," outraged the Colonists and led to rioting and resistance. The homes of British officials in America were attacked. Stamp collectors and others who tried to enforce the law were threatened with violence. The cry, "No taxation without representation" resounded throughout the colonies. Patriotic societies calling themselves the Sons of Liberty and the Daughters of Liberty were organized to boycott the sale of stamps. The Americans almost unanimously refused to pay the tax, and demanded its repeal.

Grenville, as well as many other British leaders, was in favor of enforcing the Act. The Marquis of Rockingham, who succeeded Grenville as Prime Minister, believed it would be wise to conciliate the colonies by repealing it. William Pitt, considered the most popular political figure in England, supported the contention of the colonists that the tax was not within the authority of Parliament. The law was rescinded in 1766.

This is the man who shared a great deal of responsibility for inciting the colonists to revolt, King George III.

USUAL APPEARANCE OF THE KING ABOUT 1776.

From a sketch by Gear.

The queen, like many eighteenth century (and twentieth century) wives, did not question her husband's political decisions.

QUEEN CHARLOTTE.
From a print by Worlidge

George III and his ministers started antagonizing the colonists. They hit the jackpot with the Stamp Act in 1765.

The hated postage: stamps attached by the British Government to goods sold in the American colonies. The Bettmann Archive.

Soon the Patriots began dreaming up ways of antagonizing George.

Opposition to the Stamp Act. The Pennsylvania Journal & Advertiser *sarcastically suggested affixing the Skull and Bones to imported goods. The Bettmann Archive.*

Outraged by the Stamp Act, the colonists burned the stamps in the streets. A German sympathizer gives his impression of this action.

This is an engraving by D. Berger, 1784, after D. Chodowiecki. The text, translated, reads: "The Americans resist the Stamp Act and burn the stamp paper sent from England to America, at Boston, 1764." The Bettmann Archive.

George, get off our backs. The colonists were quite clear about what they wanted.

THE HORSE AMERICA, throwing his Master.

The idea for this cartoon is said to have originated from a speech delivered by the Duke of Grafton in the House of Lords at the time that Lord North's Conciliatory Resolution, soon rejected by the Revolutionary State Congresses, was being discussed. George III is being thrown by his horse America. In one hand he is clutching a cat o' nine tails, the thongs of which are tomahawks, scalping knives, swords, and bayonets. Courtesy of the New-York Historical Society, New York City.

He did, and Parliament about-faced and capitulated, but not for long.

This popular satirical print made its appearance three days after Parliament repealed the Stamp Act. It depicts a burial procession for Miss Anne Stamp on the banks of the Thames. Executed by Benjamin Wilson, portrait painter of Benjamin Franklin, the cartoon is full of symbolic representation of the American feeling toward William Pitt who sought to avoid war with the colonies. "I think it is wrong to put in Lord Bute, who had nothing to do with the Stamp Act," Benjamin Franklin wrote his wife. "But, it is the Fashion to abuse that Nobleman, as the Author of all Mischief." Courtesy of The New-York Historical Society, New York City.

Crisis followed crisis. British-American relations deteriorated as the British sought to subordinate the colonists' welfare to British commercial interests. In 1767, under the leadership of Charles Townshend, Parliament passed the *Townshend Acts* which imposed duties on paper, lead, glass, paint, and tea brought into American ports. There were few dissenters in Parliament on this occasion, and a Board of Customs Commissioners was soon established at Boston. The colonists, however, resisted the revenue act. Rioting followed, and the Americans attempted once again to stop the importation of British goods. British troops sent to Boston to protect the Customs Commissioners became involved in clashes with the townspeople. This in turn led to the terrible Boston Massacre on March 5, 1770, in which British soldiers stationed at Boston, "jostled and stoned" by a crowd of men and boys, fired on their attackers, killing five and wounding several more. When Frederick, Lord North, called for a repeal of all duties except that on tea, Parliament yielded. Another *Tea Act* in 1773 gave the British East India Company a monopoly of the tea business in America. This time the colonists were offered tea that was cheap, but taxed, and they refused to allow it to land in their ports. When the British authorities in Boston ignored their demands, the Boston Tea Party followed.

The tea tax was as loaded as TNT, and the Patriots decided to dump it.

This lithograph recommends "a new method of macarony making as practised at Boston. For the Custom House officer's landing the Teas they tarred and feathered him just as you see. And they drench'd him so well, both behind and before, That he begg'd for God's sake they would drench him no more."

This Revolutionary War cartoon was copied on stone by D. C. Johnston from a print published in London, 1774, showing two American Revolutionists tarring and feathering a Loyalist. "Macaronies" were a group of young English dandies. The Bettmann Archive.

They gave a tea party to which the Loyalists were not invited.

The British Parliament had continued its tax on tea to show their right to aid the East India Company, and to tax the colonies. The Governor of Massachusetts refused to give clearing papers to leave the port to three British ships with cargoes of tea. On December 16, 1773, outraged American patriots, disguised as Indians, boarded the ships after nightfall, opened the cases, and threw the tea into the harbor. Courtesy of The New-York Historical Society, New York City.

Determined to prove that their authority was not to be denied, Parliament retaliated by passing the *Coercive Acts,* which the Americans called the "Intolerable Acts," to quell the unrest in America.

In March 1774, the British Parliament passed the *Boston Port Bill* designed to starve the colony of Massachusetts into submission, and abrogated the charter of the colony. The Act officially closed Boston's harbor in June 1774, and other colonies immediately rushed to the support of Boston by sending food and supplies. The time had come for united action by the colonists "for the preservation of the general and particular rights and privileges of North America." The Massachusetts assembly under the leadership of Samuel Adams issued an invitation to all the colonies to send delegates to a General Congress. On September 5, 1774, the first Continental Congress met at Philadelphia, rallying under Benjamin Franklin's slogan, "Join or Die." Cooperative resistance had begun. The Congress forbade all trade with Britain, and passed resolutions of protest and appeal which William Pitt, Lord Chatham, described as "the wisest State Papers" the world had ever seen.

Origin of the American Revolution. According to the French. The news of the American Revolution reached France via this pictorial broadside. It shows Bostonians seizing the tax collector, John Malcom, January 25, 1774. Note that the simply garbed colonists have been "transvestized" into fashionable French ladies and gentlemen.

This cartoon was drawn and engraved in copper by Francois Godefray (1729–88) in Paris, in 1774. The translation of the text reads as follows:

"After long debates, England established their taxes on June 29, 1767, in order to make valid inhibitions of trade under the inspection of officers named and paid by the king. All over they were resisted and opposed and on May 18, 1770, the Boston population arrested an employee for having seized a little building under the excuse of 'contrebande.' They undressed him and after having tarred and feathered him paraded him through the city.

John Malcom, a customs officer, was given the same treatment for the same reasons, but no one bothered to undress him. This proud tax collector having made some indiscreet remarks about the king and parliament taking revenge against the band, the majority of the population awaited an opportunity to punish him with more vindictiveness and strength. This is what happened on January 25, 1774.

On January 25, 1774, the enraged people entered his house without weapons. He wounded several of them with his sword: but the Bostonians—measured except for their vindictiveness—seized him, took him down via the window, into a cart; then he was undressed, feathered, tarred, led to the public square, beaten with whips and obliged to express his thanks for not being punished by death. Then he was taken home without further punishment." Courtesy The Bettmann Archive, Inc.

The French had their own views on the situation in America.

Dessiné et Gravé par F. Godefroy
de l'académie Imp.le et R.le de Vienne &c.

JOHN MALCOM.

Le 25 Janvier 1774 la populace irritée pénétra sans armes dans sa maison. Il blessa plusieurs personnes à coups d'épée: mais les Bostoniens, modérés jusques dans leur vengeance, le saisirent, le descendirent par la fenêtre dans une charrette; ensuite il fut dépouillé, goudronné, emplumé, mené sur la place publique, battu de verges, et obligé de remercier de ce qu'on ne le punissait point de mort: puis on le ramena chez lui sans autre mal.

ORIGINE DE LA RÉVOLUTION AMÉRICAINE.

Les Provinces de la Nouvelle Angleterre jouissaient du droit de s'imposer elles-mêmes dans leurs assemblées: les officiers du gouvernement et les juges étaient nommés par le roi, mais aux gages du peuple. L'Angleterre éprouvant des besoins de finances, et voulant les faire partager aux Américains, fit paraître un bill le 4 avril 1764, à l'effet de les taxer, au mépris des chartres sur la foi desquelles les émigrants de l'ancien monde s'étaient établis dans le nouveau. Cette démarche était d'autant plus inconsidérée, que pendant la guerre précédente, le ministère envoyant chaque année un mémoire des besoins publics à ses colonies, et la réalité de ses besoins étant discutée dans leurs assemblées, les secours d'hommes et d'argent surpassèrent toujours ce qu'on attendait de leurs facultés. C'est ce dont les actes de la Chambre des communes font foi: ils rendent aussi témoignage que les succès de cette guerre dont l'Angleterre se glorifie sont dus presque tous au zèle et à la force de ses colonies.

Après de longs débats, l'Angleterre y établit des douanes le 29 juin 1767 pour faire exécuter des prohibitions de commerce sous l'inspection de commissaires nommés et gagés par le roi. Par tout on s'opposait à l'exercice de leurs fonctians, et le 18 mai 1770 la populace de Boston arrêta un commis pour avoir saisi un petit bâtiment sous prétexte de contrebande; elle le dépouilla et l'ayant barbouillé de goudron et couvert de plumes, le promena par la Ville. John Malcom, officier des douanes, fut traité de même en 1773 pour le même motif; mais on eut le ménagement de ne le point dépouiller. Ce fier maltôtier ayant dit que le roi et le parlement le vengeraient bientôt de cette canaille, la multitude attendit qu'il lui fournît l'occasion de le punir avec plus de sévérité; ce qui arriva le 25 janvier 1774.

29

So did the eminent Dr. Franklin. He printed an unfunny caricature and hoped the British would get the message.

MAGNA *Britannia: her Colonies* REDUCED.

A CARICATURE DESIGNED BY BENJAMIN FRANKLIN.—LONDON, 1774.

Authorities on the history of cartoons and caricature are not in agreement as to whether or not this was designed by Franklin. Parton and Weitenkampf believe it was. Murrell, on the other hand, states that this print first appeared in London in 1763, as "The Colonies Reduced, designed and engraved for the Political Register." He is uncertain as to whether it was designed or even "caused to be designed" by the eminent doctor.

Benjamin Franklin appears to have had no doubts about the identity of the caricaturist. He explained the theme of the cartoon as follows:

"The Colonies (that is, Britannia's limbs) being severed from her, Britannia is seen lifting her eyes and mangled stumps to Heaven; her shield, which she is unable to wield, lies useless by her side; her lance has pierced New England; the laurel branch has fallen from the hand of Pennsylvania; the English oak has lost its head, and stands a bare trunk, with a few withered branches; briars and thorns are on the ground beneath it; the British ships have brooms at their topmost heads, denoting their being on sale; and Britannia herself is seen sliding off the world (no longer able to hold its balance), her fragments overspread with the label, Date obolum Bellisario" *(Give a farthing to Belisarius). Courtesy The Library Company of Philadelphia.*

This cartoon covers more area of the political field than any other known satirical print. Its main theme is the closing of the Boston port by England, which destroyed the British trade.

The eighteen references make it simple to identify the figures. Figure 10, "The Genius of Britain," is saying to 11, Britannia, "Why so much distressed?" and Britannia is replying, "The Conduct of those my degenerate Sons will break my Heart." In the upper right-hand corner of the print 14, "The Goddess of Liberty," addressing herself to 15, "Fame," and pointing to her "Sons," is saying, "Behold the Ardour of my Sons and let not their brave Actions be buried in oblivion." "Fame" is replying, "I will trumpet their Noble deeds from Pole to Pole."

The following, which appeared in the London Packet *on July 3–5, 1775, expresses the English concern for liberty. "There is a wide difference," said a correspondent," between North American liberty and North's American liberty; the first is natural and constitutional freedom, the latter, M————l {Ministerial} or abject slavery." Courtesy of The New-York Historical Society, New York City.*

Furious at Boston's party, Parliament punished the colonies by passing a series of "Intolerable Acts." The Boston Port Bill was one.

The able Doctor, or America Swallowing the Bitter Draught.

America, personified by a woman, is swallowing the bitter draught, the Boston Port Bill, one of the "Intolerable Acts." Courtesy of the New-York Historical Society, New York City.

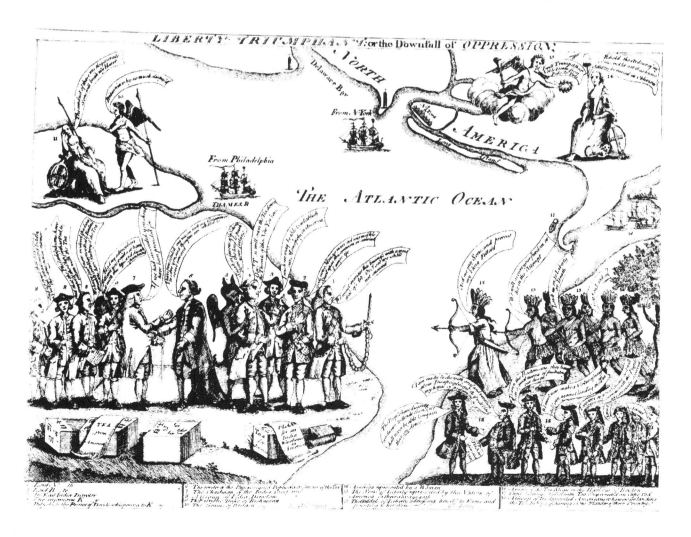

The situation in Boston, when the port was closed, was pictured by a contemporary London artist in 1774. Bostonians who opposed the Stamp Act are imprisoned in a cage attached to the Liberty Tree. They are depicted as colonial slaves, convicted of capital crimes, caged and left to starve. The gift of fish to the prisoners presumably alludes to codfish sent from Marblehead, one of many gifts to the distressed port. A group of loyalists are mocking them. Off to the side, British cannon are being readied to bring the recalcitrant Patriots to their senses. This cartoon is said to have been very popular in England. Print and caption from the Print Room, The New York Public Library.

American leaders called for united colonial action. Ben Franklin's caricature of 1754 was reproduced in several newspapers.

The first caricature to appear in America was published by Benjamin Franklin in his Pennsylvania Gazette, *May 9, 1754, under the caption "Join or Die."*

This is a political emblem with the snake divided into eight parts, each of which bears the initials of one of the New England colonies. The legend "Join or Die" had the force of what we would today call a slogan.

The caricature roused the colonists to write against their common foes, the French and Indians. Editors of the other colonial papers quickly recognized the power of a caricature or cartoon as a political weapon.

Before the end of the month it had been copied by papers in New York and Boston. Boston improved the original by putting the following words into the mouth of the snake: "Unite and Conquer."

When the Stamp Act was scheduled to go into effect, Franklin gave a return performance which was to be repeated at the outbreak of the Revolution with a new slogan, "Unite or Die," directed against the British.

The snake now had nine parts, for Georgia had joined her sister colonies. The snake became involved in a verbal duel. After the caricature was reprinted in The Pennsylvania Journal, *July 27, 1774, a writer for Loyalist* Rivington's Gazette *called it a "scandalous and saucy reflection." A corresponden of the* Journal *answered him in this fashion:*

> *To the Author of the Lines in Mr.*
> *Rivington's Paper, or the Snake depicted*
> *in some of the American Newspapers.*
>
> *"That New England's abused, and by sons of sedition,*
> *Is granted without either prayer or petition;*
> *And that 'tis 'a scandalous, saucy reflection,*
> *That merits the soundest, severest correction,*
> *Is readily granted. 'How came it to pass?'*
> *Because she is pester'd by snakes in the grass,*
> *Why, by lying and cringing, and such like pretensions,*
> *Get places once honor'd disgraced with pensions.*
> *And you, Mr. Pensioner, instead of repentance*
> *(If I don't mistake you), have wrote your own*
> *sentence;*
> *For by such snakes as this New England's abused,*
> *And the head of the serpents, 'you know, must be*
> *bruised."*
>
> *"New Jersey"*

The Sons of Liberty went into action. Town meetings were a daily occurrence.

Tories and Patriots come to blows. This picture comes from early illustrations to John Trumbull's epic poem, "M'Fingal."

Cooperative resistance against tyranny began.

1 B——
2 M——
3 Col F——
4 W——   } Super Intendants of the Butchery, from the two great Slaughter Houses.
         } Deputies to the above

5 Scotch Butchers
6 English Soldiers struck with Horror & dropping their Arm
7 The English Fleet with Scotch Commanders
8 Boston

"The Scotch Butchery," Boston, 1775. This print made its appearance the day before the battles of Lexington and Concord, in the London Chronicle. The cartoon bitterly attacks the Scottish Lords Bute and Mansfield, and other advisors to King George III. The designer of this print had no love for the Scots and held them responsible for the harsh treatment of the colonies. For instance, the thistle is used for the figurehead of the frigate firing on Boston; and the Scottish standing soldiers freely display this emblem on their standards. The English soldiers struck with horror have dropped their arms. Their action gives pictorial authenticity to reports from Boston of the desertions of British soldiers and the resignation of their officers. Courtesy of the New-York Historical Society, New York City.

This cartoon was engraved by Paul Revere for Royal American Magazine *in 1775. It was copied from* "Britannia in Distress," *which appeared in Volume IV of the* Oxford Magazine, *February 1770. The sentiments expressed in the balloons were altered to suit American consumption. From left to right, the balloons read as follows:* "Right my Lord. Penalties of that kind seem best adapted." "She must lose more Blood. Petitions are Rebellions." "Secure Her now, or it is all over with Us." "She is Mad and must be Chained!" "They will ruin her Constitution." "This is the proper fee for such a Physician." "Poor America!" *Courtesy American Antiquarian Society, Worcester, Mass.*

This engraving is an exact copy, reduced, of a caricature found by Benson Lossing at the Massachusetts Historical Society. On the back of it in script was the following explanation of the print:

"No. 1 intends the K——g of G. B., to whom the house of Commons (4) gives the Americans' money for the use of that very H. of C., and which he is endeavoring to take away with the power of the cannon. No. 2, by a Frenchman, signifies the tyranny that is intended for America. No. 3, the figure of a Roman Catholic priest with his crucifix and gibbet, assisting George in enforcing his tyrannical system of civil and religious government. Nos. 5 and 6 are honest American yeomen, who oppose an oaken staff to G———'s cannon, and determine they will not be robbed. No. 7 is poor Britannia blindfolded, falling into the bottomless pit which her infamous rulers have prepared for the Americans. Nos. 8 and 9 represent Boston in flames and Quebec triumphant, to show the probable consequence of submission to the present wicked ministerial system, that popery and tyranny will triumph over true religion, virtue and liberty."

Some Virginians were reluctant to sign the Articles of Association of 1774 wherein they agreed to a policy of non-importation from England. Tar & feathers are here shown as the alternative! In this cartoon the burgesses of Virginia are shown being forced by their constituents to sign an agreement of non-importation. Loyalists were pressed for a similar concession by the anti-British populace. Cartoon, London, 1775. Print Room, N. Y. Public Library.

In April 1774, General Thomas Gage was sent from England to become Governor of the Colony of Massachusetts and to suppress the rebellion. He brought four regiments with him to put down any possible opposition.

British officers—civil and military—tightened their grip on the colonies and sought to compel obedience to British authority. On April 18, 1775, General Gage sent a small force of soldiers to Lexington for the purpose, among other things, of seizing some military supplies of the Patriots said to be stored in and around Concord.

The Patriots bore the news of these intentions to the people even before the British had carried them out. Paul Revere on his famous ride reached Lexington around midnight. William Dawes arrived there a little later. On April 19, 1775, the Revolution which both sides had tried to avert was on.

In May, when the Second Continental Congress assembled at Philadelphia, the majority of delegates were inclined to be conciliatory toward England. They were still hopeful that she would acknowledge the American rights that had been declared earlier. By 1776 this hope had faded. The desire for independence burned in the hearts of the Patriots. In *Common Sense,* a tract published in Philadelphia, Thomas Paine called for immediate and unconditional independence for America. "Now is the seed-time of Continental union, faith and honor," he wrote, "O! ye that love mankind! Ye that dare oppose not only tyranny but the tyrant, stand forth."

British troops seized munitions and other American supplies stored at Concord. This triggered the historic battle at Lexington, where the Redcoats did a backward march.

The Retreat

From Concord to Lexington of the Army of Wild Irish Asses Defeated by the Brave American Militia

Mr. Deacon Mr. Loeings Mr. Mulikens Mr. Bonds Houses and Barn all Plunder'd and Burnt on April 19.th

according to Act June 14 1775

On the 19th of April, 1775 General Gage, determined to destroy munitions stored at Concord, sent out a detachment under cover of night and secrecy. Warren discovered the move; and Dawes and Revere carried the message.

The retreat depicted is that of Lord Percy's Irish Regiment sent out to rescue the original detachment of British forces from the New England Minute Men. There are two rows of Colonial soldiers with their Union Jacks inscribed, LIBERTY. The officer on horseback is shouting, "Come on My Brave Boys, we'll die or be free"; the officer on the right of the line bellows "We will do for this Bloody Crew!" On the ground lies a dead soldier; an assheaded officer cries "I'll Run, for they are at our heels." In the center, three files of troops led by an officer armed with a halberd are retreating behind their officer, saying "My lord, the Rebels are too hard for us, I am Wounded." In front of the houses and barn on fire common American soldiers carry off trunks, bales of goods, and a blazing torch. One says, "I'll Run, for what's in this box will be the Making of Me." Facing them Earl Percy on horseback, with drawn sword, says, "Where's the Troops agoing that I have mett {?} I am come with succour."

The British forces were saved from utter rout solely by the appearance of reinforcements under Lord Percy, under whose protection the retreat to Boston was managed. Courtesy of the New-York Historical Society, New York City.

News of Lexington brought cries of vengeance from the radicals. The Revolutionary War was on.

In May the Second Continental Congress chose George Washington as Commander-in-Chief of the Continental Army.

Muster-masters began drum-beating for recruits.

An American Officier
1778
Kail.
F. v Germann

An American Soldier.
1778
Kail.
F. v. Germann

Although the British were victorious at Bunker Hill, American morale was strengthened after the battle.

A woman caricaturist dramatized the event with an unusual coiffure.

Bunker's Hill or America's Head Dress, 1775. This caricature was executed by Mathina (Mary) Darly. It satirizes the fact that the British-claimed victory, at Bunker's Hill, found little acclaim among the people.

The London Packet *of July 26–28 of the year 1775 commented:* "Notwithstanding all the pains taken by the hirelings of Government to blacken the Americans, it does not appear even from the partial account in the *Gazette of the action of the 17th of June, that they (Americans) were either cruel, unskillful, or cowardly. They fought it out bravely to the last, carried off their dead, nay buried them in spite of their enemies' utmost efforts."* The exaggerated French coiffure depicts the redoubts at Bunker Hill over which three flags were placed: a baboon (Louis XVI of France), a goose (possibly General Israel Putnam), and two women (America and Britannia) holding out olive branches. Courtesy of the New-York Historical Society, New York City.*

The king and his henchmen planted the seeds from which a harvest of satirical cartoons erupted in England and America. Hatred of England was expressed in different ways.

The Parricide. This "Sketch of American Patriotism" was considered exceptional when it appeared in April, 1776. The daughter, America, is represented by an Indian woman holding a tomahawk and a dagger given her by John Wilkes, English political reformer. She is ready to strike Britannia, the mother, whose hands are bound, while members of the British opposition who call themselves patriots look on. The extreme Patriots in America were dismayed. Courtesy of the New-York Historical Society, New York City.

It even became dangerous for a Tory to have a shave.

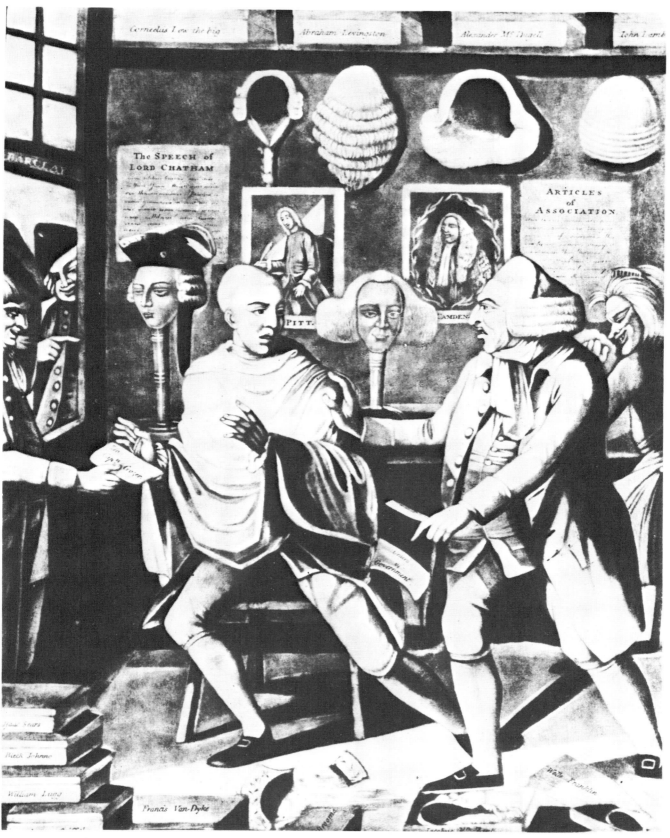

"The Patriotick Barber of New York" honors Jacob Vredenburgh, who, in 1774, when half through shaving a British naval captain learned his identity and refused to finish the job. Print and caption courtesy New York Public Library.

Who had eyes for George now?

Tearing down king's arms from above the door in the chamber of the Supreme Court Room in Independence Hall, July 8th, 1776. Print and caption courtesy The Bettmann Archive.

The Germans engraved their own cartoon on this subject.

Die Zerstörung der Königlichen Bild Säule zu Neu Yorck. | La Destruction de la Statue royale a Nouvelle York.

Destruction of the statue of George III, 1776 in Bowling Green. Line engraving by Francis Xav. Habermann. Museum of the City of New York.

The king on occasion managed to get away from it all.

George III reflecting on his gluttonous appetite. This is an English caricature by Gillray. It depicts His Royal Highness toasting muffins. The cartoon was reprinted in Germany with the following text:

Das Königliche Frühstück. Er röstet Plätzchen. O, so ein Paar war noch nie gesehen . . . von der Natur so ganz für einander geschaffen! (The royal breakfast. He toasts a muffin. O, such a pair has never been seen . . . so naturally made for each other!) The Bettmann Archive.

France and Spain had begun keeping a close watch on the developments in the thirteen American colonies as soon as it became obvious to them that the Americans were not happy with Britain's colonial policy. When news reached Europe that the two had come to blows, Vergennes, the French Prime Minister, and other forces in France urged Louis XVI to give aid to the colonists. The French king was reluctant, regarding such action as "both dishonorable conduct and potential disaster," but finally, in 1776, he was persuaded to bow to the majority, and ordered that one million livres be used to buy munitions for America. The Spanish government, which had been considering similar aid to the colonies promptly contributed the same amount of money to the cause, so that by the end of 1776 both countries were giving the colonies secret aid.

Burgoyne's defeat at Saratoga is, according to Charles and Mary Beard, rightly counted among "the decisive battles" of history. It proved that American troops, although poorly trained and supplied, had "a genius for warfare" and could "in certain circumstances" handle the British regulars.

The defeat caused panic among British officials, first because they had never anticipated anything but victories, and second because they feared an alliance between France and America might now materialize. Parliament tried to negotiate to save America for the Empire. Sufficient concessions were to be offered to the Patriots to induce them to make peace. In this way the king and Lord North thought an alliance between France and America could be averted. However, the Commissioners left for America without permission to recognize American independence or to withdraw British forces from the thirteen colonies. Consequently the British move met with total failure, because Congress refused to deal with the Commissioners until American independence had been recognized and the British military forces withdrawn.

More importantly, the defeat of Burgoyne convinced the French that the American cause was looking up, and brought France into the war. On February 6, 1778 two treaties between France and the United States were signed. In the Treaty of Amity and Commerce, France officially recognized American independence. In the Treaty of Alliance the two countries pledged mutual aid and defense. The French government declared war on England and began to take part in military and naval operations against her, and early the following year Spain joined France. Dutch merchants who had been selling munitions to the patriots at a profit now began supplying France and Spain with naval supplies and "preying" on British commerce.

England now had three external enemies, but her domestic situation improved. As a result of the entry of France and Spain into the war, members of the opposition who had favored the American cause now rallied to the defense of their own country. In his dying speech in 1778 Lord Chatham found good cause to "rejoice that the grave has not closed upon me, that I am still alive to lift up my voice against the dismemberment of this ancient and most noble monarchy."

While General William Howe was winning inconclusive victories in southern Pennsylvania, General John Burgoyne raised the white flag at Saratoga.

Reduced state of Burgoyne's army at Saratoga, 1777. In this cartoon the men of Burgoyne's army suffering from hunger and thirst, are forced to drink "Congress Water." Courtesy of the New-York Historical Society, New York City.

On Christmas Eve Washington made a surprise trip by boat across the Delaware.

Washington crosses the Delaware, December 24, 1777. General Washington had decided that since General William Howe had scattered his troops, fearing no attack from the revolutionaries, it was a good time to clip the wings of the redcoats. He resolved to make a bold effort to check the progress of the enemy. For that purpose he planned an attack on the detachment of about 1,500 Hessians at Trenton. On Christmas Eve he hoped to surprise the enemy after the holiday festivities. The Delaware River was almost blocked with floating ice when he and his men were ferried across, and it was three o'clock in the morning before the troops arrived on the Jersey side. The night was bitter cold with snow and sleet. The roads were slippery, but General Washington continued his forward thrust. At eight o'clock in the morning he reached the Hessian advanced posts which he immediately drove in. The Hessian leader, apprised of Washington's arrival soon had his men under arms and prepared for a defense. Early in the engagement, when he received a mortal wound, his men threw down their arms and surrendered. Courtesy of The New-York Historical Society, New York City.

A "circulatory letter" which erupted in the Massachusetts House of Representatives inspired Paul Revere to design and engrave a cartoon.

A WARM PLACE --- HELL

On brave RESCINDERS! to yon yawning Cell,
SEVENTEEN such Miscreants sure will startle Hell;
There puny Villains damn'd for petty Sin,
On such distinguish'd SCOUNDRELS gaze and grin:
The out done DEVIL will resign his Sway,
He never curst his MILLIONS in a day.

This caricature is believed to have been both designed and engraved by Paul Revere. It was inspired by the action of seventeen Tories in the Massachusetts House of Representatives. On February 11, 1768, the House voted to give their approval to a "Circulatory Letter" that opposed various acts of Parliament levying taxes on the colonies. Parliament was disturbed by the letter. Governor Bernard was ordered to demand that the vote of the House should be rescinded. Ninety-two members voted against this measure while seventeen were in favor of rescinding. The vote caused quite a stir in Massachusetts. Toasts were drunk to "the glorious ninety-two" and the seventeen rescinders were held up to public obloquy. The scene shows the devil with a pitchfork pushing seventeen men into the yawning, fiery jaws of a monster representing the mouth of Hell. Above is a flying devil shouting, "Push on Tim," a reference to Timothy Ruggles, an active Loyalist and one of the seventeen. Another member of the group has a calf's head. This is believed to be a reference to Dr. John Calef. Amercan Antiquarian Society.

An English cartoonist depicts the British and their "worthy" allies (the Indians) scalping Americans on western frontiers.

A Scene on the FRONTIERS as Practiced by the HUMANE BRITISH and their WORTHY ALLIES

Bring me the Scalps and the King our master will reward you —

Reward for Sixteen Scalps

*Arise Columbia's Sons and forward press.
Your country's wrongs call loudly for redress.
The Savage Indian with his Scalping Knife
Or Tomahawk may seek to take your life.*

*By bravery aw'd they'll in a dreadful fright
Shrink back for Refuge to the Woods in flight.
Their British leaders then will quickly shake
And for their wrongs shall restitution make.*

This Revolutionary War cartoon is an English copper engraving by William Charles. It shows the British with their "worthy allies" (the Indians) scalping American freedom-fighters. The Tories were a menace as far as the Patriots were concerned. They assisted the British fleets and armies as much as they could. This picture refers to the fact that the Tories led the Indians against the Western frontier settlements. They enlisted in Redcoat regiments, formed their own militia and their own provincial battalions. Courtesy The Bettmann Archive.

News of the French alliance was greeted by Americans with outbursts of joy. French cooperation meant French gold for the revolutionary treasury, without which further prosecution of the war seemed hopeless.

Orage causé par l'Impôt sur le Thé en Amérique.

Le Temps fait voir avec sa Lanterne Magique, aux quatre parties du Monde, que cet Orage que les Anglois ont excité, les foudroye eux-mêmes, et va donner à l'Amérique les moyens de se saisir du bonnet de la Liberté.

A Storm brought about by the Taxes over Tea in America, 1775. The French were interested in the Revolutionary War long before they became allies of the Americans. Here they have some comments to make about the tea controversy. This engraving was published in Paris about 1775. The text, translated, reads: "Time, with its magic lantern, reveals throughout the four corners of the world, that this storm the English have initiated, strikes them down themselves, and will give to America the means to seize the cap of liberty." ("Liberty cap" refers to the cap given to a freedman in ancient Rome at manumission.) The Metropolitan Museum of Art, Gift of William H. Huntington, 1882.

England got the jitters when Spain and Holland came to the assistance of the revolutionaries.

The Treaty of Alliance between France and the United States was a blow to Britain. Her empire, her commercial and maritime supremacy, were in danger. American independence was regarded now as of secondary importance, as Spain and Holland later joined France. There was some advantage for England, as members of the government who had favored the American cause now rallied to the defense of the country. This caricature pinpoints the outlook for Britain. The characters involved are, from left to right, Yankee Doodle of America, Monsieur Louis Baboon of France, Don Diego of Spain, and Mynheer Frog of Holland. "Sink me, but I could beat them all," says Yankee Doodle. "I have almost forgot how to fight," complains the Spaniard. "By St. J———," cries the Dutchman, "He has almost blinded me." And England complains, "This fall has hurt my back." From a British caricature in the collection of R. T. H. Halsey, New York.

The Dutch Trade with America. Assistance came to the revolutionaries from another source. Holland was a country governed by the commercial spirit. Though she was tied by treaty to England, little love was lost between the two peoples. According to Henrik Van Loon, the Dutch "wished nothing more than to see the Republic's commercial rivals in the hands of a receiver." The American war was an opportunity not to be wasted. With no fleet, America was at the mercy of England on the sea. But the Dutch had ships, munitions of war, and the desire to make a profit. A brisk smuggling trade between the Dutch West Indies and American ports sprang up, much to the annoyance of the English. Many of the more influential among the Dutch sympathized with the American cause; and private loans to the rebels were forthcoming. This cartoon depicts Dutch propaganda for the United States. The King, about to be disrobed of his royal prerogatives by two stalwart Americans, calls on the faltering North for aid. At one side are Englishmen petitioning Cromwell, who had given them such mighty support in their commercial rivalry with the Dutch, to come to their aid now, as the ministry of North is turning a deaf ear to their pleas. The Goddess of Justice, however, is about to strike the unsuspecting English. From a contemporary Dutch cartoon in the collection of R. T. H. Halsey, New York. Print Room, N. Y. Public Library.

British commerce was far from bullish.

Westm. Mag. Feb. 1778

PHILADELPHIA

A Picturesque View of the State of the Nation for February 1778.

This is a line engraving ascribed to Paul Revere. A cow symbolizes Great Britain's commerce. The Congress of America are sawing off her horns, which are her natural strength and defense. One is already gone, the other ready to go. The jolly, plump Dutchman is milking the cow with great glee. The Frenchman and the Spaniard are each "catching at their respective bowls of milk and running off laughing." The British lion lying on the ground is fast asleep. He is being trampled on by a pug dog (Holland), but seems to see nothing, feel nothing and hear nothing. An emancipated Englishman is wringing his hands at his unsuccessful attempt to awaken the lion. Both British General William Howe and his brother Richard, the Admiral, are shown in the background asleep from wine, in Philadelphia. Only one of their flagships is visible—"all the rest of the fleet invisible, nobody knows where." Courtesy of The New-York Historical Society, New York City.

Mother Britannia determined to hurdle the generation gap and sought ways to win back the devotion of daughter America. King George sent his commissioners to the colonies but the revolutionaries would have no truck with them.

THE CURIOUS ZEBRA.
alive from America! walk in Gemmen and Ladies, walk in.
London, Printed for G. Johnson as the Act directs 3 Sep.r 1778, and Sold at all the Printshops in London & Westminster

This cartoon is a delayed print on the Stamp Act. The zebra's stripes contain the names of the thirteen colonies. Four men compete for the animal, as well as the British Commissioners, who come to conciliate their former subjects and find their hay and oats rejected. English statesman George Grenville, nicknamed the "Gentle Shepherd," is placing a saddle, "Stamp Act," on the zebra, while a Frenchman and George Washington yank on the tail. Courtesy of The New-York Historical Society, New York City.

The English and American Discovery—Lord North Makes Concessions, 1778. Rumors of the French treaties had crossed the Channel. In a desperate effort to stave off a Continental war Lord North, on February 17, announced to the parliament a plan of conciliation with America, repealing the imposition of taxes on the Colonies. With nearly unanimous consent, the proposition was accepted, receiving the royal signature on March 11, 1778. But Congress, then in session at York, Pennsylvania, to forestall any wavering among the states and the people, issued an address "to the Inhabitants of the United States of America" urging continued resistance. For the Colonies were now more than ever insistent upon independence as the essential condition of peace. And the North proposals, conciliatory as they were in certain respects, did not include or even consider any recognition of independence. Congress recommended that ministers of the gospel of all denominations read or cause to be read, immediately after services, its address spurning Lord North's peace offer. The cartoon, which gives a very early representation of "Brother Jonathan," was intended to aid in bringing about a rapprochement between the warring parties. Courtesy of R. T. H. Halsey, New York.

America to Her Mistaken Mother. A pair of rebuses published by Darly and dated 6 and 11 May {1778} sum up the situation facetiously. In "Britannia to America" the former holds out an olive branch and signs herself "your friend and mother." The answer "America To Her Mistaken Mother," is headed by a print of America as a Red Indian woman with flag and shield of stripes and stars, holding it "flirtily" for the French alliance. She begins: "You silly old woman that you have sent a lure to us is very plain." "Take home your ships and soldiers . . . leave me to myself as I am at age to know my own interests without your foolish advice and know that I shall always regard you and my brothers as relations but not as friends. I am your greatly injured daughter America." Courtesy of the New-York Historical Society, New York City.

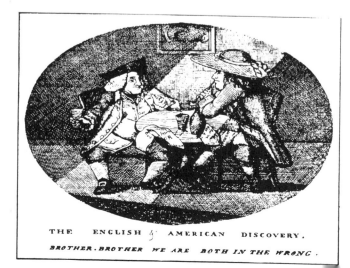

THE ENGLISH & AMERICAN DISCOVERY.

BROTHER. BROTHER WE ARE BOTH IN THE WRONG.

The colonists were particularly amused by British and American cartoons satirizing the weaknesses and predicaments of the British government and its army of occupation.

British Heroism, 1777. Writer-poet John Trumbull takes a crack at the British military in a derisive scene from his epic poem "M'Fingal." Courtesy of the New-York Historical Society, New York City.

Poor Old England Endeavoring to Reclaim His Wicked American Children and therefore is England Maim'd and forc'd to go with a Staff. Caricature etched by M. Darly, 1777. Print and caption courtesy Print Room, New York Public Library.

THE STATE TINKERS.

The National Kettle, which once was a good one, | The Master he thinks, they are wonderful Clever,
For boiling of Mutton, of Beef, & of Pudding, | And cries out in raptures, 'tis done! now or never!
By the fault of the Cook, was quite out of repair, | Yet sneering the Tinkers their old Trade pursue,
When the Tinkers were sent for, — Behold them & Stare. | In stopping of one Hole— they're sure to make Two.

Pub¹ish'd Feb² 10ᵗʰ 1780. by W. Humphrey Nº 227 Strand.

The State Tinkers, 1780. In this political cartoon the cartoonist James Gillray expressed the general contempt for the British ministry when pressure against it was strong. The witty Lord Frederick North who was for coercion of American patriots back in 1774, the incompetent Earl of Sandwich, First Lord of the Admiralty, and Lord George Germain, who followed the King's royal leadership out of conviction; are the State Tinkers who destroy a great bowl, "The National Kettle," while pretending to mend it. George III in his oriental turban looks on with a foolish smile, directed by the delighted Lord Bute, in jester's attire, just behind the monarch. Courtesy of The New-York Historical Society, New York City.

61

Armchair strategists were sure they could have done much better. A British cartoonist ridicules a British general who had once been an active fighter in the colonies.

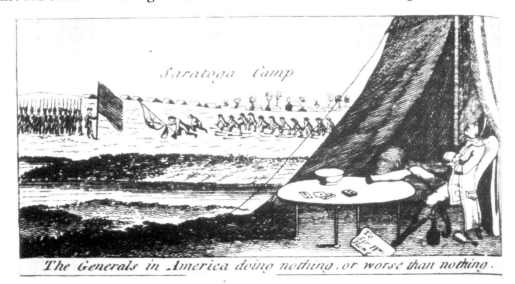

A British jibe at Sir William Howe, from Westminster Magazine, *1779. Courtesy of the New-York Historical Society, New York City.*

A British Armchair Strategist, 1779. "Beg your pardon my Dear Sir—had it from my Lord Fiddlefaddle. He'd nothing to do but cut 'em off pass the Susquehanna and proceed to Boston possess himself of Crown point—then Philadelphia would have fallen of course and a communication opened with the Northern Army—as easily as I'd open a Vein." Courtesy of the New-York Historical Society, New York City.

A View of Plymouth, or Poking Fun at Lord Amherst, ca. 1777. This cartoon was published by Humphrey in England. It shows a "Colonel Mushroom" telling Lord Amherst about the war in America. The Bettmann Archive.

If it wasn't one thing it was another.
Both Georges had their hands full getting recruits.

"Recruits," A satire on the difficulty of recruiting for service in America. London, 1780. *W. H. Bunbury, creator of this cartoon, ridicules the lowly type of men recruited for the British army.* The Public Advertiser *of January 6, 1778 made the following observation regarding recruits: "It is said the Recruiting Service goes on merrily. At Manchester it seems there have been enlisted 'One Barbers Boy, a Chimney Sweeper, a drunken Taylor, two Buttonmakers and a Rat-Catcher." Lord Barrington, Secretary of War, made a proposal in the House of Commons for plans to hire the Hessian troops. He was freely quoted as saying "notwithstanding numerous inducements and try as hard as he would he {Washington} was only able to recruit 450 men for American service, hence would be obliged to hire Germans." One newspaper correspondent had some doubt as to whether the English Regiments would be ready to "cut the Throats of their fellow Subjects in America for Six-pence a Day. After the defeat of Cornwallis American recruiters were likewise scraping the bottom of the barrel. Even a young woman managed to get mustered in. Courtesy of The New-York Historical Society, New York City.*

British victories to the south had not proved conclusive due to the action of bands of American guerilla troops. In March 1781 Cornwallis headed for Virginia. After failing to capture the American troops led by the Marquis de Lafayette, he retired to Yorktown on the Virginia coast to await the British navy, which he hoped would support him from the sea.

At this time General Washington and his French allies were planning an attack on Clinton in New York. Realizing that Cornwallis had gotten himself in a bind, Washington decided to take advantage of the situation. Happily, a French fleet under Admiral de Grasse arrived from the West Indies in time to disperse British naval forces and prevent Cornwallis's escape by sea. After attacking his redoubts at Yorktown the allies drove Cornwallis into his inner fortifications, and on October 17, after a storm prevented him from cutting his way out to the north through Gloucester, he capitulated. The surrender of all his forces was demanded, and two days later, on October 19, 1781, he and more than seven thousand men formally laid down their arms. The war had virtually come to an end.

George III, still refusing to believe that the thirteen colonies could not be conquered, insisted that the war be continued, but the British government declined to carry out his wishes.

Two years passed before a treaty of peace could be concluded between the United States and England. The final treaty was signed on September 3, 1783 and ratified in January 1784 by the Congress at Annapolis.

Things really started looking up for America when Cornwallis surrendered at York-town. The last great battle for American independence had been won.

The Surrender of Cornwallis. This wash drawing by Ramberg was executed around 1785. The Metropoli-tan Museum of Art, Bequest of Charles Allen Munn, 1924.

Another view of Cornwallis's surrender at Yorktown, which brought most of the active hostility to an end. Courtesy of the New-York Historical Society, New York City.

Let George do it, The Continental Congress declared in 1775. George did it in 1783. The Treaty of Paris was signed and the Revolutionary War was over.

Peale's picture of George Washington.

67

The Continental Army Marching Down the Bowery, 1783. On November 25, 1783, the steadfast Continental regulars, the backbone of the whole Revolutionary army, paraded through New York in a victory march. The following year they were disbanded and and had great difficulty in getting jobs. Many, hopelessly unfit through wounds or disease, were forced to beg—as were, indeed, some officers. Even among the highest ranks there was great, and mostly unrelieved, distress. On June 2, 1784, Congress reduced the army to a force of eighty men, "with officers in proportion," and even these eighty were kept only to guard the storehouses at Fort Pitt and West Point. The preamble to this masterpiece of mistaken legislation stated that "standing armies in time of peace are inconsistent with the principles of republican governments." Washington knew better. "Regular troops alone are equal to the exigencies of modern war," he said, "as well for defense as offense, and whenever a substitute is attempted it must prove illusory and ruinous. No militia will ever acquire the habits necessary to resist a regular force. The firmness requisite for the real business of fighting is only to be attained by a constant course of discipline and service." From an engraving by Lande after a drawing by Howard Pyle. From J. G. Wilson's Memorial History of the City of New York, *1892.*

Rejected by the Americans and by Prime Minister Shelburne of England, the American Loyalists were left holding the bag.

Shelb—n's Sacrifice, or the Recommended Loyalists, 1783. This cartoon is from an old print published in 1783. It is a faithful reproduction of "a Tragedy Shortly to be Performed on the Continent of America." The complete abandonment of the American Loyalists added to the unpopularity of Prime Minister Shelburne's administration, because these people had the sympathy of the British. At times, particularly in the early years of the war, the American Loyalists had been under heavy attack as it was believed they were responsible for false information given by their leaders to Lord North. They were, therefore, blamed for being instrumental in bringing on the war. Later, the feelings changed. The English Peace Commissioners pleaded for assurance of protection for the Loyalists, but the Americans were unforgiving. In this scene, as two American Indians, tomahawks in hand, pursue four Loyalists, Britannia, on the extreme right, is about to attack Shelburne with her spear. R. T. H. Halsey finds this cartoon "particularly villifying." Culver Pictures.

Not all the British shared Shelburne's views.

This print is taken from an allegorical picture by Benjamin West describing an event that took place when the War was over. Religion and Justice are extending the mantle of Britannia while she herself holds out her arm and shield to receive the Loyalists. The group comprises representatives of the Law, the Church, and Government, with other people. An Indian chief holds out one hand to Britannia, and with the other points to the Widows and Orphans of the War. In a cloud near Religion and Justice the Genii of Great Britain and America are seen in an opening glory, binding the broken faces of the two countries, emblematic of the Treaty of Peace.

At the head of the Loyalists, wearing a large wig, is Sir William Pepperell, one of their most efficient friends in England. Immediately behind him, carrying a scroll, is Dr. Franklin's son, Governor William Franklin of New Jersey, who remained loyal until the end. The two figures on the right are Benjamin West and his wife, both natives of Pennsylvania. Franklin and Joseph Galloway were among the most prominent of the loyal refugees who sought shelter in England.

Back to the salt mine. It was moving day for Congress when the seat of government was shifted to Philadelphia.

This caricature of the wealthy Pennsylvania Senator Robert Morris was inspired by the New Yorkers. They resented the role he played in having the seat of government removed from their city to Philadelphia. Congress and Senator Morris are depicted on the march. Morris is holding out a large moneybag. Numerous balloons carry the words of the different participants. Morris says, "My name is Robert Coffer R. M." In turn the Congressmen say: "We are going at the rate of 6 Dollars pr. day," "Stick to it Bobby," "Money & preferment," "This is what influences me" {He is clutching a moneybag}, "It is bad to have a gouty Constitution." To which is the reply, "I am afraid bobbys dance will not mend it." "I hope the Philadelphians will not serve as they once did {In 1783 Congress had to flee from Philadelphia because of mutiny among the soldiers}." To which another responds, "So am I for I am tired of traviling." "What will they move to prolong our next session?" And other unflattering comments go on. Print Room, N. Y. Public Library.

2

Light and Lively Literature: Prose

The history of the colonies during the seventeenth and eighteenth centuries takes on new meaning for us when we include a study of their literature.

For me the most interesting, and certainly the most readable, kinds of literature are the personal narratives including chronicles of adventure, diaries, and letters—many unpublished—which give detailed accounts of events and experiences as well as comments on people and the times. Rich in source material for writers and students of history, these subjective works help us gain insight into the values and ethics of a people of another era, and to understand the situations that confronted them in their day-to-day living. As we read, we view the political scene through their eyes, and come to share their inner conflicts and uncertainties, their purposes and goals. History is no longer facts but people, people who want a better world for themselves and their children, a world in which all men will be free and equal.

The colonists also read long tracts and essays on religion, classical and modern histories, political essays, written oratory, and some fiction. These too, even though we may find them pedagogical and wordy, are important in giving us insight into the past. It is desirable for us to know what the settlers read in order to determine what kind of people they were. Many of the men who sought to build their own new world needed to read ancient and modern histories to learn how other worlds were built. They had to have faith, too, for their own survival, when they subdued the wilderness and became steeped in theological learning. In the late seventeenth and early eighteenth century light and lively literature was deemed a waste of time, as was the theater. "Fill this country with devout and useful books," Cotton Mather urged an itinerant peddler of books and pamphlets.

Just before and during the Revolutionary War the literary word took on new significance. The development of discontent in the colonies, the rebellion of the colonists against the curtailment of their liberties, and finally their resolve to become independent gave rise to political satire from the pens of leading writers and poets. These satirical writings grew increasingly embittered and venomous on both sides.

72

Literature in the form of propaganda became an important weapon in the struggle for independence, as pamphlets and newspapers molded public opinion.

Patriot writers followed Samuel Adams's rule for literary warfare, "Keep your enemy in the wrong," and bombarded the Tories "with intermittent showers of shot and shell in the form of arguments, anathemas, jokes and jeers."

The inner conflicts of men like John Dickinson become very real to us. Although a dedicated patriot, Dickinson was one of many who did not want to see a break with England and resisted the realization that the break was inevitable. Many of the leaders were confident in the readiness of the thirteen colonies to become a nation, but others had their doubts, and they show up in these writings.

The prose writings that appear in this book were selected for their human interest, their wit, and their natural humor rather than for their literary style—although many are beautifully written. Each one in its way helps recapture the great spirit of a bygone era. We can now read with emotion and pride the stirring words of Thomas Paine:

Our citizenship in the United States is our national character. Our citizenship in any particular State is only our local distinction. By the latter we are known at home, by the former to the world. Our great title is Americans.

Essays and True Stories

Benjamin Franklin was the eighteenth century's great humorist.

A book about eighteenth-century humor would hardly be complete without a few choice selections by the great Philadelphia scientist, inventor, philanthropist, author, and publisher.

Franklin's humor is timeless. His ability to tell a joke made him useful in many a crisis.

The great doctor was, of course, one of the authors of the Declaration of Independence, and a signer as well, although he was not asked to write the document because it was feared he would conceal a joke in the middle of it. When he did sign it he declared, "We must all hang together, or assuredly we shall all hang separately."

In addition to his innumerable political and scientific accomplishments, Franklin was an authority on fornication, nudity, and intoxication. His articles on these subjects are as contemporary as many that appear in today's books and magazines. In the selections that follow he pulls no punches.

Franklin, the eighteenth century's sensuous man and an authority on fornication, here advises a young friend who had complained about his lustful inclinations.

Why a Young Man Should Choose an Old Mistress

My dear friend: I know of no medicine fit to diminish the violent natural inclinations you mention; and if I did, I think I should not communicate it to you. Marriage is the proper Remedy. It is the most natural state of Man, and therefore the State in which you are most likely to find solid Happiness. Your reasons against entering into it at present appear to me not well founded. The circumstantial Advantages you have in view by postponing it are not only uncertain, but they are small in comparison with that of the Thing itself, the being married and settled. It is the Man and Woman united that make the compleat human Being. Separate, she wants his Force of Body and Strength of Reason; he, her Softness, Sensibility, and acute Discernment. Together they are more likely to succeed in the World. A single Man has not nearly the value he would have in the State of Union. He is an incomplete Animal. He resembles the odd half of a pair of Scissars. If you get a prudent, healthy Wife, your Industry in your Profession, with her good Economy, will be a fortune sufficient.

But if you will not take this Counsel and persist in thinking a Commerce with the Sex inevitable, then I repeat my former Advice, that in all your Amours you should prefer old Women to young ones.

You call this a Paradox and demand my Reasons. They are these:

1. Because they have more Knowledge of the World, and their Minds are better stored with Observations, their Conversation is more improving, and more lastingly agreeable.

2. Because when Women cease to be handsome they study to be good. To maintain their Influence over Men, they supply the Diminution of Beauty by an Augmentation of Utility. They learn to do a thousand Services small and great, and are the most tender and useful of Friends when you are sick. Thus they continue amiable. And hence there is hardly such a thing to be found as an old Woman who is not a good Woman.

3. Because there is no Hazard of Children, which irregularly produced may be attended with much Inconvenience.

4. Because through more Experience they are more prudent and discreet in conducting an Intrigue to prevent Suspicion. The Commerce with them is therefore safer with regard to your Reputation. And with regard to theirs, if the Affair should happen to be known, considerate People might be rather inclined to excuse an old Woman, who would kindly take care of a young Man, form his Manners by her good counsels, and prevent his ruining his Health and Fortune among mercenary Prostitutes.

5. Because in every Animal that walks upright, the Deficiency of the Fluids that fill the Muscles appears first in the highest Part. The Face first grows lank and wrinkled; then the Neck; then the Breast and Arms; the lower Parts continuing to the Last as plump as ever: so that covering all above with a Basket, and regarding only what is below the Girdle, it is impossible of two Women to tell an old one from a young one. And as in the dark all Cats are grey, the Pleasure of Corporal Enjoyment with an old Woman is at least equal, and frequently superior; every Knack being, by Practice, capable of Improvement.

6. Because the Sin is less. The debauching a Virgin may be her Ruin, and make her for Life unhappy.

7. Because the Compunction is less. The having made a young Girl miserable may give you frequent bitter Reflection; none of which can attend the making an old Woman happy.

8th & lastly. They are so grateful!!

Thus much for my Paradox. But still I advise you to marry directly; being sincerely

Your affectionate Friend,
(signed) Benjamin Franklin

Ben Franklin shows a contemporary curiosity about sex, dreams, and nudity in his humorous essays.

Franklin As A Nudist

You know the cold bath has long been in vogue here as a tonic; but the shock of the cold water has always appeared to me, generally speaking, as too violent, and I have found it much more agreeable to my constitution to bathe in another element, I mean cold air. With this view I rise almost every morning, and sit in my chamber without any clothes whatever, half an hour or an hour, according to the season, either reading or writing. This practice is not in the least painful, but, on the contrary, agreeable; and, if I return to bed afterwards, before I dress myself, as sometimes happens, I make a supplement to my night's rest of one or two hours of the most pleasing sleep that can be imagined. I find no ill consequences whatever resulting from it, and that at least it does not injure my health, if it does not in fact contribute much to its preservation. I shall therefore call it for the future a bracing or tonic bath.

Franklin's views on health have a twentieth century touch.

The Art of Producing Pleasant Dreams

As a great part of our life is spent in sleep, during which we have sometimes pleasant and sometimes painful dreams, it becomes of some consequence to obtain the one kind and avoid the other; for whether real or imaginary, pain is pain and pleasure is pleasure. If we can sleep without dreaming, it is well that painful dreams are avoided. If while we sleep we can have any pleasing dream, it is, as the French say, *autant de gagné,* so much added to the pleasure of life.

To this end it is, in the first place, necessary to be careful in preserving health, by due exercise and great temperance; for, in sickness, the imagination is disturbed, and disagreeable, sometimes terrible, ideas are apt to present themselves. Exercise should precede meals, not immediately follow them, the first promotes, the latter, unless moderate, obstructs digestion. If, after exercise, we feed sparingly, the digestion will be easy and good, the body lightsome, the temper cheerful, and all the animal functions performed agreeably. Sleep, when it follows, will be natural and undisturbed; while indolence, with full feeding, occasions nightmares and horrors inexpressible; we fall from precipices, are assaulted by wild beasts, murderers, and demons, and experience every variety of distress. Observe, however, that the quantities of food and exercise are relative things; those who move much may, and indeed ought to eat more; those who use little exercise should eat little. In general, mankind, since the improvement of cookery, eat about twice as much as nature requires. Suppers are not bad, if we have not dined; but restless nights naturally follow hearty suppers after full dinners. Indeed, as there is a difference in constitutions, some rest well after these meals; it costs them only a frightful dream and an apoplexy, after which they sleep till doomsday. Nothing is more common in the newspapers, than instances of people who, after eating a hearty supper, are found dead abed in the morning.

Another means of preserving health, to be attended to, is the having a constant supply of fresh air in your bed-chamber. It has been a great mistake, the sleeping in rooms exactly closed, and in beds surrounded by curtains. No outward air that may come in to you is so unwholesome as the unchanged air, often breathed, of a close chamber. As boiling water does not grow hotter by longer boiling, if the particles that receive greater heat can escape; so living bodies do not putrefy, if the particles, so fast as they become putrid, can be thrown off. Nature expels them by the pores of the skin and the lungs, and in a free, open air they are carried off; but in a close room we receive them again and again, though they become more and more corrupt. A number of persons crowded into a small room thus spoil the air in a few minutes, and even render it mortal, as in the Black Hole at Calcutta.

For sufferers from gout this is must reading.

Dialogue between Franklin and the Gout

[*Dated at Midnight, 22 October, 1780.*]

FRANKLIN. Eh! Oh! Eh! What have I done to merit these cruel sufferings?

GOUT. Many things; you have ate and drank too freely, and too much indulged those legs of yours in their indolence.

FRANKLIN. Who is it that accuses me?

GOUT. It is I, even I, the Gout.

FRANKLIN. What! my enemy in person?

GOUT. No, not your enemy.

FRANKLIN. I repeat it; my enemy; for you would not only torment my body to death, but ruin my good name; you reproach me as a glutton and a tippler; now all the world, that knows me, will allow that I am neither the one nor the other.

GOUT. The world may think as it pleases; it is always very complaisant to itself, and sometimes to its friends; but I very well know that the quantity of meat and drink proper for a man who takes a reasonable degree of exercise, would be too much for another, who never takes any.

FRANKLIN. I take—Eh! Oh!—as much exercise—Eh!—as I can, Madam Gout. You know my sedentary state, and on that account, it would seem, Madam Gout, as if you might spare me a little, seeing it is not altogether my own fault.

GOUT. Not a jot; your rhetoric and your politeness are thrown away; your apology avails nothing. If your situation in life is a sedentary one, your amusements, your recreations, at least, should be active. You ought to walk or ride; or, if the weather prevents that, play at billiards. But let use examine your course of life. While the mornings are long, and you have leisure to go abroad, what do you do? Why, instead of gaining an appetite for breakfast, by salutary exercise, you amuse yourself with books, pamphlets, or newspapers, which commonly are not worth the reading. Yet you eat an inordinate breakfast, four dishes of tea, with cream, and one or two buttered toasts, with slices of hung beef, which I fancy are not things the most easily digested. Immediately afterward you sit down to write at your desk, or converse with persons who apply to you on business. Thus the time passes till one, without any kind of bodily exercise. But all this I could pardon, in regard, as you say, to your sedentary condition. But what is your practice after dinner? Walking in the beautiful gardens of those friends, with whom you have dined, would be the choice of men of sense; yours is to be fixed down to chess, where you are found engaged for two or three hours! This is your perpetual recreation, which is the least eligible of any for a sedentary man, because, instead of accelerating the motion of the fluids, the rigid attention it requires helps to retard the circulation and obstruct internal secretions. Wrapt in the speculations of this wretched game, you destroy your constitution. What can be expected from such a course of living but a body replete with stagnant humors, ready to fall a prey to all kinds of dangerous maladies, if I, the Gout, did not occasionally bring you relief by agitating those humors, and so purifying or dissipating them? If it was in some nook or alley in Paris, deprived of walks, that you played awhile at chess after dinner, this might be excusable; but the same taste prevails with you in Passy, Auteuil, Montmartre, or Sanoy, places where there are the finest gardens and walks, a pure air, beautiful women, and most agreeable instructive conversation; all which you might enjoy by frequenting the walks. But these are rejected for this abominable game of chess. Fie, then, Mr. Franklin! But amidst my instructions, I had almost forgot to administer my wholesome corrections; so take that twinge,—and that.

FRANKLIN. Oh! Eh! Oh! Ohhh! As much instruction as you please, Madam Gout, and as many reproaches; but pray, Madam, a truce with your corrections!

GOUT. No, Sir, no,—I will not abate a particle of what is so much for your good,—therefore—

FRANKLIN. Oh! Ehhh!—It is not fair to say I take no exercise, when I do very often, going out to dine and returning in my carriage.

GOUT. That, of all imaginable exercises, is the most slight and insignificant, if you allude to the motion of a carriage suspended on springs. By observing the degree of heat obtained by different kinds of motion, we may form an estimate of the quantity of exercise given by each. Thus, for example, if you turn out to walk in winter with cold feet, in an hour's time you will be in a glow all over; ride on horseback, the same effect will scarcely be perceived by four hours' round trotting; but if you loll in a carriage, such as you have mentioned, you may travel all day, and gladly enter the last inn to warm your feet by a fire. Flatter yourself then no longer, that half an hour's airing in your carriage deserves the name of exercise. Providence has appointed few to roll in carriages, while he has given to all a pair of legs, which are machines infinitely more commodious and serviceable. Be grateful, then, and

76

make a proper use of yours. Would you know how they forward the circulation of your fluids, in the very action of transporting you from place to place; observe when you walk, that all your weight is alternately thrown from one leg to the other; this occasions a great pressure on the vessels of the foot, and repels their contents; when relieved, by the weight being thrown on the other foot, the vessels of the first are allowed to replenish, and, by a return of this weight, this repulsion again succeeds, thus accelerating the circulation of the blood. The heat produced in any given time depends on the degree of this acceleration; the fluids are shaken, the humors attenuated, the secretions facilitated, and all goes well; the cheeks are ruddy, and health is established. Behold your fair friend at Auteuil [Madame Helvetius]; a lady who received from bounteous nature more really useful science, than half a dozen such pretenders to philosophy as you have been able to extract from all your books. When she honors you with a visit, it is on foot. She walks all hours of the day, and leaves indolence, and its concomitant maladies, to be endured by her horses. In this see at once the preservative of her health and personal charms. But when you go to Auteuil, you must have your carriage, though it is no farther from Passy to Auteuil than from Auteuil to Passy.

FRANKLIN. Your reasonings grow very tiresome.

GOUT. I stand corrected. I will be silent and continue my office; take that, and that.

FRANKLIN. Oh! Ohh! Talk on, I pray you!

GOUT. No, no; I have a good number of twinges for you to-night, and you may be sure of some more to-morrow.

FRANKLIN. What, with such a fever! I shall go distracted. Oh! Eh! Can no one bear it for me?

GOUT. Ask that of your horses; they have served you faithfully.

FRANKLIN. How can you so cruelly sport with my torments?

GOUT. Sport! I am very serious. I have here a list of offences against your own health distinctly written, and can justify every stroke inflicted on you.

FRANKLIN. Read it then.

GOUT. It is too long a detail; but I will briefly mention some particulars.

FRANKLIN. Proceed. I am all attention.

GOUT. Do you remember how often you have promised yourself, the following morning, a walk in the grove of Boulogne, in the garden de la Muette, or in your own garden, and have violated your promise, alleging, at one time it was too cold, at another too warm, too windy, too moist, or what else you pleased; when in truth it was too nothing but your insuperable love of ease?

FRANKLIN. That I confess may have happened occasionally, probably ten times in a year.

GOUT. Your confession is very far short of the truth; the gross amount is one hundred and ninety-nine times.

FRANKLIN. Is it possible?

GOUT. So possible, that it is fact; you may rely on the accuracy of my statement. You know Mr. Brillon's gardens, and what fine walks they contain; you know the handsome flight of an hundred steps, which lead from the terrace above to the lawn below. You have been in the practice of visiting this amiable family twice a week, after dinner, and it is a maxim of your own, that "a man may take as much exercise in walking a mile, up and down stairs, as in ten on level ground." What an opportunity was here for you to have had exercise in both these ways! Did you embrace it, and how often?

FRANKLIN. I cannot immediately answer that question.

GOUT. I will do it for you; not once.

FRANKLIN. Not once?

GOUT. Even so. During the summer you went there at six o'clock. You found the charming lady, with her lovely children and friends, eager to walk with you, and entertain you with their agreeable conversation; and what has been your choice? Why to sit on the terrace, satisfying yourself with the fine prospect, and passing your eye over the beauties of the garden below, without taking one step to descend and walk about in them. On the contrary, you call for tea and the chess-board; and lo! you are occupied in your seat till nine o'clock, and that besides two hours' play after dinner; and then, instead of walking home, which would have bestirred you a little, you step into your carriage. How absurd to suppose that all this carelessness can be reconcilable with health, without my interposition!

FRANKLIN. I am convinced now of the justness of poor Richard's remark, that "Our debts and our sins are always greater than we think for."

GOUT. So it is. You philosophers are sages in your maxims, and fools in your conduct.

FRANKLIN. But do you charge, among my crimes, that I return in a carriage from Mr. Brillon's?

GOUT. Certainly; for having been seated all the while, you cannot object the fatigue of the day, and cannot want, therefore, the relief of a carriage.

FRANKLIN. What, then, would you have me do with my carriage?

GOUT. Burn it, if you choose; you would at least get heat out of it once in this way; or, if you dislike that proposal, here's another for you; observe the poor peasants, who work in the vineyards and grounds about the villages of Passy, Autèuil, Chaillot, &c.; you may find every day, among these deserving creatures, four or five old men and women, bent and perhaps crippled by weight of years and too long and too great labor, After a most fatiguing day, these people have to trudge a mile or two to their smoky huts. Order your coachman to set them down. This is an act that will be good for your soul; and, at the same time, after your visit to the Brillons, if you return on foot, that will be good for your body.

FRANKLIN. Ah! how tiresome you are!

GOUT. Well, then, to my office; it should not be forgotten that I am your physician. There.

FRANKLIN. Ohhh! what a devil of a physician!

GOUT. How ungrateful you are to say so! Is it not I who, in the character of your physician, have saved you from the palsy, dropsy and apoplexy? one or other of which would have done for you long ago, but from me.

FRANKLIN. I submit, and thank you for the past, but entreat the discontinuance of your visits for the future; for, in my mind, one had better die than be cured so dolefully. Permit me just to hint, that I have also not been unfriendly to *you*. I never feed physician or quack of any kind, to enter the list against you; if, then, you do not leave me to my repose, it may be said you are ungrateful too.

GOUT. I can scarcely acknowledge that as any·objection. As to quacks, I despise them; they may kill you indeed, but cannot injure me. And as to regular physicians, they are at last convinced that the gout, in such a subject as you are, is no disease, but a remedy; wherefore cure a remedy?—but to our business,—there.

FRANKLIN. Oh! Oh!—for Heaven's sake leave me; and I promise faithfully never more to play at chess, but to take exercise daily, and live temperately.

GOUT. I know you too well. You promise fair; but after a few months of good health, you will return to your old habits; your fine promises will be forgotten like the forms of the last year's clouds. Let us then finish the account, and I will go. But I leave you with an assurance of visiting you again at a proper time and place; for my object is your good, and you are sensible now that I am your *real friend.*"

Timothy Dwight has a touching story to tell of a dog's fidelity.

[TIMOTHY DWIGHT (1752–1817) served as Chaplain of General Parsons's Connecticut Continental Brigade. He had already embarked on a successful literary career and shared the honors among the Hartford Wits with men like John Trumbull. He also carried on a theological career, was active in public affairs, and, for over twenty years, was President of Yale College.]

In the autumn, when the seige of Fort Stanwix was raised, the following occurrence took place here. Capt. Greg, one of the American officers left in the garrison, went out one afternoon with a corporal belonging to the same corps, to shoot pigeons. When the day was far advanced Greg, knowing that the savages were at times prowling round the fort, determined to return. At that moment a small flock of pigeons alighted upon a tree in the vicinity. The corporal proposed to try a shot at them; and having approached sufficiently near, was in the act of elevating his piece toward the pigeons, when the report of two muskets discharged by unknown hands at a small distance was heard. The same instant, Greg saw his companion fall and felt himself badly wounded in the side. He tried to stand but speedily fell, and in a moment perceived a huge Indian taking long strides toward him with a tomahawk in his hand. The savage struck him several blows on the head; drew his knife, cut a circle through the skin from his forehead to the crown, and then drew off the scalp with his teeth. At the approach of the savage, Greg had counterfeited the appearance of being dead with as much address as he could use, and succeeded so far as to persuade his butcher that he was really dead; otherwise measures still more effectual would have been employed to despatch him. It is hardly necessary to observe that the pain, produced by these wounds, was intense and dreadful. Those on the head were, however far the most excruciating, although that in his side was believed by him to be mortal. The savages, having finished their bloody business, withdrew.

As soon as they were fairly gone, Greg, who had seen his companion fall, determined if possible to make his way to the spot where he lay;—from a persuasion that if he could place his head upon the corporal's body it would in some degree relieve his excessive anguish. Accordingly he made an effort to rise; and, having with great difficulty succeeded, immediately fell. He was not only weak and distressed but had been deprived of the power of self-command by the tomahawk. Strongly prompted, however, by this little hope of mitigating his sufferings, he made a second attempt and again fell. After several unsuccessful efforts, he finally regained possession of his feet; and, staggering slowly through the forest, at length reached the spot where the corporal lay. The Indian who had marked him for his prey, took a surer aim than his fellow and killed him outright. Greg found him lifeless and scalped. With some difficulty he laid his own head upon the body of his companion; and, as he had hoped, found material relief from this position.

While he was enjoying this little comfort he met with trouble from a new quarter. A small dog which belonged to him and had accompanied him in his hunting, but to which he had been hitherto wholly inattentive, now came up to him in an apparent agony; and, leaping around him in a variety of involuntary motions, yelped, whined, and cried in an unusual manner, to the no small molestation of his master. Greg was not in a situation to bear the disturbance even of affection. He tried, in every way which he could think of, to force the dog from him, but he tried in vain. At length wearied by his cries and agitations and not knowing how to put an end to them, he addressed the animal as if he had been a rational being. "If you wish so much to help me go and call some one to my relief." At these words the creature instantly left him, and ran through the forest at full speed to the great comfort of his master who now hoped to die quietly.

The dog made his way directly to three men, belonging to the garrison, who were fishing at the distance of a mile from the scene of this tragedy. As soon as he came up to them, he began to cry in the same afflicting manner and, advancing near them, turned, and went slowly back toward the point where his master lay, keeping his eye continually on the men. All this he repeated several times. At length one of the men observed to his companions that there was something very extraordinary in the actions of the dog; and that, in his opinion, they ought to find out the cause. His companions were of the same mind; and they immediately set out with an intention to follow the animal whither he should lead them. After they had pursued him some distance and found nothing, they became discouraged. The sun had set; and the forest was dangerous. They therefore determined to return. The moment the dog saw them wheel about, he began to cry with increased violence; and, coming up to the men, took hold of the skirts of their coats with his teeth and attempted to pull them toward the point to which he had before directed their course. When they stopped again he leaned his back against the back part of their legs, as if endeavoring to push them onward to his master. Astonished at this conduct of the dog, they agreed after a little deliberation to follow him until he should stop. The animal conducted them directly to his master. They found him still living, and after burying the corporal as well as they could, they carried Greg to the fort. Here his wounds were dressed with the utmost care; and such assistance was rendered to him as proved the means of restoring him to perfect health. . . .

John Trumbull, leader of the Patriot Wits of Hartford, offers this tidbit.

[*Connecticut-born* JOHN TRUMBULL, *(1750–1831) was an American lawyer and poet. He became a judge first of the Connecticut Superior Court and then of the Supreme Court of Errors. He wrote a series of essays for the* Boston Chronicle *entitled "The Meddlers," from which the following advertisement is taken. It appears in the Trumbull MSS, as given in Tyler's* Literary History of the American Revolution.]

"To be Sold at Public Vendue
The Whole Estate of
Isabella Sprightly, Toast and Coquette,
(Now retiring from Business).

Imprimis, all the Tools and Utensils necessary for carrying on the Trade, viz: Several bundles of Darts and Arrows, well-pointed, and capable of doing great execution. A considerable quantity of Patches, Paint, Brushes, and Cosmetics, for plastering, painting, and whitewashing the face; a complete set of caps, 'a la mode a Paris,' of all sizes from five to fifteen inches in height; With several dozens of Cupids, very proper to be stationed on a ruby lip, a diamond eye, or a roseate cheek.

Item, as she proposes by certain ceremonies to transform one of her humble servants into a husband, and keep him for her own use, she offers for sale, Florio, Daphnis, Synthio, and Cleanthes, with several others, whom she won by a constant attendance on business during the space of four years. She can prove her indisputable right thus to dispose of them, by certain deeds of gifts, bills of sale, and attestation, vulgarly called love-letters, under their own hands and seals. They will be offered very cheap, for they are all of them broken-hearted, consumptive, or in a dying condition. Nay, some of them have been dead this half year, as they declare and testify in the above-mentioned writing.

David Humphrey tells how farmer Israel Putnam, a future Revolutionary War hero, tracks down a wolf.

[DAVID HUMPHREYS, *one of the Hartford Wits, published his* Life of General Putnam *in 1788. This is a selection from it.*

At the same time George Washington was selected by the Continental Congress as commander-in-chief, certain other generals were also appointed, among them Israel Putnam. General Putnam, formerly a successful farmer, had seen service on the frontier in the French and Indian War and was known throughout New England for several sensational exploits. A courageous, outspoken man, he was a hero to the New England troops. This tale narrates an incident of the year 1739, when Putnam moved to Pomfret, Connecticut, to take up farming.]

. . . The first years on a new farm are not, however, exempt from disasters and disappointments, which can only be remedied by stubborn and patient industry. Our farmer, sufficiently occupied in building an house and barn, felling woods, making fences, sowing grain, planting orchards, and taking care of his stock, had to encounter, in turn, the calamities occasioned by drought in summer, blast in harvest, loss of cattle in winter, and the desolation of his sheep-fold by wolves. In one night he had seventy fine sheep and goats killed, besides many lambs and kids wounded. This havoc was committed by a she wolf, which, with her annual whelps, had for several years infested the vicinity. The young were commonly destroyed by the vigilance of the hunters, but the old one was too sagacious to come within reach of gun-shot: upon being closely pursued, she would generally fly to the western woods, and return the next winter with another litter of whelps.

This wolf, at length, became such an intolerable nuisance that Mr. Putnam entered into a combination with five of his neighbors to hunt alternately until they could destroy her. Two, by rotation, were to be constantly in pursuit. It was known, that, having lost the toes from one foot, by a steel-trap, she made one track shorter than the other. By this vestige the pursuers recognized, in a light snow, the route of this pernicious animal. Having followed her to Connecticut river, and found she had turned back in a direct course towards Pomfret, they immediately returned, and by ten o'clock the next morning the blood-hounds had driven her into a den, about three miles distant from the house of Mr. Putnam. The people soon collected with dogs, guns, straw, fire, and sulphur, to attack the common enemy. With this apparatus, several unsuccessful efforts were made to force her from the den. The hounds came back badly wounded, and refused to return. The smoke of blazing straw had no effect. Nor did the fumes of burnt brimstone, with which the cavern was filled, compel her to quit the retirement. Wearied with such fruitless attempts (which had brought the time to ten o'clock at night), Mr. Putnam tried once more to make his dog enter, but in vain. He proposed to his negro man to go down into the cavern and shoot the wolf: the negro declined the hazardous service. Then it was that the master, angry at the disappointment, and declaring that he was ashamed to have a coward in his family, resolved himself to destroy the ferocious beast, lest she should escape through some unknown fissure of the rock. His neighbors strongly remonstrated against the perilous enterprize: but he, knowing that wild animals were intimidated by fire, and having provided several strips of birch-bark, the only combustible material which he could obtain that would afford light in this deep and darksome cave, prepared for his descent. Having, accordingly, divested himself of his coat and waistcoat, and having a long rope fastened round his legs, by which he might be pulled back, at a concerted signal, he entered head-foremost, with the blazing torch in his hand.

The aperture of the den, on the east side of a very high ledge of rocks, is about two feet square; from thence it descends obliquely fifteen feet, then running horizontally about ten more, it ascends gradually sixteen feet toward its termination. The sides of this subterraneous cavity are composed of smooth and solid rocks, which seem to have been divided from each other by some former earthquake. The top and bottom are also of stone, and the entrance, in winter, being covered with ice, is exceedingly slippery. It is in no place high enough for a man to raise himself upright, nor in any part more than three feet in width.

Having groped his passage to the horizontal part of the den, the most terrifying darkness appeared in front of the dim circle of light afforded by his torch. It was silent as the house of death. None but monsters of the desert had ever before explored this solitary mansion of horror. He, cautiously proceeding onward, came to the ascent, which he slowly mounted on his hands and knees, until he discovered the glaring eyeballs of the wolf, who was sitting at the extremity of the cavern. Startled at the sight of fire, she gnashed her teeth, and gave a sudden growl. As soon as he had made the necessary discovery, he kicked the rope as a signal for pulling him out. The people at the mouth of the den, who had listened with painful anxiety, hearing the growling of the wolf, and supposing their friend to be in the most imminent danger, drew him forth with such celerity that his shirt was stripped over his head, and his skin severely lacerated. After he had adjusted his clothes, and loaded his gun with nine buck-shot, holding a torch in one hand and the musket in the other, he descended the second time. When he drew nearer than before, the wolf, assuming a still more fierce and terrible appearance, howling, rolling her eyes, snapping her teeth, and dropping her head between her legs, was evidently in the attitude, and on the point of springing at him. At the critical instant he levelled and fired at her head. Stunned with the shock, and suffocated with the smoke, he immediately found himself drawn out of the cave. But, having refreshed himself, and permitted the smoke to dissipate, he went down the third time. Once more he came within sight of the wolf, who appearing very passive, he applied the torch to her nose; and perceiving her dead, he took hold of her ears, and then kicking the rope (still tied round his legs), the people above, with no small exultation, dragged them both out together . . .

Alexander Graydon has something to say about the gay rakes in the British army.

[ALEXANDER GRAYDON *was born in Bristol, Pennsylvania in 1752 and died in Philadelphia in 1818. This extract is from his* Memoirs of a Life Chiefly Passed in Pennsylvania, *1811.*]

. . . It was not alone by hostile alarms, that the good people of Philadelphia were annoyed. Their tranquillity had been likewise disturbed by the uncitizenlike conduct of a pair of British officers, who, for want of something better to do, had plunged themselves into an excess of intemperance; and in the plenitude of wine and hilarity, paraded the streets at all hours,
A la clarté de cieux dans l'ombre de la nuit,
to the no small terror of the sober and the timid. The firm of this duumxirate was Ogle and Friend, names always coupled together, like those of Castor and Pollux, or of Pylades ond Orestes. But the cement which connected them was scarcely so pure as that which had united those heroes of antiquity. It could hardly be called friendship, but was rather a confederacy in debauchery and riot, exemplified in a never-ending round of frolic and fun. It was related of Ogle, that upon hiring a servant he had stipulated with him that he should never get drunk but when his master was sober. But the fellow some time after requested his discharge, giving for his reason, that he had in truth no dislike to a social glass himself, but it had so happened, that the terms of the agreement had absolutely cut him off from any chance of ever indulging his propensity.

Many are the pranks I have heard ascribed, either conjointly or separately, to this *par nobile fratrum.* That of Ogle's first appearance in Philadelphia has been thus related to me by Mr. Will Richards, the apothecary, who, it is well known, was, from his size and manner, as fine a figure for Falstaff as the imagination can conceive. "One afternoon," said he, "an officer in full regimentals, booted and spurred, with a whip in his hand, spattered with mud from top to toe, and reeling under the effects of an overdose of liquor, made his entrance into the coffee-house, in a box of which I was sitting perusing a newspaper. He was probably under the impression that every man he was to meet would be a Quaker, and that a Quaker was no other than a licensed Simon Pure for his amusement: for no sooner had he entered, than throwing his arms around the neck of Mr. Joshua Fisher, with the exclamation of —'Ah, my dear Broadbrim, give me a kiss,' he began to slaver him most lovingly. As Joshua was a good deal embarrassed by the salutation, and wholly unable to parry the assault or shake off the fond intruder, I interfered in his behalf and effected a separation, when Ogle, turning to me, criedout, 'Ha! my jolly fellow, give me a smack of your fat chops,' and immediately fell to hugging and kissing me, as he had done Fisher. But instead of the coyness he had shown, I hugged and kissed in my turn as hard as I was able, until my weight at length brought Ogle to the floor and myself on top of him. Nevertheless, I kept kissing away, until nearly mashed and suffocated, he exclaimed, 'for heaven's sake let me up, let me up or you will smother me!' Having sufficiently tormented him and avenged Joshua Fisher, I permitted him to rise, when he seemed a good deal sobered, and finding that I was neither a Quaker nor wholly ignorant of the world, he evinced some respect for me, took a seat with me in a box, and, entering into conversation, soon discovered that, however he might be disguised by intoxication, he well knew what belonged to the character of a gentleman." "This," said Richards, "was the commencement of an acquaintance between us; and Captain Ogle sometimes called to see me, upon which occasions he always behaved with the utmost propriety and decorum."

This same coffee-house, the only one indeed in the city, was also the scene of another affray by Ogle and Friend in conjunction. I know not what particular acts of mischief they had been guilty of, but they were very drunk, and their conduct so extremely disquieting and insulting to the peaceable citizens there assembled, that being no longer able to endure it, it was judged expedient to commit them; and Mr. Chew, happening to be there, undertook, in virtue probably of his office of recorder, to write their commitment. But Ogle, facetiously jogging his elbow, and interrupting him with a repetition of the pitiful interjection of "Ah now, Mr. Chew!" he was driven from his gravity, and obliged to throw away the pen. It was then taken up by Alderman M——n with a determination to go through with the business, when the culprits reeling round him, and Ogle, in particular, hanging over his shoulder and reading after him as he wrote, at length with irresistible effect hit upon an unfortunate oversight of the alderman. "Ay," says he, "my father was a justice of peace too, but he did not spell that word as you do. I remember perfectly well, that instead of an *s* he always used to spell *circumstance* with a *c*." This sarcastic thrust at the scribe entirely turned the tide in favor of the rioters; and the company being disarmed of their resentment, the alderman had no disposition to provoke further criticism by going on with the *mittimus*.

The irregularities of these gay rakes were not more eccentric than diversified; and the more extravagant they could render them, the better. At one time they would drive full tilt through the streets in a chair; and upon one of these occasions, on approaching a boom which had been thrown across the street, in a part that was undergoing the operation of paving, they lashed forward their steed, and sousing against the spar with great violence, they were consequently hurled from their seats, like Don Quixote in his temerarious assault of the windmills. At another time, at Doctor Orme's, the apothecary, where Ogle lodged, they, in emulation of the same mad hero at the puppet show, laid about them with their canes upon the defencelsss bottles and phials, at the same time assaulting a diminutive Maryland parson, whom, in their frolic, they kicked from the street door to the kitchen. He was a fellow lodger of Ogle's; and, to make him some amends for the roughness of this usage, they shortly after took him drunk to the dancing assembly, where, through the instrumentality of this unworthy son of the Church, they contrived to excite a notable hubbub. Though they had escaped, as already mentioned, at the coffee-house, yet their repeated malfeasances had brought them within the notice of the civil authority; and they had more than once been in the clutches of the mayor of the city. This was Mr. S——, a small man of a squat, bandy-legged figure; and hence, by way of being revenged on him, they bribed a negro with a precisely similar pair of legs, to carry him a billet, which imported, that as the bearer had in vain searched the town for a pair of hose that might fit him, he now applied to his honor to be informed where he purchased *his* stockings.

I have been told that General Lee, when a captain in the British service, had got involved in this vortex of dissipation; and, although afterward so strenuous an advocate for the civil rights of the Americans, had been made to smart severely for their violation, by the mayor's court of Philadelphia.

The common observation, that when men become soldiers they lose the character and feelings of citizens, was amply illustrated by the general conduct of the British officers in America. Their studied contempt of the *mohairs,* by which term all those who were not in uniform were distinguished, was manifest on all occasions: and it is by no means improbable that the disgust then excited, might have more easily ripened into that harvest of discontent which subsequent injuries called forth, and which terminated in a subduction of allegiance from the parent land.

Nathaniel Ames dreamed of our times. If he had foreseen the reality of our "great cities" he would have had a nightmare.

A Prophecy for North America

[NATHANIEL AMES *was born in Bridgewater, Massachusetts in 1708 and died at Dedham, Massachusetts in 1764. He was well-known for his excellent Almanacs, and his predictions of eclipses. The following prophecy is from his Almanac of 1758.*]

Thirdly, of the future state of North America.—Here we find a vast stock of proper materials for the art and ingenuity of man to work upon:—Treasures of immense worth; concealed from the poor ignorant aboriginal natives! The curious have observed that the progress of human literature (like the sun) is from the east to the west; thus has it travelled through Asia and Europe, and now is arrived at the eastern shore of America.

As the celestial light of the Gospel was directed here by the finger of God, it will doubtless finally drive the long, long night of heathenish darkness from America. So arts and sciences will change the face of nature in their tour from hence over the Appalachian Mountains to the western ocean; and as they march through the vast desert, the residence of wild beasts will be broken up, and the obscene howl cease forever; instead of which the stones and trees will dance together in the music of Orpheus,—the rocks will disclose their hidden gems,—and the inestimable treasures of gold and silver be broken up. Huge mountains of iron ore are already discovered; and vast stores are reserved for future generations.

This metal, more useful than gold and silver, will employ millions of hands, not only to form the martial sword and peaceful share alternately, but an infinity of utensils improved in the exercise of art and handicraft among men. Nature through all her works has stamped authority on this law, namely, "That all fit matter shall be improved to its best purpose." Shall not then those vast quarries that teem with mechanic stone,—those for structure be piled into great cities,—and those for sculpture into statues to perpetuate the honor of renowned heroes; even those who shall now save their country? O! ye unborn inhabitants of America! should this page escape its destined conflagration at the year's end, and these alphabetical letters remain legible,—when your eyes behold the sun after he has rolled the seasons round for two or three centuries more, you will know that in Anno Domini 1758, we dreamed of your times.

Diaries and Personal Narratives

Sidelights on the Revolutionary War are given by two participants. Doctor Thacher's diary is valuable source material.

[*Dr.* JAMES THACHER *(1754–1844), a surgeon in the American Infantry, came from Barnstable on Cape Cod, Massachusetts. He kept a diary throughout his years of service. In the first extract from the diary in 1781, he describes the surrender of Cornwallis.*]

17th. The whole of our works are now mounted with cannon and mortars; not less than one hundred pieces of heavy ordnance have been in continual operation during the last twenty-four hours. The whole peninsula trembles under the incessant thunderings of our infernal machines; we have leveled some of their works in ruins, and silenced their guns; they have almost ceased firing. We are so near as to have a distinct view of the dreadful havoc and destruction of their works, and even see the men in their lines tore to pieces by the bursting of our shells. But the scene is drawing to a close. Lord Cornwallis, at length realizing the extreme hazard of his deplorable situation, and finding it in vain any longer to resist, has this forenoon come to the humiliating expedient of sending out a flag, requesting a cessation of hostilities for twenty-four hours, that commissioners may be appointed to prepare and adjust the terms of capitulation. Two or three flags passed in the course of the day, and General Washington consented to a cessation of hostilities for two hours only, that his lordship may suggest his proposals as a basis for a treaty, which being in part accepted, a suspension of hostilities will be continued till to-morrow.

18th. It is now ascertained that Lord Cornwallis, to avoid the necessity of a surrender, had determined on the bold attempt to make his escape in the night of the 16th, with a part of his army into the country. His plan was to leave sick and baggage behind, and to cross with his effective force over to Gloucester Point, there to destroy the French legion and other troops, and to mount his infantry on their horses and such others as might be procured, and thus push their way to New York by land. A more preposterous and desperate attempt can scarcely be imagined. Boats were secretly prepared, arrangements made, and a large proportion of his troops actually embarked and landed on Gloucester Point, when, from a moderate and calm evening, a most violent storm of wind and rain ensued. The boats with the remaining troops were all driven down the river, and it was not till the next day that his troops could be returned to the garrison at York.

[*In this second extract the surgeon describes the dramatic celebration of the birth of the French Dauphin at West Point. He gives the date as May 31, 1782, but according to the most recent history of West Point,* The River and the Rock *by David Richard Palmer, the event took place on June 10 of that year.*]

May 30th. Great preparations are making at West Point, to celebrate the birth of the young Dauphin of France; being in alliance with his Most Christian Majesty, propriety requires that we should celebrate the joyous event of the birth of his first son. His excellency General Washington has, in general orders, given an invitation to all officers of the army, and they are requested to invite any friends or acquaintance they may have in the country to participate in the grand festival.

June 1st. Yesterday was celebrated the birth of the Dauphin of France, by a magnificent festival. The edifice under which the company assembled and partook of the entertainment was erected on the plain at West Point. The situation was romantic, and the occasion novel and interesting. Major Villefranche, an ingenious French engineer, has been employed with one thousand men about ten days in constructing the curious edifice. It is composed of the simple materials which the common trees in this vicinity afford. It is about six hundred feet in length and thirty feet wide, supported by a grand colonnade of one hundred and eighteen pillars, made of the trunks of trees. The covering of the roof consists of boughs, or branches of trees curiously interwoven, and the same materials form the walls, leaving the ends entirely open. On the inside, every pillar was encircled with muskets and bayonets, bound round in a fanciful and handsome manner, and the whole interior was decorated with evergreens, with American and French military colors, and a variety of emblems and devices, all adjusted in such style as to beautify the whole interior of the fabric. This superb structure, in symmetry of proportion, neatness of workmanship, and elegance of arrangement, has seldom perhaps been surpassed on any temporary occasion; it affected the spectators with admiration and pleasure and reflects much credit on the taste and ability of Major Villefranche. Several appropriate mottos decorated the grand edifice, pronouncing benedictions on the Dauphin and happiness to the two allied nations. The whole army was paraded on the contiguous hills on both sides of the river, forming a circle of several miles in open view of the public edifice, and at the given signal of firing three cannon, the regimental officers all left their commands, and repaired to the building to partake of the entertainment which had been prepared by order of the commander-in-chief. At five o'clock, dinner being on the table, his excellency General Washington and lady and suite, the principal officers of the army and their ladies, Governor Clinton and his lady, and a number of respectable characters from the states of New York and New Jersey, moved from Major-General McDougall's quarters through the line formed by Colonel Crane's regiment of artillery to the arbor, where more than five hundred gentlemen and ladies partook of a magnificent festival. A martial band charmed our senses with music, while we feasted our appetites and gazed with admiration on the illustrious guests and the novel spectacle exhibited to our view. The cloth being removed, thirteen appropriate toasts were drank, each one being announced by the discharge of thirteen cannon and accompanied by music. The guests retired from the table at seven o'clock, and the regimental officers repaired to their respective commands. The arbor was, in the evening, illuminated by a vast number of lights, which being arranged in regular and tasteful order, exhibited a scene vieing in brilliancy with the starry firmament. The officers having rejoined their regiments, thirteen cannon were again fired as a prelude to a general *feu de joie,* which immediately succeeded throughout the whole line of the army on the surrounding hills; and being three times repeated, the mountains resounded and echoed like tremendous peals of thunder, and the flashing from thousands of fire-arms in the darkness of evening, could be compared only to the most vividflashes of lightning from the clouds. The *feu de joie* was immediately followed by three shouts of acclamation and benediction for the Dauphin, by the united voices of the whole army on all sides. At half-past eleven o'clock, the celebration was concluded by the exhibition of fire-works, very ingeniously constructed of various figures. His Excellency General Washington was unusually cheerful. He attended the ball in the evening, and with a dignified and graceful air, having Mrs. Knox for his partner, carried down a dance of twenty couples in the arbor on the green grass. . . .

June 23d. The officers of our regiment prepared an entertainment and invited a respectable party. At three o'clock we repaired to an arbor erected for the occasion, under which a long table was spread and a variety of dishes arranged in proper style; we prided ourselves on our camp dinner, as being almost on a par with that of a country gentlemen. A band of military music attended, and we finished with toasts and songs in social glee."

Private Hargrove of World War II and Private Martin of '76 had a few things in common.

[JOSEPH PLUMB MARTIN *was a young soldier in the revolutionary army. The following is excerpted from his war memoir,* A Narrative of Some of the Adventures, Dangers and Sufferings of a Revolutionary Soldier, *first published in 1830.*]

I remember the stir in the country occasioned by the stamp act, but I was so young that I did not understand the meaning of it; I likewise remember the disturbances that followed the repeal of the stamp act, until the destruction of the tea at Boston and elsewhere; I was then thirteen or fourteen years old, and began to understand something of the works going on. . . .

Time passed smoothly on with me till the year 1774 arrived, the smell of war began to be pretty strong, but I was determined to have no hand in it, happen when it might; I felt myself to be a real coward. What—venture my carcass where bullets fly! that will never do for me. Stay at home out of harm's way, thought I, it will be as much to your health as credit to do so. But the pinch of the game had not arrived yet; I had seen nothing of war affairs, and consequently was but a poor judge in such matters.

. . . The winter of this year passed off without any very frightening alarms, and the spring of 1775 arrived. Expectation of some fatal event seemed to fill the minds of most of the considerate people throughout the country. I was ploughing in the field about half a mile from home, about the twenty-first day of April, when all of a sudden the bells fell to ringing, and three guns were repeatedly fired in succession down in the village; what the cause was we could not conjecture. I had some fearful forbodings that something more than the sound of a carriage wheel was in the wind. I set off to see what the cause of the commotion was. I found most of the male kind of the people together; soldiers for Boston were in requisition. A dollar deposited upon the drum head was taken up by some one as soon as placed there, and the holder's name taken, and he enrolled, with orders to equip himself as quick as possible. My spirits began to revive at the sight of the money offered; the seeds of courage began to sprout. . . .

The men that had engaged "to go to war" went as far as the next town, where they received orders to return, as there was a sufficiency of men already engaged, so that I should have had but a short campaign had I gone.

During the winter of 1775–6, by hearing the conversation and disputes of the good old farmer politicians of the times, I collected pretty correct ideas of the contest between this country and the mother country, (as it was then called). I thought I was as warm a patriot as the best of them; the war was waged; we had joined issue, and it would not do to "put the hand to the plough and look back."

. . . I one evening went off with a full determination to enlist at all hazards. When I arrived at the place of rendezvous I found a number of young men of my acquaintance there; the old bantering began—come, if you will enlist I will, says one, you have long been talking about it, says another—come, now is the time. Thinks I to myself, I will not be laughed into it or out of it, at any rate; I will act my own pleasure arter all. But what did I come here for to-night? Why, to enlist; then enlist I will. So seating myself at the table, enlisting orders were immediately presented to me; I took up the pen, leaded it with the fatal charge, made several mimic imitations of writing my name, but took especial care not to touch the paper with the pen until an unlucky wight who was leaning over my shoulder gave my hand a stroke, which caused the pen to make a woeful scratch on the paper.

. . . I was now, what I had long wished to be, a soldier; I had obtained my heart's desire; it was now my business to prove myself equal to my profession. Well, to be short, I went, with several others of the company, on board a sloop, bound to New-York: arrived at New-York; marched up into the city, and joined the rest of the regiment that were already there. . . .

I was called out every morning at reveille beating, which was at daybreak, to go to our regimental parade, in Broad-street, and there practice the manual exercise, which was the most that was known in our new levies, if they knew even that. I was brought to an allowance of provisions, which while we lay in New-York was not bad: if there was any deficiency it could in some measure be supplied by procuring some kind of sauce; but I was a stranger to such living. . . .

Soon after my arrival at New-York, a forty-four gun ship (the Phoenix), and a small frigate (the Rose, I think) came down the North or Hudson River (they had been sometime in the river), and passed the city in fine stile [sic], amidst a cannonade from all our fortifications, in and near the city. I went into what was then called the grand battery, where I had a complete view of the whole affair. Here I first heard the muttering of cannon shot, but they did not disturb my feelings so much as I apprehended they would before I had heard them; I rather thought the sound was musical, or at least grand. . . .

. . . I was stationed in Stone-street, near the southwest angle of the city; directly opposite to my quarters was a wine cellar, there were in the cellar at this time, several pipes of Madeira wine. By some means the soldiers had "smelt it out." Some of them had, at mid-day, taken the iron grating from a window in the back yard, and one had entered the cellar, and by means of a powder-horn divested of its bottom, had supplied himself, with wine, and was helping his comrades, through the window, with a "delicious draught," when the owner of the wine, having discovered what they were about, very wisely, as it seemed, came into the street and opened an outer door to the cellar in open view of every passenger; the soldiers quickly filled the cellar, when he, to save his property, proposed to sell it, at what he called a cheap rate, I think a dollar a gallon. In one corner of the cellar lay a large pile of oil flasks, holding from half a gallon to a gallon each, they were empty and not very savory neither, as they had lain there till the oil which adhered to the sides and bottoms had become quite rancid. While the owner was drawing for his purchasers on one side of the cellar, behind him on the other side, another set of purchasers were drawing for themselves, filling those flasks. As it appeared to have a brisk sale, especially in the latter case, I concluded I would take a flask amongst the rest, which, I accordingly did, and conveyed it in safety to my room, and went back into the street to see the end. The owner of the wine soon found out what was going forward on his premises, and began remonstrating, but he preached to the wind; finding that he could effect nothing, with them, he went to Gen. Putnam's quarters, which was not more than three or four rods off; the General immediately repaired in person to the field of action; the soldiers getting wind of his approach hurried out into the street, when he, mounting himself upon the doorsteps of my quarters, began "harangueing the multitude," threatening to hang every mother's son of them. Whether he was to be the hangman or not, he did not say; but I took every word he said for gospel, and expected nothing else but to be hanged before the morrow night. I sincerely wished him hanged and out of the way, for fixing himself upon the steps of our door; but he soon ended his discourse, and came down from his rostrum, and the soldiers dispersed, no doubt much edified. I got home as soon as the General had left the coast clear, took a draught of the wine, and then flung the flask and the remainder of the wine out of my window, from the third story, into the water cistern in the back yard, where it remains to this day for aught I know. . . .

I remained in New-York two or three months . . . in the latter part of the month of August, I was ordered upon a fatigue party; we had scarcely reached the grand parade, when I saw our sergeant-major directing his course up Broadway, towards us, in rather an unusual step for him; he soon arrived and informed us, and then the commanding officer of the party, that he had orders to take off all belonging to our regiment and march us to our quarters, as the regiment was ordered to Long-Island, the British having landed in force there. We were soon ordered to our regimental parade, from which, as soon as the regiment was formed, we were marched off for the ferry. At the lower end of the street were placed several casks of sea-bread, made, I believe, of canel and peas-meal, nearly hard enough for musket flints; the casks were unheaded and each man was allowed to take as many as he could, as he marched by. As my good luck would have it, there was a momentary halt made; I improved the opportunity thus offered me, as every good soldier should upon all important occasions, to get as many of the biscuits as I possibly could; no one said any thing to me, and I filled my bosom, and took as many as I could hold in my hand, a dozen or more in all, and when we arrived at the ferry-stairs I stowed them away in my knapsack. We quickly embarked on board the boats; as each boat started, three cheers were given by those on board, which was returned by the numerous spectators who thronged the wharves; they all wished us good luck, apparently; although it was with most of them, perhaps, nothing more than ceremony. We soon landed at Brooklyn, upon the Island, marched up the ascent from the ferry, to the plain. We now began to meet the wounded men, another sight I was unacquainted with, some with broken arms, some with broken legs, and some with broken heads. The sight of these a little daunted me, and made me think of home, but the sight and thought vanished together. We marched a short distance, when we halted to refresh ourselves. Whether we had any other victuals besides the hard bread I do not remember, but I remember my gnawing at them. . . . One of the soldiers complaining of thirst to his officer; look at that man, said he, pointing to me, he is not thirsty, I will warrant it. I felt a little elevated to be stiled [sic] a man. While resting here, which was not more than twenty minutes or half an hour, the Americans and British were warmly engaged within sight of us. . . .

The officers of the new levies wore cockades of different colours to distinguish them from the standing forces, as they were called; the field officers wore red, the captains white, and the subaltern officers green. While we were resting here our Lieutenant-Colonel and Major, (our Colonel not being with us), took their cockades from their hats; being asked the reason, the Lieutenant-Colonel replied, that he was willing to risk his life in the cause of his country, but was unwilling to stand a particular mark for the enemy to fire at. He was a fine officer and a brave soldier.

We were soon called upon to fall in and proceed. We had not gone far, about half a mile, when I heard one in the rear ask another where his musket was; I looked round and saw one of the soldiers stemming off without his gun, having left it where we last halted; he was inspecting his side as if undetermined whether he had it or not, he then fell out of the ranks to go in search of it: one of the company, who had brought it on (wishing to see how far he would go before he missed it) gave it to him. The reader will naturally enough conclude that he was a brave soldier. Well, he was a brave fellow for all this accident, and received two severe wounds, by musket balls, while fearlessly fighting for his country at the battle of White Plains. . . .

CAMPAIGN OF 1777

The spring of 1777 arrived; I had got recruited during the winter, and began to think again about the army. In the month of April, as the weather warmed, the young men began to enlist.

As I had time to reflect, I began sorely to repent. The next day I met the sergeant and told him that I repented my bargain; he endeavored to persuade me to stick to it, but I could then say—No—He told me that he would speak to his Captain about the matter, and as I had taken no bounty money, he thought that he would dismiss me.

The inhabitants of the town were about this time put into what were called squads, according to their rateable property. Of some of the most opulent, one formed a squad,—of others, two or three, and of the lower sort of the people, several formed a squad. Each of these squads were to furnish a man for the army, either by hiring or by sending one of their own number.

I had an elbow relation, a sort of (as the Irishman said) cousin-in-law, who had been in the army the two preceding campaigns, and now had a Lieutenant's commission in the standing army. He was continually urging my grandparents to give their consent for me to go with him. He told the old gentleman a power of fine stories and made him promises, respecting his behaviour to me, which he never intended to perform, until he obtained my grandsire's consent, and at length, after much persuasion, my consent likewise.

One of the above-mentioned squads, wanting to procure a man, the Lieutenant told them that he thought they might persuade me to go for them, and they accorly [sic] attacked me, front rear and flank. I thought, as I must go, I might as well endeavour to get as much for my skin as I could;— accordingly, I told them that I would go for them and fixed upon a day when I would meet them and clinch the bargain. The day, which was a muster-day of the militia of the town, arrived;—I went to the parade, where all was liveliness, as it generally is upon such occasions; but poor I felt miserably; my execution-day was come. I kept wandering about till the afternoon, among the crowd, when I saw the Lieutenant, who went with me into a house where the men of the squad were, and there I put my name to enlisting indentures for the last time. And now I was hampered again. The men gave me what they agreed to, I forgot the sum, perhaps enough to keep the blood circulating during the short space of time which I tarried at home after I had enlisted. They were now freed from any further trouble, at least for the present, and I had become the scape-goat for them.

. . . Our troops, not long after this, marched to join the main army in Pennsylvania. . . .

We . . . crossed the Delaware . . . between Burlington and Bristol. Here we procured a day's ration of southern salt pork . . . and a pound of sea bread. We marched a little distance and stopped "to refresh ourselves," we kindled some fires in the road, and some broiled their meat; as for myself, I ate mine raw. We quickly started on and marched till evening, when we went into a wood for the night. We did not pitch our tents; and about midnight it began to rain very hard which soon put out all our fires, and we had to lie and "weather it out." The troops marched again before day; I had sadly sprained my ankle the day before, and it was much swelled. My lieutenant told me to stay where I was until day and then come on. Just as I was about to start off, our Brigadier General and suite passed by and seeing me there alone, stopped his horse and asked what I did there, I told him that Lieutenant S. ordered me to remain there till daylight. Says he, Lieutenant S.——deserves to have his throat cut, and then went on. . . . I hobbled on as well as I could.

. . . we joined the grand army near Philadelphia, and the heavy baggage being sent back to the rear of the army, we were obliged to put us up huts by laying up poles and covering them with leaves; a capital shelter from winter storms. . . .

About this time the whole British army left the city, came out, and encamped, or rather lay, on Chesnut-hill in our immediate neighborhood; we hourly expected an attack from them; we had a commanding position and were very sensible of it. We were kept constantly on the alert, and wished nothing more than to have them engage us, for we were sure of giving them a drubbing, being in excellent fighting trim, as we were starved and as cross and ill-natured as curs. The British, however, thought better of the matter, and after several days manoeuvering on the hill, very civilly walked off into Philadelphia again.

Starvation seemed to be entailed upon the army and every animal connected with it. The oxen, brought from New-England for draught, all died, and the southern horses fared no better; even the wild animals that had any concern with us, suffered. . . .

. . . The army was now not only starved but naked; the greatest part were not only shirtless and barefoot, but destitute of all other clothing, especially blankets. I procured a small piece of raw cowhide and made myself a pair of moccasons [sic], which kept my feet (while they lasted) from the frozen ground, although, as I well remember, the hard edges so galled my ancles [sic], while on a march, that it was with much difficulty and pain that I could wear them afterwards; but the only alternative I had, was to endure this inconvenience or to go barefoot, as hundreds of my companions had to, till they might be tracked by their blood upon the rough frozen ground. But hunger, nakedness and sore shins were not the only difficulties we had at the time to encounter;—we had hard duty to perform and little or no strength to perform it with.

The army continued at or near the Gulf for some days, after which we marched for the Valley Forge in order to take up our winter-quarters. . . .

CAMPAIGN OF 1778

. . . We left our winter cantonments, crossed the Schuylkill and encamped on the left bank of that river, just opposite to our winter-quarters. We had lain there but a few days when we heard that the British army had left Philadelphia and were proceeding to New-York through the Jerseys. We marched immediately in pursuit. . . .

It was extremely hot weather, and the sandy plains of that part of New-Jersey did not cool the air to any great degree, but we still kept close to the rear of the British army; deserters were coming over hourly to us, but of stragglers we took only a few. . . .

. . . The following circumstance gave me cause to laugh as well as all the rest who heard it. We halted in a wood for a few minutes in the heat of the day, on the ascent of a hill, and were lolling on the sides of the road, when there passed two old men, both upon one horse that looked as if the crows had bespoken him. I did not know but Sancho Panza had lost his Dapple and was mounted behind Don Quixote upon Rosinante and bound upon some adventure with the British. However, they had not long been gone past us before another, about the same age and complexion, came stemming by on foot. Just as he had arrived where I was sitting, he stopped short, and looking toward the soldiers, said, "Did you see two old horses riding a Dutchman this road up?—Hoh!" The soldiers set up a laugh, as well as they might, and the poor old Dutchman finding he had gone "dail foremost" in his question, made the best of his way off out of hearing of us. We this night turned into a new ploughed field, and I laid down between two furrows and slept as sweet as though I had lain upon a bed of down. . . .

CAMPAIGN OF 1779

. . . About the middle of this month (December) we crossed the Hudson, at King's ferry, and proceeded into New-Jersey, for winter-quarters. . . .

. . . Our destination was at a place in New-Jersey, called Baskinridge. It was cold and snowy, we had to march all day through the snow and at night take up our lodgings in some wood, where, after shovelling away the snow, we used to pitch three or four tents facing each other, and then join in making a fire in the centre. Sometimes we could procure an armful of buckwheat straw to lie upon, which was deemed a luxury. Provisions, as usual, took up but a small part of our time, though much of our thoughts.

We arrived on our wintering ground in the latter part of the month of December, and once more, like the wild animals, began to make preparations to build us a "city for habitation." The soldiers, when immediately going about the building of their winter huts, would always endeavour to provide themselves with such tools as were necessary for the business (it is no concern of the reader's, as I conceive, by what means they procured their tools), such as crosscut-saws, handsaws, frows, augers, &c. to expedite the erection and completion of their dwelling-places. . . .

CAMPAIGN OF 1780

The winter of 1779 and '80 was very severe; it has been denominated "the hard winter," and hard it was to the army in particular, in more respects than one. The period of the revolution has repeatedly been styled "the times that tried men's souls." I often found that those times not only tried men's soul's [sic], but their bodies too; I know they did mine, and that effectually.

Sometime in the month of January there happened a spell of remarkably cold weather; in the height of the cold, a large detachmene from the army was sent off on an expedition against some fortifications held by the British on Staten Island. The detachment was commanded by Major-General John Sullivan. It was supposed by our officers that the bay before New-York was frozen sufficiently to prevent any succours being sent to the garrisons in their woods. It was therefore determined to endeavour to surprise them and get possession of their fortifications before they could obtain help. Accordingly, our troops were all conveyed in sleighs and other carriages; but the enemy got intelligence of our approach (doubtless by some tory) before our arrival on the island. When we arrived we found Johnny Bull prepared for our reception; he was always complaisant, especially when his own honour or credit was concerned; we accordingly found them all waiting for us—so that we could not surprise them. . . .

CAMPAIGN OF 1782

The arm of British power in America being dislocated by the capture of Lord Cornwallis and his myrmidons, we had not much to disturb us on account of the enemy; I fared rather better than I did when I was here on my journey to Mud Island in 1777. Our duty was not very hard, but I was a soldier yet, and had to submit to soldier's rules and discipline, and soldier's fare.

Either here, or just before, our officers had enlisted a recruit; he had lately been discharged from the New-Jersey line. After enlisting with us, he obtained a furlough to visit his friends; but receiving no money when he engaged with us (which was, I believe, the sole motive of his entering the service at this time) and obtaining his ends in getting home, he took especial care to keep himself there; at least, till he could get another opportunity to try his luck again, which he accordingly did, by enlisting in a corps of new levies in his own State—New-Jersey. My Captain hearing where he was, and how engaged, sent me with two men to find him out, and bring him back to his duty. . . .

. . . One of our Captains and another of our men being about going that way on furlough, I and my two men set off with them. We received, that day, two or three rations of fresh pork and hard bread. We had no cause to call this pork "carrion," or "hogmeat," for, on the contrary, it was so fat, and being entirely fresh, we could not eat it at all. The first night of our expedition, we boiled our meat; and I asked the landlady for a little sauce, she told me to go to the garden and take as much cabbage as I pleased, and that, boiled with the meat, was all we could eat. The next morning we proceeded; it was cool weather, and about six inches deep of snow on the ground. After two or three days journeying, we arrived in the neighbourhood of the game that we were in pursuit of. It was now sundown; and our furloughed Captain and man, concluded to stop for the night; here we fell in with some soldiers of the corps that our man belonged to. Our captain inquired if they knew such a man, naming him; they equivocated and asked many questions concerning our business. Our officious Captain answered them so much to their satisfaction that Mr. Deserter took so good care of himself that I could not find him, and I cared but little about it. I knew he would get nothing with us, if we caught him, but a striped jacket; and as we concluded the war was nearly ended, we thought it would be of little service to him, nor his company any to us.

The Captain put me and my two men into the open cold kitchen of a house that they said, had sometime or other, been a tavern; but as it was in the vicinity of the place where I passed the winter of 1779–80, I was acquainted with several of the inhabitants in the neighbourhood, and accordingly sent one of my men to a house hard by, the master of which I knew to be a fine man, and obtained his leave to lodge there. We had a good warm room to sit and lodge in, and as the next day was thanksgiving, we had an excellent supper. In the morning, when we were about to proceed on our journey, the man of the house came into the room and put some bread to the fire to toast; he next produced some cider, as good and rich as wine, then giving each of us a large slice of his toasted bread, he told us to eat it and drink the cider, —observing that he had done so for a number of years and found it the best stimulater [sic] imaginable. We again prepared to go on, having given up the idea of finding the deserter. Our landlord then told us that we must not leave his house till we had taken breakfast with him; we thought we were very well dealt by already, but concluded not to refuse a good offer. We therefore staid [sic] and had a genuine New-Jersey breakfast, consisting of buckwheat slapjacks, flowing with butter and honey, and a capital dish of chockolate [sic]. We then went on, determined not to hurry ourselves, so long as the thanksgiving lasted.

91

We found a good dinner at a farmer's house; but I thought that both the good man and his lady looked at us as if they would have been as well pleased with our room as our company; however, we got our dinners and that was quite sufficient for us. At night we applied for lodging at a house near the road; there appeared to be none but females in the house, two matronly ladies and two misses. One of the women said she would have no objection to our staying there through the night, were it not that a woman in the house was then lying at the point of death (I had often heard this excuse made before); we readily perceived her drift, and, when turning to go away, one of the men told her that he did not wish to stay, "for," said he, "if old Corpus should chance to come in the dark, for the sick woman, he might in his haste mistake and take me." The woman smiled and we went on. . . .

In the month of September, while we lay here [opposite West Point] and our tents were pitched about promiscuously, by reason of the ruggedness of the ground, our Captain had pitched his marquee in an old gravel pit, at some distance from the tents of the men. One day, two or three of our young hotheads told me that they and some others of the men, whom they mentioned, were about to have some fun with "the old man," as they generally called the Captain. I inquired what their plans were, and they informed me that they had put some powder into a canteen and were going to give him a bit of a hoist. I asked them to let me see their apparatus, before they put their project in execution; accordingly, they soon showed me a wooden canteen with more, as I judged, than three pounds of gunpowder in it, with a stopper of touch-wood for a fuze [sic], affixed to it, all, they said, in prime order. I told them they were crazy, that the powder they had in the canteen would 'hoist' him out of time; but they insisted upon proceeding,—it would only frighten him, they said, and that was all they wished to do,—it would make him a little more complaisant. I then told them that if they persisted in their determination and would not promise me on the spot to give up their scheme, I would that instant go to the Captain and lay the whole affair before him. At length, after endeavouring, without effect, to obtain my consent to try a little under his berth, they concluded to give up the affair altogether; and thus, I verily believe, I saved the old man's life; although I do not think they meant any thing more than to frighten him.

CAMPAIGN OF 1783

The winter set in rather early for that part of the country, and not over gentle. We had a quarters guard and a magazine guard to keep; the magazine was situated on one of the highest hills, or rather ledges, on the island. In a cold northeast snow storm it would make a sentry shake his ears to stand two hours before the magazine. We likewise kept a small guard to protect the slaughter-house, about half the winter, the Invalids kept it the other half. All this made the duty of our little corps (of less than seventy men) rather hard. . . . .

. . . . Some time in the latter part of the month of February, our officers were about to send off some men to Newburgh, ten or twelve miles up the river, to bring down some clothing. As the ice in the river had not been broken up (although it began to be thin and rotten), several of the non-commissioned officers solicited the job for the sake of a frolic. We readily obtained permission, and seven or eight of us set off in the morning on the ice, with a large hand-sled to bring the clothing upon. About a mile and a half above West Point there was a large rent in the ice, quite across the river, in some places not more than a foot or two wide, in others, eight or ten. We crossed this place very easily, and went on, when we met an officer coming down the river, picking his way among the holes in the ice. He asked us, what troops we belonged to. We told him. He bid us be careful, for, said he, "you are too good looking men to be drowned." We thanked him for his compliment, and passed on. . . . When we came to New-Windsor, about three or four miles below Newburgh, we conceited we were growing thirsty. We concluded, thereupon, to go on shore and get something to make us breathe freer. We could not get any thing but cider, but that was almost as good and as strong as wine. We drank pretty freely of that, and set off again. It was now nearly sun down, and we had about seven miles to travel. Just before we had arrived at the before mentioned rent in the ice, we overtook a sleigh drawn by two horses and owned by a countryman that I was acquainted with. He had in his sleigh a hogshead of rum, belonging to a suttler on West Point. There were two or three other citizens with him, one of whom was, to appearance, sixty or seventy years of age. When we arrived at the chasm in the ice, the teamster untackled his horses in order to jump them over, and we stopped to see the operation performed. He forced them both over at once; and when they struck the ice on the other side, they both went through breaking the ice for a rod round. The poor man was in a pitiful taking: he cried like a child. Some of our party told him to choke them out. He had but little faith in the plan; we, however, soon got his leading reins, which happened to be strong new cords, and fixed one round each of the horse's necks, with a slip noose. They did not require much pulling before they both sprang out upon the ice together. The owner's tune now turned; he was as joyful as he had been sad before. The next thing was, to get the sleigh and rum over. We got it to a narrow spot in the chasm, and all hands taking hold, we ran it over; but when the hinder ends of the sleigh-runners came near the edge of the ice, they, with their own weight, broke the ice as bad as the horses had done before. The sleigh arrived safe on the other side, but we were, mostly, upon the broken floating ice; but by the aid of Providence, we all survived the accident. The old man that I mentioned, happened to be on the same fragment of ice with me; when I had stepped off, I saw him on the edge of the piece, settling down gradually in the water, without making the least exertion to help himself. I seized him by the shoulder, and at one flirt, flung him upon the solid ice. He appeared as light as a bag of feathers. He was very thankful, and said I had saved his life; and I am not quite sure that I did not. After we had got matters regulated again, we must take a sip of their rum with them. They soon got the bung from the hogshead, the only way they had in their power to get at the good creature. We each took a hearty pull at it, for soldiers are seldom backward in such cases. The rum soon began to associate with the cider, and between them, they contrived to cut some queer capers amongst us; for we had not gone far, before one of our corporals hauled up, or rather upset. We laid him upon the sled, and hauled him to the wharf at West Point, where we landed. There was a sentry on the wharf, and as we had to go some distance to deliver the clothing to our commanding officer, we left our disabled corporal in the care of the sentry, with a strict charge not to let him stir from the place, for fear that he might blunder off the wharf and break his neck on the ice. We were gone an hour or more. When we returned we found the poor prisoner in a terrible chafe with the sentinel for detaining him, for the guard had been true to his trust. We then released him from his confinement, and he walked with us as well as he could, across the river, to our barracks, where, during the night, he settled his head. If the reader says there was no "suffering of a Revolutionary Soldier" in this affair; I say, perhaps there was not; but there was an 'adventure'. . . .

. . . Time thus passed on to the nineteenth of April, when we had general orders read which satisfied the most skeptical, that the war was over, and the prize won for which we had been contending through eight tedious years. But the soldiers said but very little about it, their chief thoughts were more closely fixed upon their situation as it respected the figure they were to exhibit upon leaving the army and becoming citizens. Starved, ragged and meagre, not a cent to help themselves with, and no means or method in view to remedy or alleviate their condition; this was appaling [*sic*] in the extreme. All that they could do, was to make a virtue of necessity and face the threatening evils with the same resolution and fortitude that they had for so long a time faced the enemy in the field.

. . . . At length the eleventh day of June, 1783, arrived. "The old man," our Captain came into our room, with his hands full of papers, and first ordered us to empty all our cartridge boxes upon the floor (this was the last order he ever gave us) and then told us that if we needed them, we might take some of them again; they were all immediately gathered up and returned to our boxes. Government had given us our arms, and we considered the ammunition as belonging to them, and he had neither right nor orders to take them from us. He then handed us our discharges, or rather furloughs, for they were in appearance no other than furloughs, permission to return home, but, to return to the army again, if required. This was policy in government; to discharge us absolutely in our present pitiful forlorn condition, it was feared, might cause some difficulties, which might be too hard for government to get easily over.

The powder in our cartridges was soon burnt. Some saluted the officers with large charges, others only squibbed them, just as each one's mind was affected toward them. Our "old man" had a number of these last mentioned symbols of honour and affection, presented him. Some of the men were not half so liberal in the use of powder as they were when they would have given him a canteen full at once. . . .

93

The Remembrancer of Christopher Marshall

[CHRISTOPHER MARSHALL's *Diary,* or *Remembrancer, covers the years 1774–1781 inclusive. Marshall retired from his successful business as a druggist prior to the start of the war. With ample time for leisure he held various positions of responsibility during the war years. He was on friendly and confidential terms with many leading men in the Continental Congress and the new government of Pennsylvania. Because of his active role on the side of the Whigs during the war, Marshall was cut off from the Society of Friends. He believed that the members of the Society who actively supported Britain departed as much from the doctrine and discipline of the Society as he had! What makes Marshall's Diary particularly interesting is the inclusion of references to simple day-by-day activities that continue throughout the war years. The extracts that follow are in chronological order:*]

1774

January 9th. Very little news has transpired this week, except an observation on the conduct of Bostonians. See Pennsylvainia Journal, No. 1623. * *

18th. Sundry resolves were passed by our Assembly respecting the riots in the county of Northumberland; also, some resolutions were laid before the House from Maryland.

20th. This day was published a scheme for a Society of Innoculating for the Small Pox.

March 23d. Account of [the] destruction of tea in Boston reached London about [the] 20th of January, and our tea ship sent back arrived at Dover the 25th same month. . . .

June 8th. Cloudy weather, and so continued all day. I rose before five, breakfasted, and went on the commons past seven. Came back past nine: then by ten went again and staid till past two, viewing the parade of the three battalions [of] militia of the City and Liberties, with the artillery company, (with two twelve-pounders and four six-pound brass field pieces), a troop of light horse, several companies of light infantry, rangers, and riflemen, in the whole, above two thousand men, who joined in one brigade, and went through their manual exercises, firings, and maneuvres, & c. & c., in the presence of General Lee, the Continental Congress, and several thousand spectators, then all marched into town to the Coffee House.

1775

July 2d. * * Afternoon, two o'clock, an alarm spread of a man of war, full of troops, seen at Bambay Hook, coming up. This alarmed the City, but it proved to be a false report. * *

7th. * * To Grace Hastings'; stayed there till church was done, there being a sermon preached at Christ Church to the First Battalion of the City Militia, by Jacob Duche.

9th. * * It is said that some day last week, there was a meeting of the Quakers in this city, wherein it was agreed that a collection should be set afoot in that society, for the relief of the necessitous of all religious denominations in New England who are reduced to losses and distresses in this time of public calamity, to be distributed among them by a committee of their brethren in New England, and to this, it is said, they recommended to their brethren in their several meetings in New Jersey, to subscribe for [the] said purpose. In the evening came Colonel Dyer [Silas] Deane, and [John] Jay, three of the delegates, * * * who all stayed and supped, and spent the evening very agreeably, till near ten o'clock, it being a fine serene night. . . .

July 14th. * * The many and various accounts of the slain at Bunker's Hill reconciled, by an account of the return made to General Washington on the fourth instant—of the Provincials, viz., one hundred and thirty-eight killed, three thousand and one wounded, and seven missing, and the best account he had received of the regulars was, that eight hundred were killed, and seven hundred wounded.

16th. * * After two, Charles and his wife, and daughter Betsey, came in the chair; just stopped and bid us farewell. They were going to Bristol, to try the water on account of son Charles's health. * * * After they were gone, Samuel and John Adams, two of the delegates, came; stayed some time.

17th. * * Stayed at home till near six; took a walk to the College yard, to see the Dutch butcher ask pardon of one of the companies for speaking disrespectfully of their proceedings. * *

July 20th. * * This being the memorable day in which an unjust and cruel ministry took away all our sea trade, as far as their inveterate malice could reach: the morning was pleasant; fine sunshine, yet cool and agreeable weather, although a melancholy appearance presented, as all the houses and shops in our neighborhood were shut, and to appearance more still than a First Day produced, as there was no riding abroad visiting, as is generally on First Day.

* * * Most families attended divine worship in the different churches and meeting houses of this city. I went to Christ Church, where an excellent sermon was preached on the occasion, from Psalm—, unto a large and crowed auditory, amongst whom were, I presume, all the delegates. It was an awful meeting, as numbers of wet eyes demonstrated their attention. * * * This afternoon, Robert Taylor called at my house, who said there was nigh two hundred of their militia came up this morning from their parts to church, in their uniforms, as he was. He is a lieutenant.

24th. * * Accounts are that on the eighth instant, two hundred volunteers, from the Rhode Island and Massachusetts forces, had burnt and destroyed the regulars' guard-house . . . this done without [the] loss of one of our men. This was an advanced post, and gave the regulars an opportunity of discovering our operations at Roxbury. On the eleventh instant, a party of men from the Roxbury Camp went to Long Island, in Boston harbour, and brought off fifteen of the regular prisoners, between twenty and thirty horned cattle, and about one hundred sheep. The prisoners were sent from the headquarters yesterday, to Concord. The same account says that General Gage's Troops are much dispirited, that they are very sickly, and are heartily disposed to leave off dancing any more to the tune of Yankee Doodle, and that General Gage had sent many reputable housekeepers in Boston, to prison, for refusing to work a day's work on board of the men of war, and the fortifications.

July 25th. * * Account was brought last night, that a vessel from Hispaniola had brought and landed, for our use, seven tons of gunpowder, being about one hundred and thirty casks; put under the care of the Committee of Safety. * *

26th. * * It's said that a person was sent to prison this forenoon, for attempting to spike the guns in the State House Yard. Account is arrived from Georgia that the people there, hearing of a parcel of gunpowder's being on board a ship just arrived from London, went, landed and secured it for their own use. It's said that it amounted to thirteen thousand pounds, and that the Georgians have appointed delegates to attend the Continental Congress, and [who] are daily expected. A gentleman who got off [from] Boston, July 10th, says that the inhabitants were numbered, and amounted to six thousand five hundred and seventy-three—soldiers, women and children. Three hundred Tories are chosen to patrol the Spring Mill; that last Second Day a heavy firing was heard, which by report, was an engagement in the Jerseys between our forces there and the enemy, but was not decided as both maintained their ground in order to renew the fight next morning, * * * that our out-scouts near Fair Hill, had attacked and driven the enemy's pickets into the City; waited in hopes they would have been succoured, and so have brought on a general engagement, as our army was ready to have engaged, had the enemy come out, but they contented themselves with remaining in their lines.

November 30th. * * This morning James Young, Esq., set out for camp, on a commission from the President and Council, he, with Col. Bayard, being appointed to enquire into the complaints made that the troops of this State are in a ragged condition, while the other troops are well equipped; also to see sundry clothes distributed amongst them that are in real want, from a parcel now collecting in this county, some of which are sent and more going, and also to make a true report to Council of the state of our army, and of the reasons of the complaints made respecting the scarcity of provisions. * *

December 2nd. * * Yesterday were read in Council, the Thirteen Articles of Confederation and Perpetual Union of the United States; also a letter from Robert Morris to the President and Council, requesting the enlargement of John Brown, and proposing to be his security in any sum that they should require. The same was put to vote, and carried unanimously that he should still be retained a prisoner. * *

3rd. * * Gen. Howe left Philadelphia [on the] Fourth instant at eleven at night, with his army, consisting of ten thousand men, marched towards Germantown, attacked and drove [in] our picket guard, which being reinforced, returned, drove their advanced guard back, killed near twenty, amongst which, a Brigadier General, Captain, &c; took sixteen prisoners; that we lost Gen. Irvin, who was wounded and taken prisoner, one Colonel, one Captain, twelve or fourteen privates killed, and maintained our post that night; that next day a general engagement, it was thought, was unavoidable, as the two armies lay in sight of each other; and that the enemy had burnt Beggar's town in their front. . . .

December 4th. * * After dinner I carried a few lines written to the Speaker of the House of Assembly, signifying my intentions of resigning my seat in the Committee of Safety. Now the doing [of] this arose from an information R. Whitehill gave me at dinner, that the House in his absence this forenoon had passed a Resolve that they would desire the President and Council immediately to dissolve the Council of Safety. This was what induced me to take the start of them, and decline in time. * *

5th. * * Baron De Holtzendorff's Aide-de-Camp; come from camp, but brought no news except that he thought that our troops were to go soon into winter quarters. * * * The beginning of this week, three Delegates, viz: [Elbridge] Gerry, Jones and Robert Morris, set out by order of Congress to head-quarters, in order to consult only with Gen. Washington, on the present critical affairs of the army, the commissaries and other officers, &c.

6th. * * Visited early by Col. Roberdeau. Stayed in solid conversation till past ten. Gave him Seventeen hundred and five Dollars, left me by my sons Christopher and Charles, in order to get them changed by Congress, if suitable and convenient, for the same number of Dollars, these having been defaced by lying in a damp place, which entirely took away all the names and numbers that were done with red ink. . . .

December 8th. * * Then came Norton Pryor, who brought a letter from son Charles, giving account * * * that both armies were in sight of each other, Howe's occupying Germantown, and Washington's Chestnut Hill, Whitemarsh, &c. (He and horse stayed all night, as he, after trial, could find no entertainment in the town.) Spent the evening in conversation respecting the difficulties attending our friends in and about Philadelphia, till near ten.

December 10th. * * Yesterday, about noon, came into town, from the Northward, about four hundred soldiers of the Regiment of Col. ———, in order to be innoculated for the small pox; went into barracks. They brought with them, it's said, about one hundred English prisoners that had been taken at different times. * *

11th. * * News of the day, it's said, is that Gen. Howe, after giving out in Philada. that he was going with his army to drive Gen. Washington and his army over the Blue Mountains, after marching his whole army up to Chestnut Hill and staying there some days, last First Day night decamped and returned to Philada. on the Second Day, leaving behind him about two hundred of his men, in slain and taken prisoners. It's said they have pillaged and carried with them every thing that came in their way that was portable and of any value, besides burning [and] destroying many houses and effects, also taking with them, by force, all the boys they could lay their hands on, above the age of ten years. Thus, this time, has the great boaster succeeded in this vainglorious expedition, to the eternal shame of him and of all his boasting Tory friends. It's said that last week, Joseph Galloway was proclaimed in Philada. Governor of this Province, by the knot of Tories there; that John Hall, cooper, is to be tried for his life for cursing George the Third, as is Robert Riché for writing to Gen. Washington, (some say it was to Riché's wife) giving them an account of the fortifying of the City, &c.

Our Founding Fathers had plenty of monetary problems. There was never enough. Continental money, like the current dollar, had to be depreciated.

By some letters intercepted, there appears to be a combination between the Friends sent into Virginia by the President and Council and some inhabitants of Lancaster, in order to depreciate the Continental currency. . . . This discovery has obliged the Board of War to send all the Quaker prisoners to Staunton in Augusta County, and Owen Jones to close confinement, without the use of pen, ink and paper, except in presence of the Lieutenant of the County or his deputy, and the other Friends to the same restriction, unless they take an affirmation that they will neither act, speak, nor write any thing that is against the Independancy of the United States of America. . . .

12th. * * News of the day is that Gen. Howe is come out again from Philadelphia, with his army; crossed [the] Schuylkill at Middle Ferry, marched up Lancaster Road to the Sorrel Horse, thirteen miles from the City, and there rested yesterday.

December 13th. * * Some people pretended to have heard a firing of cannon this morning. * * * This is a strange age and place, in which I now dwell, because nothing can be had cheap but lies, falsehood, and slanderous accusation. Love and Charity, the badge of Christianity, is not so much as named amongst them. . . .

14th. * * Near twelve, came to pay me a visit the French Engineer, Baraset De Kermorvan, who came by my son Christopher's from camp, and is going to York Town. He brought me a letter from him of the twelfth instant, that gave us an agreeable account that all their family were in good health, but to counterbalance, mentioned that they had met with fearful alarms since the enemy left town, it's said with their whole army, in order to attack Washington's army at Chestnut Hill, but are now returned to town, finding his army too strong in that situation to engage him. This, Howe was informed of by a deserter from Col. Proctor's Regiment of Artillery; that they had taken in with them some cattle, and it's reported, a quantity of forage, although our people pursued them; and, by a person since come out of town, who says that twenty-five wagons, with killed and wounded, were brought in. * *

15th. * * Upon the rumour yesterday of Gen. Howe's army's being on the Lancaster Road, it's said that the papers and records belonging to the Executive Council were packed up and sent by wagons to York Town; it's said that the English army is returned into Philadelphia and that our army is on this side of [the] Shuylkill. Our Assembly continues sitting here. It's said that a spirited letter is penned by them to send to Congress to morrow, respecting the report of our troops' going into winter quarters, as the enemy are attempting to, and does, ravage the country for a number of miles' extent around Philada.

December 16th. * * The circumstances of affairs of [a] public nature make a very gloomy appearance. Our City, with its virtuous inhabitants that could not escape, in the hands of cruel taskmasters; the country around ravaged, stripped and destroyed, with houses, barns, &c., burnt and levelled with the ground by the same band of banditti worse than savages; no priests nor prophets, but such as are delineated by Jeremiah in his Lamentations. The thoughts of these things, and having my children with their lovely offspring in the very jaws of these enemies, afflict me sorely, break my peace and disturb my rest, but here I must stop, because the Lord is good and does not afflict willingly. The cause is of our side; we have grossly offended; yet spare us, O Lord my God! Spare thy people and bless thine inheritance, for Jesus Christ's sake. . . .

21st. . . . No news of any moment to be depended upon, except General orders from head quarters, encouraging the army to build huts and to content themselves where they are now. * *

22nd. * * In [the] afternoon, returned the three men and two wagons from York Town, as went last. They called to get some sustenance, as they could get none on the road from York Town till here. After refreshing themselves, they set out for home just at dusk. * *

December 25th. * * Yesterday came to this town from York, Gen. Conway, on his way down to head quarters, and also to propose two Brigadier Generals in the room of Gen. Potter [and] Gen. Armstrong, who propose to go from the army unto their own homes. No company dined with us to day, except Dr. Phyle, one of our standing family. We had a good roast turkey, plain pudding, and minced pies. * *

26th. * * This evening Col. Proctor called, drank tea, stayed some time, giving a relation of the sufferings of the back inhabitants, through the inroads now making by the Indians and the soldiery from Fort Detroit.

27th. * * I spent the evening at home examining part of [the] History of Ephrata, brought me by Peter Miller for my inspection and correction. There appears to be no kind of news to be depended upon, but as for lies, this place is really pregnant and brings forth abundance daily, I might safely say, hourly.

Marshall is pessimistic about the military situation.

28th. * * Our affairs wear a very gloomy aspect. Great part of our army gone into winter quarters; those in camp wanting breeches, shoes, stockings, [and] blankets, and by accounts brought yesterday, were in want of flour, yet being in the land of plenty; our farmers having their barns and barracks full of grain; hundreds of barrels of flour lying on the banks of the Susquehannah perishing for want of care in securing it from the weather, and from the danger of being carried away, if a freshet should happen in the river; fifty wagon loads of cloths and ready made clothes for the soldiery in the Clothier General's store in Lancaster; (this I say from the demand made by John Mease to the President a few days past, when the enemy was expected to be coming this way, for this number of wagons to take away these stores,) our enemies revelling in balls, attended with every degree of luxury and excess in the City; rioting and wantonly using our houses, utensils and furniture; all this [and] a numberless number of other abuses we endure from that handful of banditti, to the amount of six or seven thousand men, headed by that monster of rapine, Gen. Howe. Add to this their frequent excursions round about for twenty miles together, destroying and burning what they please, pillaging, plundering men and women, stealing boys above ten years old, deflowering virgins, driving into the City for their use, droves of cattle, sheep [and] hogs; poultry, butter, meal, meat, cider, furniture and clothing of all kinds, loaded upon our own horses. All this is done in the view of our Generals and our army, who are careless of us, but carefully consulting where they shall go to spend the winter in jollity, gaming and carousing. O tell not this in France or Spain! Publish it not in the streets of London, Liverpool or Bristol, lest the uncircumcised there should rejoice, and shouting for joy, say "America is ours, for the rebels are dismayed and afraid to fight us any longer! O Americans, where is now your virtue? O Washington, where is your courage?" * * * News to-day is that Col. Bull, on the twenty-fifth instant, made an excursion into Fourth street in Philadelphia, with two thousand militia [and] alarmed the City by firing off some pieces of cannon into the air, whereby some of the balls fell about Christ Church. He then made a good retreat back to his station, without the loss of one man. It's further said that it alarmed Gen. Howe. . . . . . Gen. Howe has ordered all the fire buckets that can be found in the City to be put aboard his fleet. . . .

December 29th. * * It's said that Gen. Sullivan, on the retreat of Gen. Howe's army on Christmas Day from Darby, on the alarm given by Cols. Bull, Antis and ———— (in three divisions, instead of one under Col. Bull as above, but all militia,) took thirteen provision wagons loaded from the enemy. * * * Visited in the evening by Dr. Yeardwell, who told me they had made a hospital at Ephrata, in which were near two hundred and forty-seven sick and wounded men. * *

31st. * * Visited by Jedediah Snowden and Benja. Harbeson, for me to sign a petition they were carrying about, for the purpose of requesting the Assembly to call out the whole force of this State, immediately, while there is a prospect of this severe cold weather's lasting, in order to attack Gen. Howe in and out of our City, and thereby entirely ruin his army, and rid the Colonies of such cruel monsters. I then went to writing or, more properly, correcting the Annals of Ephrata, and so continued till bed time, near eleven o'clock. * *

Marshall's diary for 1778 gives an idea of the chores of a revolutionary housewife.*

* These excerpts from Marshall's diary were found in Alice Morse Earle's *Colonial Dames and Wives*, The Riverside Press, Cambridge, 1895 pp. 258-75.

As I have in this memorandum taken scarcely any notice of my wife's employments, it might appear as if her engagements were very trifling; the which is not the case but the reverse. And to do her justice which her services deserved, by entering them minutely, would take up most of my time, for this genuine reason, how that from early in the morning till late at night she is constantly employed in the affairs of the family, which for four months has been very large; for besides the addition to our family in the house, it is a constant resort of comers and goers which seldom go away with dry lips and hungry bellies. This calls for her constant attendance, not only to provide, but also to attend at getting prepared in the kitchen, baking our bread and pies, meat &c. and also the table. Her cleanliness about the house, her attendance in the orchard, cutting and drying apples of which several bushels have been procured; add to which her making of cider without tools, for the constant drink of the family, her seeing all our washing done, and her fine clothes and my shirts, the which are all smoothed by her; add to this, her making of twenty large cheeses, and that from one cow, and daily using with milk and cream, besides her sewing, knitting &c. Thus she looketh well to the ways of her household, and eateth not the bread of idleness; yea she also stretcheth out her hand, and she reacheth forth her hand to her needy friends and neighbors. I think she has not been above four times since her residence here to visit her neighbors; nor through mercy has she been sick for any time, but has at all times been ready in any affliction to me or my family as a faithful nurse and attendant both day and night. . . .

. . . My tender wife keeps busily engaged and looks upon every Philadelphian who comes to us as a person suffering in a righteous cause; and entitled to partake of her hospitality which she administers with her labor and attendance with great freedom and alacrity. . . .

My dear wife meets little respite all the day, the proverb being verified, that Woman's Work is never done.

I owe my health to the vigilance, industry and care of my wife who really has been and is a blessing unto me. For the constant assiduity and press of her daily and painful labor in the kitchen, the Great Lord of the Household will reward her in due time.

Mrs. Marshall was also a "nonsuch gardner, working bravely in her garden," and a "first class butter-maker," who constantly supplied her poor neighbors with milk, still managing always to have cream to spare for her dairy.
The Marshalls had a servant problem, though. They had a particularly difficult time with Poll, a bound girl.
Mr. Marshall noted it in his diary for September 13, 1775.

After my wife came from market (she went past 5) she ordered her girl Poll to carry the basket with some necessaries to the place, as she was coming after her, they intending to iron the clothes. Poll accordingly went, set down the basket, came back, went and dressed herself all clean, short calico gown, and said she was going to school; but presently after the negro woman Dinah came to look for her, her mistress having mistrusted she had a mind to play truant. This was about nine, but madam took her walk, but where —she is not come back to tell.

Sept. 16. I arose before six as I was much concern'd to see my wife so afflicted as before on the bad conduct of her girl Poll who is not yet returned, but is skulking and running about town. This I understand was the practice of her mother who for many years before her death was a constant plague to my wife, and who left her this girl as a legacy, and who by report as well as by own knowledge, for almost three years has always been so down to this time. About eight, word was brought that Poll was just taken by Sister Lynn near the market, and brought to their house. A messenger was immediately dispatched for her, as she could not be found before, though a number of times they had been hunting her.

Over the years, Poll kept taking what Marshall calls "cruises," "driving strokes of impudence," visiting friends, strolling around the streets, "faring up and down the country. . . ."

This night our girl was brought home. I suppose she was hunted out, as it is called, and found by Ruth on the Passyunk Road. Her mistress was delighted upon her return, but I know of nobody else in house or out. I have nothing to say in the affair, as I know of nothing that would distress my wife so much as for me to refuse or forbid her being taken into the house.

". . . I arose by four as my wife had been up sometime at work cleaning house, and as she could not rest on account of Poll's not being yet return'd. The girl's frolics always afflict her mistress, so that to me it's plain if she does not mend, or her mistress grieve less for her, that it will shorten Mrs. Marshall's days considerably; besides our house wears quite a different face when Miss Poll is in it (although all the good she does is not worth half the salt she eats). As her presence gives pleasure to her mistress, this gives joy to all the house, so that in fact she is the cause of peace or uneasiness in the home.

Finally the "jaded, harassed, and conscientious" wife went away for a visit. Marshall was left to face the domestic situation. No sooner had the mistress gone than young Poll took off. Marshall writes on the 23d:

I roused Charles up at daylight. Found Miss Poll in the straw house. She came into the kitchen and talked away that she could not go out at night but she must be locked out. If that's the case she told them she would pack up her clothes and go quite away; that she would not be so served as her Mistress did not hinder her staying out when she pleased, and the kitchen door to be opened for her when she came home and knocked. The negro woman told me as well as she could what she said. I then went out and picked up her clothes that I could find. I asked her how she could behave so to me when I had conducted myself so easy towards her even so as to suffer her to sit at table and eat with me. This had no effect upon her. She rather inclined to think that she had not offended and had done nothing but what her mistress indulged her in. I told her before Betty that it was not worth my while to lick her though she really deserved it for her present impudence; but to remember I had taken all her clothes I could find except what she had on, which I intended to keep; that if she went away Charles with the horse should follow her and bring her back and that I would send a bellman around the borough of Lancaster to cry her as a runaway servant, wicked girl, with a reward for apprehending her.

As a result of Marshall's reproofs and threats Miss Poll ran away that very night. Marshall was outraged:

Charles arose near daybreak and I soon after, in order to try to find my nightly and daily plague, as she took a walk again last night. Charles found her. We turned her upstairs to refresh herself with sleep. . . .

[Two days later] After breakfast let our Poll downstairs where she has been kept since her last frolic. Fastened her up again at night. I think my old enemy Satan is much concerned in the conduct and behavior of that unfortunate girl. He knows her actions give me much anxiety and indeed at times raise my anger so I have said what should have been avoided, but I hope for the future to be more upon my guard and thus frustrate him in his attempts.

Mrs. Marshall's return was heralded with joy by her spouse. As for Poll—

Notwithstanding such heavy weather overhead and exceeding dirty under foot our Poll after breakfast went to see the soldiers that came as prisoners to Burgoyne's army. Our trull returned this morning. Her mistress gave her a good sound whipping. This latter was a variety.

100

At last, with "her head dressed in tiptop fashion" Poll rolled off in a coach to Yorktown without pausing to bid adieu to "her vanquished master."

Letters

Letter-writing was the popular form of communication among our Founding Fathers and their wives on any and every subject.
John Adams as diarist and letter-writer recalls some resolutions of his youth.
[*Extracts from his diaries, n.d.*]

Good-sense will make us remember that others have as good a right to think for themselves, and to speak their own opinions, as we have; that another man's making a silly speech does not warrant my ill-nature and pride in grasping the opportunity to ridicule him and show my wit; a puffy, vain, conceited conversation never fails to bring a man into contempt, although his natural endowments be ever so great, and his application and industry ever so intense; no accomplishments, no virtues, are a sufficient atonement for vanity and a haughty overbearing temper in conversation; and such is the humor of the world, the greater a man's parts, and the nobler his virtues in other respects, the more derision and ridicule does this one vice and folly throw him into. Good-sense is generally attended with a very lively sense and delight in applause; the love of fame in such men is generally much stronger than in other people, and this passion, it must be confessed, is apt to betray men into impertinent exertions of their talents, sometimes into censorious remarks upon others, often into little meannesses to sound the opinions of others, and, oftenest of all, into a childish affectation of with and gayety. I must own myself to have been, to a very heinous degree, guilty in this respect; when in company with persons much superior to myself in years and place, I have talked to show my learning; I have been too bold with great men, which boldness will, no doubt, be called self-conceit; I have made ill-natured remarks upon the intellectuals, manners, practice, etc., of other people; I have foolishly aimed at wit and spirit, at making a shining figure in gay company; but, instead of shining brighter, I only clouded the few rays that before rendered me visible. Such has been my unhappy fate. I now resolve, for the future, never to say an ill-natured thing concerning ministers or the ministerial profession; never to say an envious thing concerning governors, judges, ministers, clerks, sheriffs, lawyers, or any other honorable or lucrative offices or officers; never to affect wit upon laced waistcoats, or large estates, or their possessors; never to show my own importance or superiority by remarking the foibles, vices, or inferiority of others. But I now resolve, as far as lies in me, to take notice chiefly of the amiable qualities of other people; to put the most favorable construction upon the weaknesses, bigotry, and errors of others, etc.; and to labor more for an inoffensive and amiable, than for a shining and invidious character. . . .

He comes out unequivocally against affectation.

Pretensions to wisdom and virtue, superior to all the world, will not be supported by words only. If I tell a man I am wiser and better than he or any other man, he will either despise, or hate, or pity me, perhaps all three. I have not conversed enough with the world to behave rightly. I talk to Paine about Greek; that makes him laugh. I talk to Samuel Quincy about resolution, and being a great man, and study, and improving time; which makes him laugh. I talk to Ned about the folly of affecting to be a heretic; which makes him mad. I talk to Hannah and Esther about the folly of love; about despising it; about being above it; pretend to be insensible of tender passions; which makes them laugh. I talk to Mr. Wibird about the decline of learning; tell him I know no young fellow, who promises to make a figure; cast sneers on Dr. Marsh, for not knowing the value of old Greek and Roman authors; ask when will a genius rise that will shave his beard, or let it grow rather, and sink himself in a cell in order to make a figure? I talked to Parson Smith, about despising gay dress, grand buildings and estates, fame, etc., and being contented with what will satisfy the real wants of nature.

All this is affectation and ostentation. It is affectation of learning, and virtue, and wisdom, which I have not; and it is a weak fondness to show all that I have, and to be thought to have more than I have. Besides this, I have insensibly fallen into a habit of affecting wit and humor; of shrugging my shoulders and moving and distorting the muscles of my face; my motions are stiff and uneasy, ungraceful; and my attention is unsteady and irregular. These are reflections on myself, that I make; they are faults, defects, fopperies, and follies, and disadvantages. Can I mend these faults and supply these defects? . . . .

Adams writes stirringly to Abigail of the birth of the United States, and sees the "rays of ravishing light and glory in its future."

To His Wife, on the Birth of the New Nation

Yesterday, the greatest question was decided, which ever was debated in America, and a greater, perhaps, never was nor will be decided among men. A resolution was passed without one dissenting colony, "that these United Colonies are, and of right ought to be, free and independent States, and as such they have, and of right ought to have, full power to make war, conclude peace, establish commerce, and to do all other acts and things which other States may rightfully do." You will see in a few days a Declaration setting forth the causes which have impelled us to this mighty revolution, and the reasons which will justify it in the sight of God and man. A plan of confederation will be taken up in a few days.

When I look back to the year 1761, and recollect the argument concerning writs of assistance in the superior court, which I have hitherto considered as the commencement of this controversy between Great Britain and America, and run through the whole period, from that time to this, and recollect the series of political events, the chain of causes and effects, I am surprised at the suddenness as well as greatness of this revolution. Britain has been filled with folly, and America with wisdom. At least, this is my judgment. Time must determine. It is the will of Heaven that the two countries should be sundered forever. It may be the will of Heaven that America shall suffer calamities still more wasting, and distresses yet more dreadful. If this is to be the case, it will have this good effect at least. It will inspire us with many virtues, which we have not, and correct many errors, follies and views which threaten to disturb, dishonor, and destroy us. The furnace of affliction produces refinement, in States as well as individuals. And the new governments we are assuming in every part will require a purification from our vices, and an augmentation of our virtues, or they will be no blessings. The people will have unbounded power, and the people are extremely addicted to corruption and venality, as well as the great. But I must submit all my hopes and fears to an overruling Providence, in which, unfashionable as the faith may be, I firmly believe.

Had a Declaration of Independency been made seven months ago, it would have been attended with many great and glorious effects. We might, before this hour, have formed alliances with foreign States. We should have mastered Quebec, and been in possession of Canada. You will perhaps wonder how such a declaration would have influenced our affairs in Canada, but if I could write with freedom, I could easily convince you that it would, and explain to you the manner how. Many gentlemen in high stations and of great influence have been duped by the ministerial bubble of commissioners to treat. And in real, sincere expectation of this event, which they so fondly wished, they have been slow and languid in promoting measures for the reduction of that province. Others there are in the colonies who really wished that our enterprise in Canada would be defeated, that the colonies might be brought into danger and distress between two fires, and be thus induced to submit. Others really wished to defeat the expedition to Canada, lest the conquest of it should elevate the minds of the people too much to hearken to those terms of reconciliation, which, they believed, would be offered us. These jarring views, wishes, and designs, occasioned an opposition to many salutary measures, which were proposed for the support of that expedition, and caused obstructions, embarrassments, and studied delays, which have finally lost us the province.

All these causes, however, in conjunction, would not have disappointed us, if it had not been for a misfortune which could not be foreseen, and, perhaps, could not have been prevented—I mean the prevalence of the small-pox among our troops. This fatal pestilence completed our destruction. It is a frown of Providence upon us, which we ought to lay to heart.

But, on the other hand, the delay of this declaration to this time has many great advantages attending it. The hopes of reconciliation, which were fondly entertained by multitudes of honest and well-meaning, though weak and mistaken people, have been gradually and, at last, totally extinguished. Time has been given for the whole people maturely to consider the great question of independence, and to ripen their judgment, dissipate their fears, and allure their hopes, by discussing it in newspapers and pamphlets, by debating it in assemblies, conventions, committees of safety and inspection, in town and county meetings, as well as in private conversations, so that the whole people, in every colony of the thirteen, have now adopted it as their own act. This will cement the union, and avoid those heats, and perhaps convulsions, which might have been occasioned by such a declaration six months ago.

But the day is past. The second day of July, 1776, will be the most memorable epocha in the history of America. I am apt to believe that it will be celebrated by succeeding generations as the great anniversary festival. It ought to be commemorated, as the day of deliverance, by solemn acts of devotion to God Almighty. It ought to be solemnized with pomp and parade, with shows, games, sports, guns, bells, bonfires, and illuminations, from one end of this continent to the other, from this time forward, forevermore.

You will think me transported with enthusiasm, but I am not. I am well aware of the toil, and blood, and treasure, that it will cost us to maintain this declaration, and support and defend these States. Yet, through all the gloom, I can see the rays of ravishing light and glory. I can see that the end is more than worth all the means, and that posterity will triumph in that day's transaction, even although we should rue it, which I trust in God we shall not.

PHILADELPHIA, 3 *July,* 1776.

He proudly writes Doctor Rush of Abigail's patriotic acceptance of the news that he has become a member of the House of Representatives.

To Benjamin Rush, on Mrs. Adams's Patriotism

When I went home to my family in May, 1770, from the town meeting in Boston, which was the first I had ever attended, and where I had been chosen in my absence, without any solicitation, one of their representatives, I said to my wife, "I have accepted a seat in the House of Representatives, and thereby have consented to my own ruin, to your ruin, and the ruin of our children. I give you this warning that you may prepare your mind for your fate." She burst into tears, but instantly cried out in a transport of magnanimity, "Well, I am willing in this cause to run all risks with you, and be ruined with you, if you are ruined." These were times, my friend, in Boston, which tried women's souls as well as men's. . . . . .

QUINCY, 12 *April,* 1809.

On July 31, 1777 Abigail reported to her husband John an astonishing action of female teatotalers in Boston.

There is a great scarcity of sugar and coffee, articles which the female part of the State is very loath to give up, especially whilst they consider the scarcity occasioned by the merchants having secreted a large quantity. There had been much rout and noise in the town for several weeks. Some stores had been opened by a number of people, and the coffee and sugar carried into the market and dealt out by pounds. It was rumored that an eminent stingy wealthy merchant (who is a bachelor) had a hogshead of coffee in his store which he refused to sell the committee under six shillings per pound. A number of females, some say a hundred, some say more, assembled with a cart and trunks, marched down to the warehouse and demanded the keys which he refused to deliver. Upon which one of them seized him by his neck and tossed him into the cart. Upon his finding no quarter, he delivered the keys when they tipped up the cart and discharged him; then opened the warehouse, hoisted out the coffee themselves, put into the trunks, and drove off. It was reported that he had personal chastisements among them, but this I believe was not true. A large concourse of men stood amazed, silent spectators of the whole transaction.

Oh terpsichore Oh mores! The first dance Abigail Adams saw on the stage almost brought on the vapors.

[From a Letter to Mrs. Cranch, Auteuil, February 20, 1785.]

This day eight months I sailed for Europe, since which many new and interesting scenes have presented themselves before me. I have seen many of the beauties, and some of the deformities, of this old world. I have been more than ever convinced, that there is no summit of virtue, and no depth of vice, which human nature is not capable of rising to, on the one hand, or sinking into, on the other. I have felt the force of an observation, which I have read, that daily example is the most subtile of poisons. I have found my taste reconciling itself to habits, customs, and fashions, which at first disgusted me. The first dance which I saw upon the stage shocked me; the dresses and beauty of the performers were enchanting; but, no sooner did the dance commence, than I felt my delicacy wounded, and I was ashamed to be seen to look at them. Girls, clothed in the thinnest silk and gauze, with their petticoats short, springing two feet from the floor, poising themselves in the air, with their feet flying, and as perfectly showing their garters and drawers as though no petticoat had been worn, was a sight altogether new to me. Their motions are as light as air, and as quick as lightning; they balance themselves to astonishment. No description can equal the reality. They are daily trained to it, from early infancy, at a royal academy, instituted for this purpose. You will very often see little creatures, not more than seven or eight years old, as undauntedly performing their parts as the eldest among them. Shall I speak a truth, and say that repeatedly seeing these dances has worn off that disgust, which I at first felt, and that I see them now with pleasure? Yet, when I consider the tendency of these things, the passions they must excite, and the known character, even to a proverb, which is attached to an opera girl, my abhorrence is not lessened, and neither my reason nor judgment has accompanied my sensibility in acquiring any degree of callousness. The art of dancing is carried to the highest degree of perfection that it is capable of. At the opera, the house is neither so grand, nor of so beautiful architecture, as the French theatre, but it is more frequented by the beau monde, who had rather be amused than instructed. The scenery is more various and more highly decorated, the dresses more costly and rich. And O! the music, vocal and instrumental; it has a soft, persuasive power, and a dying sound. Conceive a highly decorated building, filled with youth, beauty, grace, ease, clad in all the most pleasing and various ornaments of dress, which fancy can form; these objects singing like cherubs to the best tuned instruments, most skilfully handled, the softest, tenderest strains; every attitude corresponding with the music; full of the god or goddess whom they celebrate; the female voices accompanied by an equal number of Adonises. Think you that this city can fail of becoming a Cythera, and this house the temple of Venus?

"When music softens, and when dancing fires,"

it requires the immortal shield of the invincible Minerva, to screen youth from the arrows which assail them on every side.

As soon as a girl sets her foot upon the floor of the opera, she is excommunicated by the Church, and denied burial in holy ground. She conceives nothing worse can happen to her; all restraint is thrown off, and she delivers herself to the first who bids high enough for her. But let me turn from a picture, of which the outlines are but just sketched; I would willingly veil the rest, as it can only tend to excite sentiments of horror.

Benjamin Franklin's letter to Samuel Mather has a few nostalgic anecdotes.

I RECEIVED your kind letter, with your excellent advice to the people of the United States, which I read with great pleasure, and hope it will be duly regarded. Such writings, though they may be lightly passed over by many readers, yet, if they make a deep impression on one active mind in a hundred, the effects may be considerable. Permit me to mention one little instance, which though it relates to myself, will not be quite uninteresting to you. When I was a boy, I met with a book, entitled *"Essays to do Good,"* which I think was written by your father. It had been so little regarded by a former possessor, that several leaves of it were torn out; but the remainder gave me such a turn of thinking, as to have an influence on my conduct through life; for I have always set a greater value on the character of a *doer of good,* than on any other kind of reputation; and if I have been, as you seem to think, a useful citizen, the public owes the advantage of it to that book.

You mention your being in your seventy-eighth year; I am in my seventy-ninth; we are grown old together. It is now more than sixty years since I left Boston, but I remember well both your father and grandfather, having heard them both in the pulpit and seen them in their houses. The last time I saw your father was in the beginning of 1724, when I visited him after my first trip to Pennsylvania. He rereived me in his library, and on my taking leave showed me a shorter way out of the house through a narrow passage, which was crossed by a beam overhead. We were still talking as I withdrew, he accompanying me behind, and I turning partly towards him, when he said hastily, *"Stoop, stoop!"* I did not understand him, till I felt my head hit against the beam. He was a man that never missed any occasion of giving instruction, and upon this he said to me, *"You are young, and have the world before you;* STOOP *as you go through it, and you will miss many hard thumps."* This advice, thus beat into my head, has frequently been of use to me; and I often think of it, when I see pride mortified, and misfortunes brought upon people by their carrying their heads too high.

                                            B. FRANKLIN

PASSY, 12 *May,* 1784.

Letters from a Farmer

[JOHN DICKINSON *(1732–1808) of Delaware was a member of the Pennsylvania Assembly in 1764, of the Provincial Congress of 1765, and also of the first Continental Congress. He wrote the principal part of the state papers of that Congress. Although an ardent patriot he opposed the Declaration of Independence because he did not feel the Congress was strong enough, and was a loyal British subject until Parliament began to abuse the rights of the colonists and impose duties on commodities without their consent. While he originally had thought that independence would be a "fatal calamity," he tried to save the rights of Americans as men.*

In the latter part of 1767 a series of essays appeared in a Philadelphia newspaper, under the title Letters From A Farmer. *Though published anonymously they were quickly recognized as the work of Dickinson.*

Under the guise of a patriot Anglo-American farmer Dickinson dealt with the problems facing the colonists and the rising American dispute. As the letters appeared from week to week in the Philadelphia paper, they were eagerly read by the people. For the benefit of those not within the area they were reproduced in 21 of the 25 newspapers then published in America. Less than a month after the last letter was printed they were all collected and issued as a pamphlet, of which at least eight editions were published in different parts of America. The American people expressed their gratitude by offering a vote of thanks to him at town meetings, political associations, and grand juries. He was the popular toast at public banquets. Songs of praise were written about him. These essays were also widely read in England.

Dickinson's work was unequalled in literary merit during the Revolutionary War era. In the words of Moses Coit Tyler, the Farmer's Letters were on the whole, "the most brilliant event in the literary history of the American Revolution."]

In Letter I, Dickinson considered the recent Acts of Parliament.

LETTERS

FROM A

FARMER,

IN

PENNSYLVANIA,

To the INHABITANTS

OF THE

BRITISH COLONIES.

PHILADELPHIA

PRINTED; AND LONDON RE-PRINTED FOR J. ALMON
OPPOSITE BURLINGTON-HOUSE IN PICCADILLY.
MDCCLXXIV.

Title page from a 1774 edition of John Dickinson's Letters from a Farmer, *originally published serially in a Philadelphia newspaper in 1767. Rare Book Division, New York Public Library.*

My Dear Countrymen,

I AM a FARMER, settled, after a variety of fortunes, near the banks of the river *Delaware*, in the province of *Pennsylvania*. I received a liberal education, and have been engaged in the busy scenes of life: but am now convinced, that a man may be as happy without bustle as with it. My farm is small, my servants are few, and good; I have a little money at interest; I wish for no more: my employment in my own affairs is easy; and with a contented grateful mind, I am compleating the number of days allotted to me by Divine Goodness.

Being master of my time, I spend a good deal of it in a library, which I think the most valuable part of my small estate; and being acquainted with two or three gentlemen of abilities and learning, who honour me with their friendship, I believe I have acquired a greater share of knowledge in history, and the laws and constitution of my country, than is generally attained by men of my class; many of them not being so fortunate as I have been, in the opportunities of getting information.

From infancy I was taught to love humanity and liberty. Inquiry and experience have since confirmed my reverence for the lessons then given me, by convincing me more fully of their truth and excellence. Benevolence towards mankind excites wishes for their welfare, and such wishes endear the means of fulfilling them. Those can be found in liberty alone, and therefore her sacred cause ought to be espoused by every man, on every occasion, to the utmost of his power. As a charitable but poor person does not withold his *mite,* because he cannot relieve *all* the distresses of the miserable, so let not any honest man suppress his sentiments concerning freedom, however small their influence is likely to be. Perhaps he may "touch some wheel" [Pope] that will have an effect greater than he expects.

These being my sentiments, I am encouraged to offer to you, my countrymen, my thoughts on some late transactions, that in my opinion are of the utmost importance to you.

He declares the act suspending the legislation of New York a threat to American freedom.

Conscious of my defects, I have waited some time, in expectation of seeing the subject treated by persons much better qualified for the talk; but being therein disappointed, and apprehensive that longer delays will be injurious, I venture at length to request the attention of the public, praying only for one thing,—that is, that these lines may be *read* with the same zeal for the happiness of British America, with which they were *wrote.*

With a good deal of surprise I have observed, that little notice has been taken of an act of parliament, as injurious in its principle to the liberties of these colonies, as the STAMP-ACT was: I mean the act for suspending the legislation of New-York.

The assembly of that government complied with a former act of parliament, requiring certain provisions to be made for the troops in America, in every particular, I think, except the articles of salt, pepper, and vinegar. In my opinion they acted imprudently, considering all circumstances, in not complying so far as would have given satisfaction, as several colonies did: but my dislike of their conduct in that instance, has not blinded me so much, that I cannot plainly perceive, that they have been punished in a manner pernicious to American freedom, and justly alarming to all the colonies.

If the BRITISH PARLIAMENT has a legal authority to order, that we shall furnish a single article for the troops here, and to compel obedience to that order; they have the same right to order us to supply those troops with arms, cloaths, and every necessary, and to compel obedience to that order also; in short, to lay *any burdens* they please upon us. What is that but *taxing* us at a *certain sum,* and leaving to us only the *manner* of raising it? How is this mode more tolerable than the STAMP-ACT? Would that act have appeared more pleasing to AMERICANS, if being ordered thereby to raise the sum total of the taxes, the mighty privilege had been left to them, of saying how much should be paid for an instrument of writing on paper, and how much for another on parchment?

An act of parliament commanding us to do a certain thing, if it has any validity, is a tax upon us for the expense that accrues in complying with it, and for this reason, I believe, every colony on the continent, that chose to give a mark of their respect for GREAT-BRITAIN, in complying with the act relating to the troops, cautiously avoided the mention of that act, lest their conduct should be attributed to its supposed obligation."

He saw no real advantage to the repeal of the Stamp Act if the colonies were to lose other privileges.

The matter being thus stated, the assembly of *New-York* either had, or had not, a right to refuse submission to that act. If they had, and I imagine no AMERICAN will say, they had not, then the parliament had no *right* to compel them to execute it.—If they had not *that right,* they had *no right* to punish them for not executing it; and therefore had *no right* to suspend their legislation, which is a punishment. In fact, if the people of *New-York* cannot be legally taxed, but by their own representatives, they cannot be legally deprived of the privileges of making laws, only for insisting on that exclusive privilege of taxation. If they may be legally deprived, in such a case, of the privilege of making laws, why may they not, with equal reason, be deprived of every other privilege? Or why may not every colony be treated in the same manner, when any of them shall dare to deny their assent to any impositions that shall be directed? Or what signifies the repeal of the STAMP-ACT, if these colonies are to lose their *other* privileges, by not tamely surrendering that of *taxation?*

There is one consideration arising from this suspicion, which is not generally attended to, but shews its importance very clearly. It was not *necessary* that this suspension should be caused by an act of parliament. The crown might have restrained the governor of *New-York,* even from calling the assembly together by its prerogative in the royal governments. This step, I suppose, would have been taken, if the conduct of the assembly of *New-York,* had been regarded as an act of disobedience *to the crown alone:* but it is regarded as an act of "disobedience to "the authority of the BRITISH LEGISLATURE." This gives the suspension a consequence vastly more affecting. It is a parliamentary assertion of the *supreme authority* of the *British legislature* over these colonies in *the part of taxation;* and is intended to COMPEL *New-York* unto a submission to that authority. It seems therefore to me as much a violation of the liberty of the people of that province, and consequently of all these colonies, as if the parliament had sent a number of regiments to be quartered upon them, till they should comply. For it is evident, that the suspension is meant as a compulsion; and the *method* of compelling is totally different. It is indeed probable, that the fight of red coats, and the beating of drums, would have been most alarming, because people are generally more influenced by their eyes and ears than by their reason: but whoever seriously considers the matter, must perceive, that a dreadful stroke is aimed at the liberty of these colonies: for the cause of *one* is the cause *of all.* If the parliament may lawfully deprive *New-York* of any of its rights, it may deprive any of all the other colonies of their rights; and nothing can possibly so much encourage such attempts, as a mutual inattention to the interest of each other. To divide, and thus to destroy, is the first political maxim in attacking those who are powerful by their union . . . .

With concern I have observed, that two assemblies of this province have sat and adjourned, without taking any notice of this act. It may perhaps be asked, what would have been proper for them to do? I am by no means fond of inflammatory measures. I detest them.—I should be sorry that any thing should be done which might justly displease our Sovereign or our mother-country. But a firm, modest exertion of a free spirit, should never be wanting on public occasions. It appears to me, that it would have been sufficient for the assembly, to have ordered our agents to represent to the King's ministers, their sense of the suspending act, and to pray for its repeal. Thus we should have borne our testimony against it; and might therefore reasonably expect, that on a like occasion, we might receive the same assistance from the other colonies.

"Concorda res parvae crescunt.

Small things grow great by concord.—

A FARMER

In a later letter, he condemned the British Parliament for imposing duties on the colonists to raise a revenue.

Beloved Countrymen,

THERE is another late act of parliament, which seems to me to be as destructive to the liberty of these colonies, as that inserted in my last letter; that is, the act for granting the duties on paper, glass, &c. It appears to me to be unconstitutional.

The parliament unquestionably possesses a legal authority to *regulate* the trade of *Great-Britain,* and all its colonies. Such an authority is essential to the relation between a mother country and its colonies; and necessary for the common good of all. He who considers these provinces as states distinct from the *British Empire,* has very slender notions of *justice,* or of *their interests.* We are but parts of *a whole;* and therefore there must exist a power somewhere, to preside, and preserve the connection in due order. This power is lodged in the parliament; and we are as much dependent on *Great-Britain,* as a perfectly free people can be on another.

I have looked over *every statute* relating to these colonies, from their first settlement to this time; and I find every one of them founded on this principle, till the STAMP-ACT administration.* *All before* are calculated to preserve or promote a mutually beneficial intercourse between the several constituent parts of the empire; and though many of them imposed duties on trade, yet those duties were always imposed with design to restrain the commerce of one part that was injurious to another, and thus to promote the general welfare. The raising a revenue thereby was never intended. Thus, the King, by his judges in his courts of justice, imposes fines, which all together amount to a considerable sum, and contribute to the support of government: but this is merely a consequence arising from restrictions, which only meant to keep peace and prevent confusion; and surely a man would argue very loosely, who should conclude from hence, that the King has a right to levy money in general upon his subjects; never did the *British parliament,* till the period above-mentioned, think of imposing duties in America; FOR THE PURPOSE OF RAISING A REVENUE. Mr. *Grenville's* sagacity first introduced this language, in the preamble to the 4th of Geo. III. Ch. 15, which has these words—"And whereas it is just and necessary that A REVENUE BE RAISED IN YOUR MAJESTY'S SAID DOMINIONS IN AMERICA, *for defraying the expences of defending, protecting, and securing the same:* We your Majesty's most dutiful and loyal subjects, THE COMMONS OF GREAT BRITAIN, in parliament assembled, being desirious to make some provision in the present session of parliament, towards raising the said revenue in America, have resolved to give and grant unto your Majesty the several rates and duties herein after mentioned," &c.

A few months after came the *Stamp-act,* which reciting this, proceeds in the same strange mode of expression, thus—"And whereas it is just and necessary, that provision be made FOR RAISING A FURTHER REVENUE WITHIN YOUR MAJESTY'S DOMINION IN AMERICA, towards defraying the said expences, we your Majesty's most dutiful and loyal subjects, the COMMONS OF GREAT-BRITAIN, &c. GIVE AND GRANT," &c. as before.

The last act, granting duties upon paper, &c. carefully pursues these modern precedents. The preamble is, "Whereas it is expedient that a revenue should be raised in your Majesty's dominions in America, for making a more certain and adequate provision for the defraying the charge of the administration of justice, and the support of civil government in such provinces, where it shall be found necessary; and towards the further defraying the expences of defending, protecting and securing the said dominions, we your Majesty's most dutiful and loyal subjects, the COMMONS OF GREAT-BRITAIN, &c. give and grant," &c. as before."

Dickinson expressed indignation over the imposition of duties on commodities the colonists are forced to buy from Britain.

Here we may observe an authority expressly claimed to impose duties on these colonies; not for the regulation of trade; not for the preservation or promotion of a mutually beneficial intercourse between the several constituent parts of the empire, heretofore the *sole objects* of parliamentary institutions; *but for the single purpose of levying money upon us.*

This I call a most dangerous innovation. It may perhaps be objected, that *Great-Britain* has a right to lay what duties she pleases upon her † exports, and it makes no difference to us whether they are paid here or there.

To this I answer. These colonies require many things for their use, which the laws of *Great-Britain* prohibit them from getting any where but from her. Such are paper and glass.

Why was the *Stamp-act* then so pernicious to freedom? It did not enact, that every man in the colonies *should* buy a certain quantity of paper—No: it only directed, that no instrument of writing should be valid in law, if not made on stamp paper, &c.

The makers of that act knew full well, that the confusions that would arise upon the disuse of writings would COMPEL the colonies to use the stamp paper, and therefore to pay the taxes imposed. For this reason the *Stamp-act* was said to be a law THAT WOULD EXECUTE ITSELF. For the very same reason, the last act of parliament, if it is granted to have any force here, will execute itself, and will be attended with the very same consequences to *American Liberty.*

That we may be legally bound to pay any *general* duties on these commodities, relative to the regulation of trade, is granted; but we being *obliged by her laws* to take them from Great-Britain, any *special* duties imposed on their exportation *to us only, with intention to raise a revenue from us only,* are as much *taxes* upon us, as those imposed by the *Stamp-act.*

What is the difference in *substance* and *right,* whether the same sum is raised upon us by the rates mentioned in the Stamp-act, on the *use* of the paper, or by these duties, on the *importation* of it. It is nothing but the edition of a former book, with a new title page.

Suppose the duties were made payable in *Great-Britain?*

It signifies nothing to us, whether they are to be paid here or there. Had the *Stamp-act* directed, that all the paper should be landed in *Florida,* and the duties paid there, before it was brought to the *British Colonies,* would the act have raised less money upon us, or have been less destructive of our rights? By no means: for as we were under a necessity of using the paper, we should have been under the necessity of paying the duties. Thus in the present case, a like *necessity* will subject us, if this act continues in force, to the payment of the duties now imposed.

Some persons perhaps may say, that this act lays us under no necessity to pay the duties imposed, because we may ourselves manufacture the articles on which they are laid; whereas by the Stamp-act no instrument of writing could be good, unless made on British paper, and that too stamped.

No money should be demanded of the colonists without their consent.

Such an objection amounts to no more than this, that the injury resulting to these colonies, from the total disuse of British paper and glass, will not be *so afflicting* as that which would have resulted from the total disuse of writing among them; for by that means even the stamp-act might have been eluded. Why then was it universally detested by them as slavery itself? Because it presented to these devoted provinces nothing but a choice of calamities, imbittered by indignities, each of which it was unworthy of freemen to bear. But is no injury a violation of right but the *greatest* injury? If the eluding the payment of the duties imposed by the Stamp-act, would have subjected us to a more dreadful inconvenience than the eluding the payment of those imposed by the late act; does it therefore follow, that the last is no violation of our rights, though it is calculated for the same purpose that the other was; that is, *to raise money upon us,* WITHOUT OUR CONSENT?

This would be making *right* to consist, not in exemption from *injury*, but from a certain *degree of injury*.

But the objectors may further say, that we shall sustain no injury at all by the disuse of British paper and glass. We might not, if we could make as much as we want. But can any man, acquainted with America, believe this possible? I am told there are but two or three *glass-houses* on this continent, and but very few *paper-mills;* and suppose more should be erected, a long course of years must elapse, before they can be brought to perfection. This continent is a country of planters, farmers, and fishermen; not of manufacturers. The difficulty of establishing particular manufactures in such a country, is almost insuperable; for one manufacture is concerned with others in such a manner, that it may be said to be impossible to establish one or two without establishing several others. The experience of many nations may convince us of this truth.

Inexpressible therefore must be our distresses in evading the late acts, by the disuse of British paper and glass. Nor will this be the extent of our misfortunes, if we admit the legality of that act.

Great-Britain has prohibited the manufacturing iron and steel in these colonies, without any objection being made to her right of doing it. The like right she must have to prohibit any other manufacture among us. Thus she is possessed of an undisputed *precedent* on that point. This authority, she will say, is founded on the *original intention* of settling these colonies; that is, that she should manufacture for them, and that they should supply her with materials. The *equity* of this policy, she will also say, has been universally acknowledged by the colonies, who never have made the least objection to statutes for that purpose; and will further appear by the *mutual benefits* flowing from this usage, ever since the settlement of these colonies.

Our great advocate, Mr. PITT, in his speeches on the debate concerning the repeal of the *Stamp-act*, acknowledged, that Great-Britain could restrain our manufactures. His words are these—"This kingdom, as the supreme governing and legislative power, has *always* bound the colonies by her regulations and *restrictions* in trade, in navigation, in *manufactures*——in every thing *except that of taking their money out of their pockets*, WITHOUT THEIR CONSENT." Again he says, "We may bind their trade, CONFINE THEIR MANUFACTURES, and exercise every power whatever, except that of taking money out of their pockets, WITHOUT THEIR CONSENT.

Here then, let my countrymen ROUSE themselves, and behold the ruin hanging over their heads! If they ONCE admit, that Great-Britain may lay duties upon her exportations to us, *for the purpose of levying money on us only,* she then will have nothing to do, but to lay those duties on the articles which she prohibits us to manufacture—and the tragedy of American liberty is finished. We have been prohibited from procuring manufactures, in all cases, any where but from Great-Britain, (excepting linens, which we are permitted to import directly from Ireland;) we have been prohibited, in some cases, from manufacturing for ourselves: we are therefore exactly in the situation of a city besieged, which is surrounded by the works of the besiegers in every part *but one*. If *that* is closed up, no step can be taken, *but to surrender at discretion*. If Great-Britain can order us to come to her for necessaries we want, and can order us to pay what taxes she pleases before we take them away, or when we have them here, we are as abject slaves, as France and Poland can shew in wooden shoes, and with uncombed hair.

From what has been said, I think this uncontrovertible conclusion may be deduced, that when a ruling state obliges a dependent state to take certain commodities from her alone, it is implied in the nature of that obligation; and is essentially requisite to give it the least degree of justice; and is inseparably united with it, in order to preserve any share of freedom to the dependent state; that those commodities should never be loaded with duties for the sole purpose of levying money on the dependent state.

The place of paying the duties imposed by the late act, appears to me therefore to be totally immaterial. The single question is, whether the parliament can legally impose duties to be paid *by the people of these colonies, only* FOR THE SOLE PURPOSE OF RAISING A REVENUE, *on commodities which she obliges us to take from her alone*; or, in other words, whether the parliament can legally take money out of our pockets, without our consent? If they can, our boasted liberty is but

"*Vox et praterea nihil.*"

A sound, and nothing else.

A FARMER

If you can plow through the flowery language, the euphemisms, and the exaggeration of Ann Bleecker's prose, you will find excitement, human interest, and adventure.

The Posthumous Works
of
Ann Eliza Bleecker

THE

POSTHUMOUS WORKS

O F

ANN ELIZA BLEECKER,

I N

PROSE AND VERSE.

To which is added,

A COLLECTION OF ESSAYS,

PROSE AND POETICAL,

B Y

MARGARETTA V. FAUGERES.

NEW-YORK:
Printed by T. and J. Swords, No. 27, William-Street.
— 1793 —

Title page from a 1793 edition of Ann Eliza Bleecker's Posthumous Works, *edited by her daughter Margaretta V. Faugeres.*

[ANN ELIZA BLEECKER *was born October 1752, the youngest child of Brandt Schuyler. She was an avid reader and began writing poetry at an early age. Uncertain of her ability, she refused to show anyone but her most intimate acquaintances her writings, and destroyed them as soon as they were read. Eliza developed into a lively, beautiful young woman, "tall, graceful and elegant." In 1769 she married John J. Bleecker of New Rochelle. They eventu-*

112

ally moved to Tomhanick, a charming village eighteen miles above Albany, where Mr. Bleecker built their home. Ann Eliza's widowed mother and her half sister Susan Ten Eyck lived with the Bleeckers until 1777. That year put an end to the peace and tranquillity the family had known, as Mr. Bleecker, hearing of the approach of Burgoyne, went off to find a place for them to live in Albany. Ann Eliza was left alone with her children and a young mulatto servant, her mother and Susan having left sometime earlier. John had been gone but a day when she learned the British were within two miles of the village, "burning and murdering all before them." Taking her two daughters, Abella, a baby, and Margaretta, aged four, and the young mulatto girl, Ann Eliza abandoned her home. In her mother's Posthumous Works, *which she later edited, Margaretta describes the scene they faced.]*

The roads were crouded with carriages loaded with women and children, but none could afford her assistance—distress was depictured on every countenance, and tears of heartfelt anguish moistened every cheek. They passed on—no one spoke to another—and no sound but the dismal creaking of burdened wheels and the trampling of horses interrupted the mournful silence. After a tedious walk of four or five miles, she obtained a seat for the children upon one of the waggons, and she walked on to *Stony-Arabia*, where she expected to find many friends; but she was deceived—no door was open to *her*, whose house by many of them had been made use of as a home—she wandered from house to house, and at length obtained a place in the garret of a rich old acquaintance, where a couple of blankets, stretched upon some boards, were offered her as a bed; she, however, sat up all night and wept, and the next morning Mr. BLEECKER coming from *Albany*, met with them and returned to that city, from whence they set off with several other families by water. At twelve miles below *Albany* little ABELLA was taken so ill that they were obliged to go on shore, where she died. The *impressions* this event made on Mrs. BLEECKER's mind were never effaced.

[On November 23, 1783 Ann Eliza Bleecker died. The writings she left were but a small part of what she had written. She seldom kept copies of her poems and most of them were lost. Several of her political and satirical pieces shared a similar fate. Some of her letters, however, survived and were saved by her daughter Margaretta Faugeres. The political sentiments revealed her patriotism. "Many are faulty," her daughter writes, "but their merits are more numerous than their defects. They are interesting, easy reading."]

Letters from Ann Bleecker express the full range of emotions.

My Dear Girl,

. . . As you desire to know how we are circumstanced, in compliance with your request, I must again wound your feelings with a lamentable story: therefore, sadden your countenance accordingly; and I stipulate, that between every paragraph you shall pause and make a moral reflection.

The tories have visited many of our neighbours in a hostile manner, under the disguise of Indians. This struck a panic over the stoutest of us; but yesterday they seized an old man, and proposed the plundering of our house to him; he declined it, though a disaffected person himself, and acquainted us with our danger; also, that the banditti were thirty in number. You may guess (but 'tis likely you will not) that our disorder on this exceeded the confusion of AGRAMONTA's camp: every thing topsey-turvy, every one hurrying to secrete some little bundle in an unsuspected vacancy, and one dreadful apprehension expelling another; for SUSAN and I ventured up in a loft without light, where spectres have been gamboling for at least a dozen centuries—by report.

We still remain greatly alarmed, and never undress for bed. However, we have passed the preceding season in security and pleasure; we have frequently had sociable dances, which by way of eminence we stile a ball. The most disagreeable of our hours are when we admit politics in our female circle: this never fails of opening a field of nonsensical controversy among our ladies.

I expect shortly to remove to *Tomhanick* again, where conversing with my absent friends will be my chief amusement; and as I highly value a sensible intelligent writer, I wish I knew how to bribe cousin to favour me with her letters also.

You have omitted, my dear, to mention a syllable of your good mamma and Mrs. B. but even that is a presumption of their welfare. Please to tender my regards to them, and accept of Mr. BLEECKER'S. My little PEGGY begs leave to kiss your hands; and I am, dear girl, with unaffected sincerity, your

ANN ELIZA BLEECKER.

Cojemans, April 12, 1779

Married couples of the eighteenth century did not always live happily ever after. After a squabble with her spouse Ann Eliza Bleecker suffers from a Freudian sense of guilt.

To Mr. B------.
Wednesday Evening, July 12, 1779.

MY DEAR,

I could not see the folly and deformity of my impetuous behaviour this morning, while blinded by passion; but after you was gone, when I felt lonesome, and had leisure for reflection, when my fever returned, and I missed that tender solicitude which always alleviated my pain when you was near, I cannot describe how exquisite a compunction seized me; I have been lost the whole day in sorrow. Good God! how inconsistent is the human mind! obstinate in passion, and stormy as the *Caspian;* then again soft and yielding to persuasion, as snow before the warm influence of a summer heaven; and yet perhaps this great agitation of the spirits is meant to keep them from subsiding into a state of insensibility, as strong winds prevent the waters of a lake from stagnating.

I hope health and pleasure will attend you in your journey, and sometimes I hope you will call in my idea to amuse your silent hours when you ride alone through the lofty forest, or along the bank of some placid river, or over some flowery mead, whose glowing gems glitter beneath the crystal globules of morning; these objects inspire love and softness, and it is in such moments I would fain have you think of me. My head aches, I must lie down.

Thursday Evening, July 22.

I HAVE been very sick, and kept my bed all day. Your absence increases my disorder: O how solitary am I in this great city! Adieu, I am too unwell to sit up.

Friday Evening, July 23.

I FIND myself better. Mrs. V. S. paid us a visit this afternoon: after tea she persuaded me to walk out; the evening was lovely, the sun shone with a peculiar softness through the humid atmosphere, and the glassy *Hudson* blushed at the brightness of the painted heaven; (pardon my poetical phrenzy;) but not the blushing river, nor glowing skies, nor smiling sun could conquer my invincible melancholy. Here am I returned in as great a humour for moralizing as ever PLATO was: however, I shall quit troubling you to-night with my reflections, and perhaps to-morrow a more agreeable subject may occur. You see I continue writing till some opportunity bids me close the dull journal. Good night.

ANN ELIZA BLEECKER.

To Miss V------.

. . . Your very kind letters came to hand last night, as SUSAN and I were sitting disconsolate and apprehensive by the fire-side; but on perusing them, we insensibly forgot our gloomy situation, and got so engaged among our *R------* friends, that we passed the remainder of the evening in merrier chat than we had many preceding ones.

To-day we have been informed of Governor CLINTON's advantage over the enemy at *Canajohare:*

no doubt the papers will give you the particulars before this can reach you: but rejoice with us, my cousin, at this event, which will probably put a period to this northern massacre. I have wrote M---- a lamentable epistle, which I would suppress had I time to write another: but our terrors are not quite subsided; and as I lately boasted of our heroism, I am ready now to write in a strain of palinody, and make a formal recantation. . . . . .

ANN ELIZA BLEECKER

October 19.

Ann Bleecker's postal problems have an unpleasantly familiar ring.

To Miss V------,

MY DEAR PEGGY,

I AM wholly discouraged from writing any more to your quarter: our letters, I am sensible, are lost on the way, as I have not received a line from you or M---- since early last fall. This interruption must certainly be the consequence of an impertinent curiosity in some people, who break every seal they meet with, and then destroy the letters for fear of detection. If this should fall into such hands, I must observe to the gentlemen (few ladies being capable of such ungenerosity) that such a proceeding betrays a want of common honesty and common humanity in them. A period is put to many tender friendships by those impertinents, each party resenting being neglected by the other.

I hope, my dear, this mild winter presents you with every elegant pleasure. The army being in your vicinage, must certainly be productive of entertainment. S---- is at *Albany,* and I believe as sedentary as if she was at *Tomhanick* I expect her with Captains H---- and B------ to-morrow, when we shall ramble together through our forest while the snow lasts.---Shall we never see each other? This unlucky *New-York*---it is almost ominous to mention it; but I often think of it with tears, and the longer I am divided from it, the closer my affections are drawn to it.

I have spent the winter quite lonesome, Mr. B------- being always absent on public business, but is now detained in the chimney corner by a broken shin. I hear no more of K----; we have lately wrote to her, but cannot expect to receive from her such gay communicative letters any more, as she used to send us from *R------.* I hope she finds it agreeable. . . . .

To Miss T** E***.

December, 1781.

MY DEAREST SUSAN,

OUR mutual sufferings, through a remarkable train of unfortunate events, have so endeared you to me, that I bear your absence with sorrow and anxiety. After your departure my poor PEGGY was seized with a putrid fever, which almost sent her into eternity: my feelings on this occasion were exquisitely painful; but blessed be God this cloud also passed over my head, and she recovers finely after two relapses.

Would you believe it, my dear, we are again at *Tomhanick,* in my old apartment, agreeably situated in the neighbourhood of Mr. and Mrs. B-----, who live in the west part of my house. *Albany* became insupportable to me; I would rather have lived in ROLANDO'S Cavern, than in that unsociable, illiterate, stupid town; I prefer solitude to such company; but I miss you, my sister, in every part of this house; the hall, the little room, &c. continually remind me of the pleasant hours we have passed together in this unenvied retirement. Will you not return before spring? Ah! SUSAN, if you do not I shall begin the labours of our flower beds with a heavy heart; your favourite lillies will droop; nor shall I have courage to disengage your pinks from entangling weeds: endeavor, my dear, to come up; I am sure we shall be happy together. I received your obliging present, for which I sincerely thank you, and hope you enjoy all possible felicity in *Jersey,* whose present gaity is suitable to your youth and sprightliness; as for my disposition, depressed by calamities, worn out with sorrows, the pensive softness of a rural life accords best with it.------

Again I am left solitary: Mr. B------ went this morning on an expedition against the illegitimate Vermonters, (or new claimants) with Col. R------, from the Manor, who arrived here last night with his regiment, and eat up all my ducks and sausages. The new claimants are collected at *Sinchoick*, and form a little army: they have miserably mauled poor F---- and R------, who keep their beds. Our small force there increases daily, and begins to brow-beat the enemy: in short, we are all anarchy and confusion: heaven only knows when it will end.

January 2, 1782.

I CONCLUDE my journal after a long interval; but, dear SUSAN, so many occurrences have intervened, that I have had scarce time to breathe; our house has been a perfect garrison for several weeks. Our men intended, last Sunday, to storm JACKSON's house, where the tories were collected; but they capitulated: however, we are all in arms. Mr. B------ went plenipo to *Bennington* some days ago, where I attended him: we had an interview with all their great *Sakemakers*; but the issue was no way favourable to the whigs.

We firmly believe these commotions will be suppressed before spring; when I shall take it as an instance of your affection if you can relish our rustic life, and come up among us; if not, I shall submit and grieve. Dear sister, I thank you for your letter and present, though I never received the latter. CATY's goodwill and present I regard with affection, and with her all health and happiness.

How shall I drop my pen! Adieu, dear girl; we have kept your birth-day yesterday, with some agreeable neighbours, and had a dance in the evening. I am glad you are happy, which is a great and capital satisfaction to your entirely affectionate

ANN ELIZA BLEECKER.

George Washington's letters are self-revealing, witty and often personal.

[In a letter to Dr. John Cochran from West Point, August 16, 1779, Washington described a military dinner party.]

Dear Doctor: I have asked Mrs. Cochran and Mrs. Livingston to dine with me to-morrow; but am I not in honor bound to apprise them of their fare? As I hate deception, even where the imagination only is concerned, I will. It is needless to premise, that my table is large enough to hold the ladies. Of this they had ocular proof yesterday. To say how it is usually covered, is rather more essential; and this shall be the purport of my letter.

Since our arrival at this happy spot, we have had a ham, sometimes a shoulder of bacon, to grace the head of the table; a piece of roast beef adorns the foot; and a dish of beans, or greens, almost imperceptible, decorates the centre. When the cook has a mind to cut a figure, which I presume will be the case to-morrow, we have two beef-steak pies, or dishes of crabs, in addition, one on each side of the centre dish, dividing the space and reducing the distance between dish and dish to about six feet, which without them would be near twelve feet apart. Of late he has had the surprising sagacity to discover, that apples will make pies; and it is a question, if, in the violence of his efforts, we do not get one of apples, instead of having both of beef-steaks. If the ladies can put up with such entertainment, and will submit to partake of it on plates, once tin but now iron (not become so by the labor of scouring), I shall be happy to see them; and am, dear Doctor, yours, etc.

In advising Bushrod Washington, a favorite nephew, George shows evidence of being a square.

[From a letter to Bushrod Washington, Newburgh, January 15, 1783.]

REMEMBER, that it is not the mere study of the law, but to become eminent in the profession of it, that is to yield honor and profit. The first was your choice; let the second be your ambition. Dissipation is incompatible with both; the company, in which you will improve most, will be least expensive to you; and yet I am not such a stoic as to suppose that you will, or to think it right that you should, always be in company with senators and philosophers; but of the juvenile kind let me advise you to be choice. It is easy to make acquaintances, but very difficult to shake them off, however irksome and unprofitable they are found, after we have once committed ourselves to them. The indiscretions, which very often they involuntarily lead one into, prove equally distressing and disgraceful.

Be courteous to all, but intimate with few; and let those few be well tried before you give them your confidence. True friendship is a plant of slow growth, and must undergo and withstand the shocks of adversity before it is entitled to the appellation.

Let your heart feel for the afflictions and distresses of every one, and let your hand give in proportion to your purse; remembering always the estimation of the widow's mite, but, that it is not every one who asketh, that deserveth charity; all, however, are worthy of the inquiry, or the deserving may suffer.

Do not conceive that fine clothes make fine men, any more than fine feathers make fine birds. A plain, genteel dress is more admired, and obtains more credit, than lace and embroidery, in the eyes of the judicious and sensible.

The last thing, which I shall mention, is first in importance; and that is, to avoid gaming. This is a vice, which is productive of every possible evil; equally injurious to the morals and health of its votaries. It is the child of avarice, the brother of iniquity, and the father of mischief. It has been the ruin of many worthy families, the loss of many a man's honor, and the cause of suicide. To all those who enter the lists, it is equally fascinating. The successful gamester pushes his good fortune, till it is overtaken by a reverse. The losing gamester, in hopes of retrieving past misfortunes, goes on from bad to worse, till grown desperate he pushes at everything and loses his all. In a word, few gain by this abominable practice, while thousands are injured.

Perhaps you will say, "My conduct has anticipated the advice," and "Not one of the cases applies to me." I shall be heartily glad of it. It will add not a little to my happiness, to find those to whom I am so nearly connected pursuing the right walk of life. It will be the sure road to my favor, and to those honors and places of profit, which their country can bestow; as merit rarely goes unrewarded. I am, dear Bushrod, your affectionate uncle.

And when it comes to giving advice to a woman, particularly on matrimony, he is very reticent.

[A letter to Lund Washington from Rocky Hill, September 20, 1783.]

DEAR LUND: Mrs. Custis has never suggested in any of her letters to Mrs. Washington (unless ardent wishes for her return, that she might then disclose it to her, can be so construed) the most distant attachment to D. S.; but, if this should be the case, and she wants advice upon it, a father and mother, who are at hand and competent to give it, are at the same time the most proper to be consulted on so interesting an event. For my own part, I never did, nor do I believe I ever shall, give advice to a woman, who is setting out on a matrimonial voyage; first, because I never could advise one to marry without her own consent; and, secondly, because I know it is to no purpose to advise her to refrain, when she has obtained it. A woman very rarely asks an opinion or requires advice on such an occasion, till her resolution is formed; and then it is with the hope and expectation of obtaining a sanction, not that she means to be governed by your disapprobation, that she applies. In a word, the plain English of the application may be summed up in these words; "I wish you to think as I do; but, if unhappily you differ from me in opinion, my heart, I must confess, is fixed, and I have gone too far *now* to retract."

If Mrs. Custis should ever suggest anything of this kind to me, I will give her my opinion of the *measure,* not of the *man,* with candor, and to the following effect. "I never expected you would spend the residue of your days in widowhood; but in a matter so important, and so interesting to yourself, children, and connections, I wish you would make a prudent choice. To do which, many considerations are necessary; such as the family and connections of the man, his fortune (which is not the *most* essential in my eye), the line of conduct he has observed, and the disposition and frame of his mind. You should consider what prospect there is of his proving kind and affectionate to you; just, generous, and attentive to your children; and how far his connections will be agreeable to you; for when they are once formed, agreeable or not, the die being cast, your fate is fixed." Thus far, and no farther, I shall go in my opinions. I am, dear Lund, etc.

He is nonetheless overjoyed when a friend gets hooked.

{Letter to the Marquis de Chastellux.—Mount Vernon, 25 April, 1788.]

MY DEAR MARQUIS: In reading your very friendly and acceptable letter, which came to hand by the last mail, I was, as you may well suppose, not less delighted than surprised to meet the plain American words, "my wife." A wife! Well, my dear Marquis, I can hardly refrain from smiling to find you are caught at last. I saw, by the eulogium you often made on the happiness of domestic life in America, that you had swallowed the bait, and that you would as surely be taken, one day or another, as that you were a philosopher and a soldier. So your day has at length come. I am glad of it, with all my heart and soul. It is quite good enough for you. Now you are well served for coming to fight in favor of the American rebels, all the way across the Atlantic Ocean, by catching that terrible contagion, domestic felicity, which, like the small-pox or the plague, a man can have only once in his life, because it commonly lasts him (at least with us in America; I know not how you manage these matters in France), for his whole lifetime. And yet, after all, the worst wish which I can find in my heart to make against Madame de Chastellux and yourself, is, that you may neither of you ever get the better of this same domestic felicity, during the entire course of your mortal existence.

If so wonderful an event should have occasioned me, my dear Marquis, to write in a strange style, you will understand me as clearly as if I had said, what in plain English is the simple truth, "Do me the justice to believe, that I take a heart-felt interest in whatsoever concerns your happiness." And, in this view, I sincerely congratulate you on your auspicious matrimonial connection. I am happy to find that Madame de Chastellux is so intimately connected with the Duchess of Orleans; as I have always understood that this noble lady was an illustrious example of connubial love, as well as an excellent pattern of virtue in general.

While you have been making love under the banner of Hymen, the great personages in the north have been making war under the inspiration, or rather under the infatuation, of Mars. Now, for my part, I humbly conceive that you have acted much the best and wisest part; for certainly it is more consonant to all the principles of reason and religion, natural and revealed, to replenish the earth with inhabitants, than to depopulate it by killing those already in existence. Besides, it is time for the age of knight-errantry and mad heroism to be at an end. Your young military men, who want to reap the harvest of laurels, do not care, I suppose, how many seeds of war are sown; but for the sake of humanity it is devoutly to be wished, that the manly employment of agriculture, and the humanizing benefits of commerce, would supersede the waste of war and the rage of conquest; that the swords might be turned into ploughshares, the spears into pruning-hooks, and, as the Scriptures express it, the "the nations learn war no more."

Now I will give you a little news from this side of the water, and then finish. As for us, we are plodding on in the dull road of peace and politics. We, who live in these ends of the earth, only hear of the rumors of war like the roar of distant thunder. It is to be hoped that our remote local situation will prevent us from being swept into its vortex.

The constitution, which was proposed by the federal convention, has been adopted by the States of Massachusetts, Connecticut, New Jersey, Pennsylvania, Delaware, and Georgia. No State has rejected it. The convention of Maryland is now sitting, and will probably adopt it; as that of South Carolina is expected to do in May. The other conventions will assemble early in the summer. Hitherto there has been much greater unanimity in favor of the proposed government, than could have reasonably been expected. Should it be adopted, and I think it will be, America will lift up her head again, and in a few years become respectable among the nations. It is a flattering and consolatory reflection, that our rising republics have the good wishes of all the philosophers, patriots, and virtuous men in all nations; and that they look upon them as a kind of asylum for mankind. God grant that we may not disappoint their honest expectations by our folly or perverseness.

With sentiments of the purest attachment and esteem, I have the honor to be, my dear Marquis, etc.

P.S. If the Duc de Lauzun is still with you, I beg you will thank him, in my name, for his kind remembrance of me, and make my compliments to him.

May 1st.—Since writing the above, I have been favored with a duplicate of your letter in the handwriting of a lady, and cannot close this without acknowledging my obligations for the flattering postscript of the fair transcriber. In effect, my dear Marquis, the characters of this interpreter of your sentiments are so much fairer than those, through which I have been accustomed to decipher them, that I already consider myself as no small gainer by your matrimonial connection; especially as I hope your amiable amanuensis will not forget sometimes to add a few annotations of her own to your original text.

General Washington longed for retirement but his devoted people wouldn't let him go back to the farm. They wanted him as their leader. George responded to their pleas but set limitations.

[*From a Letter to Henry Lee—Mount Vernon, 22 September, 1778.*]

You are among the small number of those, who know my invincible attachment to domestic life, and that my sincerest wish is to continue in the enjoyment of it solely until my final hour. But the world would be neither so well instructed, nor so candidly disposed, as to believe me uninfluenced by sinister motives, in case any circumstance should render a deviation from the line of conduct I had prescribed to myself indispensable.

Should the contingency you suggest take place, and (for argument's sake alone let me say it) should my unfeigned reluctance to accept the office be overcome by a deference for the reasons and opinions of my friends, might I not, after the declarations I have made (and Heaven knows they were made in the sincerity of my heart), in the judgment of the impartial world and of posterity, be chargeable with levity and inconsistency, if not with rashness and ambition? Nay farther, would there not be some apparent foundation for the two former charges? Now justice to myself and tranquillity of conscience require, that I should act a part, if not above imputation, at least capable of vindication. Nor will you conceive me to be too solicitous for reputation. Though I prize as I ought the good opinion of my fellow citizens, yet, if I know myself, I would not seek or retain popularity at the expense of one social duty or moral virtue.

While doing what my conscience informed me was right, as it respected my God, my country, and myself, I could despise all the party clamor and unjust censure, which might be expected from some, whose personal enmity might be occasioned by their hostility to the government. I am conscious, that I fear alone to give any real occasion for obloquy, and that I do not dread to meet with unmerited reproach. And certain I am, whensoever I shall be convinced the good of my country requires my reputation to be put in risk, regard for my own fame will not come in competition with an object of so much magnitude. If I declined the task, it would lie upon quite another principle. Notwithstanding my advanced season of life, my increasing fondness for agricultural amusements, and my growing love of retirement, augment and confirm my decided predilection for the character of a private citizen, yet it would be no one of these motives, nor the hazard to which my former reputation might be exposed, nor the terror of encountering new fatigues and troubles, that would deter me from an acceptance; but a belief, that some other person, who had less pretence and less inclination to be excused, could execute all the duties full as satisfactorily as myself.

He refused to have an "uneasy head" and scotched the idea of his wearing a crown. President, Yes. Monarch, No!

[Letter to Colonel Lewis Nicola, Newburgh, May 22, 1782. In answer to a suggestion of an American Monarchy of which he should be the head.]

Sir: With a mixture of great surprise and astonishment, I have read with attention the sentiments you have submitted to my perusal. Be assured, Sir, no occurrence in the course of the war has given me more painful sensations, than your information of there being such ideas existing in the army, as you have expressed, and I must view with abhorrence and reprehend with severity. For the present the communication of them will rest in my own bosom, unless some further agitation of the matter shall make a disclosure necessary.

I am much at a loss to conceive what part of my conduct could have given encouragement to an address, which to me seems big with the greatest mischiefs that can befall my country. If I am not deceived in the knowledge of myself, you could not have found a person to whom your schemes are more disagreeable. At the same time, in justice to my own feelings, I must add that no man possesses a more sincere wish to see ample justice done to the army than I do; and, as far as my powers and influence, in a constitutional way, extend, they shall be employed to the utmost of my abilities to effect it, should there be any occasion. Let me conjure you, then, if you have any regard for your country, concern for yourself or posterity, or respect for me, to banish these thoughts from your mind, and never communicate, as from yourself or any one else, a sentiment of the like nature. I am, Sir, your most obedient servant.

3

Light and Lively Literature:
Ballads and Songs without Music

Writers of Ballads, witnesses to graphic events, wrote history in verse. Their compositions described the more picturesque and stirring incidents of the war.

Newspapers of the Revolutionary period, broadsides, and almanacs brought to the people of America thousands of ballads, songs and poems. They fall into two groups. In the first are anonymous and unattributed poems, all of which are better known for their quantity than their quality. The second group comprises poems by such distinguished writers of the period as John Trumbull, Philip Freneau, Francis Hopkinson, and Timothy Dwight.

It is to be expected that poems written by a people burgeoning into nationhood and imbued with a revolutionary passion would abound with an overwhelming patriotism that frequently borders on chauvinism. Characteristics shared by the two groups of ballads are their expressions of love for their country and their almost fanatical hatred of England.

Those songs and ballads which caught on at the time, and have been widely sung to this day, are not necessarily the most deserving of praise. The better-known ballads rather than the better ballads very likely were the first—perhaps the only—to be included in early nineteenth century anthologies, schoolbooks and the like, and as a result they are the ones that are remembered.

I have included an unusually large number of ballads and songs because I feel that, while they may fail individually, as a collection they present such a vivid portrait of the times that they are almost as documentary as the cartoons. We should not judge them according to their artistic merit but accept them as outpourings from the hearts and souls of dedicated men and women. These passionate expressions are part of our heritage—part of the Spirit of '76, the spirit of independence and nationhood.

The Ballad of Valley Forge.

IT was a night in winter,
   Some seventy years ago;
The bleak and barren landscape
   Was blurred with driving snow.

You caught a glimpse of uplands,
   And guessed where valleys lay:
The trees were broken shadows,
   A house was something gray.

Print Room, New York Public Library.

122

Bonfires illuminated the hills when the hated Stamp Act was repealed. People went wild with joy both physical and lyrical.

The Repeal
1766

[*The Stamp Act was passed on January 10, 1765, and repealed on February 22 the next year. News of its repeal was hailed with joy. The following is declared, in the papers of the day, to have been spoken at "a mirthful celebration of the free inhabitants of Northampton, Virginia."*]

In Greece and Rome renowned for art and arms,
Whose every bosom felt fair Freedom's charms,
Those manly breasts which generous ardor fired,
When public weal their swords or care required;
When peace abroad their conquering arms procured,
At home, when wisdom, Liberty secured:
Greatly unbending o'er the social bowl,
Indulged the transports of a genial soul.
So we, nor second to those sons of Fame,
In love of freedom, tho' of humbler name;
Or dauntless courage, bravely to oppose
Domestic tyranny, or foreign foes;—
We, who far foremost *here,* a virtuous few,
Dare to our country and ourselves be true;
Who dare, in spite of ev'ry venal frown,
Assert our rights, and lawless power disown;
Spite of each parasite, each cringing slave,
Each cautious dastard, each oppressive knave;
Each gibing Ass, *that reptile of an hour,*
The supercilious pimp of abject slaves in power;
Spite of those empty boasters, who conceal
Their coward fear with circumspection's veil,
Are met, to celebrate in festive mirth
The day that gives our *second* freedom birth;
That tells us, *Britain's Grenvilles* never more
Shall dare usurp unjust, illegal power,
Or threat *America's* free sons with chains,
While the least spark of ancient fire remains;
While records bid the virtuous sons admire
The godlike acts of each intrepid sire.
Exult *America!* each dauntless son
Will ever keep fair Liberty their own;
Will base submission, servile fear despise,
And Freedom's *substance,* not her *shadow* prize.
  Triumph America! thy patriot voice
Has made the greatest of mankind rejoice,
Immortal PITT!—O ever glorious name!

Far, far unequalled in the rolls of fame!
What breast, for virtue is by all approved,
And freedom even by Asia's slaves beloved,—
What breast but glows with gratitude to thee,
Boast of mankind, great prop of Liberty!
To thee, the best of parents and of friends,
America with grateful homage bends,
Her thanks, her love, unable to express,
To thee, great patron of her happiness.

. . . .

Would 'twere in pity to mankind decreed,
That still a PITT should to a PITT succeed:
Bid peaceful commerce reassume her seat;
Bid BRITISH navies whiten ev'ry coast,
And BRITISH freedom ev'ry country boast.
Let us then, emulous of each great name
Conspicuous in the ancient page of fame,
Resolve, that freedom to our sons be sped,
Not worse than when our valiant fathers bled:
Emerging glorious from our late distress,
Let ev'ry bosom hail returning peace:
This day let nought but jocund mirth employ,
Relax each brow, and give a loose to joy.

. . . .

Seven thousand Bostonians and their neighbors decided the tea should not be landed. Ballad writers let it be known where they stood.

The Taxed Tea
1773
A New Song

[*A number of people disguised as Indians went to Boston's harbor and began ransacking the three ships which harbored the "pestilential teas." In about two hours they broke up 342 chests of tea and dumped their contents into the sea.*

This song appeared in the Pennsylvania Packet *under the name "A New Song," it was to be sung to the tune of "Hozier's Ghost."*]

As near beauteous Boston lying,
  On the gently swelling flood,
Without jack or pendant flying,
  Three ill-fated tea-ships rode.

Just as glorious Sol was setting,
  On the wharf, a numerous crew,
Sons of freedom, fear forgetting,
  Suddenly appeared in view.

Armed with hammers, axe and chisels,
  Weapons new for warlike deed,
Towards the herbage-freighted vessels,
  They approached with dreadful speed.

.   .   .   .

"Soon," they cried, "your foes you'll banish,
  Soon the triumph shall be won;
Scarce shall setting Phoebus vanish,
  Ere the deathless deed be done."

Quick as thought the ships were boarded,
  Hatches burst and chests displayed;
Axes, hammers help afforded;
  What a glorious crash they made.

.   .   .   .

Captains! once more hoist your streamers,
  Spread your sails, and plough the wave;
Tell your masters they were dreamers,
  When they thought to cheat the brave.

Taxation nettled the colonists.

Taxation of America
by
Pieter St. John
1778

While I relate my story,
  Americans give ear;
Of Britain's fading glory
  You presently shall hear;
I'll give a true relation,
  Attend to what I say
Concerning the taxation
  Of North America.

There are two mighty speakers,
  Who rule in Parliament,
Who ever have been seeking
  Some mischief to invent;
'Twas North and Bate, his father,
  The horrid plan did lay
A mighty tax to gather
  In North America.

They searched the gloomy regions
  Of the infernal pit,
To find among their legions,
  One who excelled in wit;

To ask of him assistance,
    Or tell them how they may
Subdue without resistance
    This North America.

Old Satan the arch-traitor,
    Who rules the burning lake,
Where his chief navigator
    Resolved a voyage to take;
For the Britannic ocean
    He launches far away,
To land he had no notion
    In North America.

He takes his seat in Britain,
    It was his soul's intent
Great George's throne to sit on,
    And rule the Parliament;
His comrades were pursuing
    A diabolic way,
For to complete the ruin,
    Of North America.

Tories at home and abroad became great targets for Patriot poets and songsters. They pulled no punches when attacking the ruling powers in England, as well as the new generals who came to America to end the rebellion.

Gage's Proclamation
1774

[*Thomas Hutchinson was recalled to England early in 1774, and General Gage appointed his successor as governor of Massachusetts Bay. On his arrival at Boston in May of that year, Gage immediately issued a proclamation, calling upon the inhabitants to be loyal and again return to the friendship of an injured sovereign, assuring them at the same time that the royal authority would be supported at all hazards. This proclamation was versified in many parts of the colonies, and in various instances published as a ballad. The following first appeared in the* Virginia Gazette *as a "friendly warning."*]

A PROCLAMATION.

AMERICA! thou fractious nation,
Attend thy master's proclamation!
Tremble! for know, I, Thomas Gage,
Determin'd came the war to wage.

With the united powers sent forth,
Of Bute, of Mansfield, and of North;
To scourge your insolence, my choice,
While England mourns and Scots rejoice!

Bostonia first shall feel my power,
And gasping midst the dreadful shower
Of ministerial rage, shall cry,
Oh, save me, Bute! I yield! and die.

.   .   .   .

Rejoice! ye happy Scots rejoice!
Your voice lift up, a mighty voice,
The voice of gladness on each tongue,
The mighty praise of Bute be sung.

The praise of Mansfield, and of North,
Let next your hymns of joy set forth,
Nor shall the rapturous strain assuage,
Till sung's your own proclaiming Gage.

Whistle ye pipes! ye drones drone on.
Ye bellows blow! Virginia's won!
Your Gage has won Virginia's shore,
And Scotia's sons shall mourn no more.

Hail Middlesex! oh happy county!
Thou too shalt share thy master's bounty,
Thy sons obedient, naught shall fear,
Thy wives and widows drop no tear.

.   .   .   .

To Murray bend the humble knee;
He shall protect you under me;
His generous pen shall not be mute,
But sound your praise thro' Fox to Bute.

By Scotchmen lov'd, by Scotchmen taught,
By all your country Scotchmen thought;
Fear Bute, fear Mansfield, North and me,
And be as blest as slaves can be.

[*Gage's proclamations were frequently paraphrased in rhyme and otherwise ridiculed. One of the parodies, from the Massachusetts Spy, September, 1774, reveals the fearlessness of the Boston press in a town filled with armed troops sent to put down the rising rebellion.*]

Tom Gage's Proclamation,
Or blustering Denunciation
(Replete with Defamation)
Threatening Devastation
And speedy Jugulation
Of the New English Nation,
Who shall his pious ways shun.

.   .   .   .

Thus graciously the war I wage,
As witnesseth my hand—
                    TOM GAGE.

[When the general Continental Congress met in Philadelphia September 5, 1774, and information as to its firm proceedings reached Massachusetts, the Patriots assumed a bolder tone. Gage summoned the House of Representatives to meet at Salem to proceed to business according to the new order of things under the late act of Parliament. Town meetings were held, but so revolutionary were their proceedings, that Gage countermanded his order for the Assembly. His right to countermand was denied and most of the members elect, ninety in all, met at Salem on the day appointed. Gage, of course, was not there, and as nobody appeared to open the court or administer the oaths, they resolved themselves into a provincial Congress, adjourned to Concord, and there organized by choosing John Hancock president and Benjamin Lincoln, later a Revolutionary general, secretary. This poem appeared in the Massachusetts Spy, September 5, 1774.]

"A sample of gubernatorial eloquence, as lately
exhibited to the company of cadets."

Your Colonel H-n-k, by neglect
Has been deficient in respect;
As he my sovereign toe ne'er kissed,
'Twas proper he should be dismissed;
I never was and never will
By mortal man be treated ill.
I never was nor ever can
Be treated ill by mortal man.
Oh had I but have known before
That temper of your factious corps,
It should have been my greatest pleasure
To have prevented that bold measure.
To meet with such severe disgrace—
My standard flung into my face!
Disband yourselves! so cursed stout!
O had I, had I, turned you out!

The Blasted Herb
India Tea
1774

[This ballad has been attributed to MESHECH WEARE, who was president of the State of New Hampshire in 1776. It first appeared in Fowle's Gazette, July 22, 1774. Soon after it was adapted to a sacred air, and published in a broadside.]

ROUSE every generous thoughtful mind,
  The rising danger flee,
If you would lasting freedom find,
  Now then abandon tea.

Scorn to be bound with golden chains,
  Though they allure the sight;
Bid them defiance, if they claim
  Our freedom and birth-right.

128

Shall we our freedom give away,
   And all our comfort place
In drinking of outlandish tea,
   Only to please our taste?

Forbid it Heaven, let us be wise,
   And seek our country's good;
Nor ever let a thought arise,
   That tea should be our food.

Since we so great a plenty have,
   Of all that's for our health;
Shall we that blasted herb receive,
   Impoverishing our wealth?

   .   .   .   .

Adieu! away, oh tea! begone!
   Salute our taste no more;
Though thou art coveted by some
   Who're destined to be poor.

A Lady's Adieu to Her Tea Table

[*Without benefit of Women's Lib, Revolutionary War ladies seem to have managed rather well. The majority of them were intensely patriotic. One of their number, the daring Deborah Sampson of Massachusetts, made the army. Others served the cause at home. Through poems about and by the ladies it becomes obvious that they made themselves heard —particularly on the subjects of homespun and tea. One patriotic dame revealed her feelings and motives in blank verse.*]

Farewell the teaboard with its gaudy equipage
Of cups and saucers, creambucket, sugar tongs,
The pretty tea-chest, also lately stored
With Hyson, Congo and best double-fine.
Full many a joyous moment have I sat by ye
Hearing the girls tattle, the old maids talk scandal,
And the spruce coxcomb laugh at—maybe—nothing.
Though now detestable
Because I am taught (and I believe it true)
Its use will fasten slavish chains upon my country
To reign triumphant in America.

Virginia Banishing Tea
1774

[*Many urgent appeals were made to the colonists after the destruction of the tea at Boston, calling upon them to abstain from the use of all imported commodities, and to confine themselves to the fragrant herbs and other productions of their own fields and forests. The following poetical appeal was written by a young lady of whom all that is known is that she was, according to a contemporary observer, "a native of Virginia, endowed with all the graces of a*

BEGONE, pernicious, baneful tea,
  With all Pandora's ills possessed,
Hyson, no more beguiled by thee
  My noble sons shall be oppressed.

To Britain fly, where gold enslaves,
  And venal men their birth-right sell;
Tell *North* and his bribed clan of knaves,
  Their bloody acts were made in hell.

. . . .

But we oppose, and will be free,
  This great good cause we will defend;
Nor bribe, nor Gage, nor North's decree,
  Shall make us "at his feet to bend."

. . . .

Our king we love, but North we hate,
  Nor will to him submission own;
If death's our doom, we'll brave our fate,
  But pay allegiance to the throne.

Then rouse, my sons! from slavery free
Your suffering homes; from God's high wrath;
Gird on your steel; give *liberty*
To all who follow in our path.

Mercy Warren takes a friendly poke at the members of her sex who have determined to give up all imports from Great Britain.

Woman's Trifling Needs

[MERCY OTIS WARREN (1728–1814) *was born in Barnstable, Massachusetts and lived there until her marriage to James Warren, a young merchant of Plymouth who later became paymaster general of the Continental Army and, after the war, a member of the governor's council. Mercy Warren was a friend and correspondent of leading political figures of her day, including John Adams and Thomas Jefferson. Her natural bent for satire is revealed in her poems and plays,* The Adulateur, *in which the satire is aimed chiefly at Thomas Hutchinson, a governor of the colony of Massachusetts, and* The Group, *which deals with the abrogation of the charter of Massachusetts and the arrogation by the King of the Assembly's right to elect a Council—an action strongly resented by the people.*

The following poem was sent to John Winthrop after the patriotic resolution of the ladies of Edenton, North Carolina, to drink no more tea. In fine satire Mrs. Warren comments upon the widespread determination of American women to give up all imports from Great Britain except the necessities of life.]

130

An inventory clear
Of all she needs Lamira offers here.
Nor does she fear a rigid Catos frown
When she lays by the rich embroidered gown
And modestly compounds for just enough—
Perhaps some dozen of more slighty stuff.
With lawns and lutestrings, blond and mecklin laces,
Fringes and jewels, fans and tweezer cases,
Gay cloaks and hats of every shape and size,
Scarfs, cardinals and ribbons of all dyes.
With ruffles stamped, and aprons of tambour,
Tippets and handkerchiefs at least three score;
With finest muslins that far India boasts,
And the choice herbage from Chinesan coast.
(But while the fragrant hyson leaf regales
Who'll wear the home-spun produce of the vales?
For if 'twould save the nation from the curse
Of standing troops—or name a plague still worse,
Few can this choice delicious draught give up,
Though all Medea's poison fill the cup.)
Add feathers, furs, rich satins and ducapes
And head dresses in pyramidal shapes,
Sideboards of plate and porcelain profuse,
With fifty dittos that the ladies use.
So weak Lamira and her wants are few,
Who can refuse, they're but the sex's due.
In youth indeed an antiquated page
Taught us the threatening of a Hebrew page
Gainst wimples, mantles, curls and crisping pins,
But rank not these among our modern sins,
For when our manners are well understood
What in the scale is stomacher or hood?
Tis true we love the courtly mien and air
The pride of dress and all the debonair,
Yet Clara quits the more dressed negligé
And substitutes the careless polanê
Until some fair one from Britannia's court
Some jaunty dress or newer taste import,
This sweet temptation could not be withstood,
Though for her purchase paid her father's blood.

.   .   .   .

Can the stern patriot Clara's suit deny?
'Tis Beauty asks, and Reason must comply.

But the men had only "Sweet Applause" for the outbursts of Patriotism exhibited by the "Exalted Fair."

"*Young Ladies in Town*"
A Poem from the Massachusetts Gazette
November 9, 1767

[*The ladies were assured by the men that they would be more alluring in "decent plain Dresses made in their own Country than in gaudy butterfly, vain, fantastic, and expensive Dresses brought from Europe." It was also suggested that ladies should accept none but Patriots as suitors. The women agreed to make any sacrifices required of them provided their spouses give up their "beloved Punch, renounce going so often to Taverns, and become more kind and loving Sweethearts and Husbands." The ladies gave the assurance that "Most gladly we aside our Tea wo'd lay, Could we more Pleasure gain some other Way."*]

Young ladies in town and those that live round
    Let a friend at this season advise you.
Since money's so scarce and times growing worse,
    Strange things may soon hap and surprise you.
First then throw aside your high top knots of pride
    Wear none but your own country linen.
Of economy boast. Let your pride be the most
    To show cloaths of your own make and spinning.
What if homespun they say is not quite so gay
    As brocades, yet be not in a passion,
For when once it is known this is much wore in town,
    One and all will cry out 'T is the fashion.
And as one and all agree that you'll not married be
    To such as will wear London factory
But at first sight refuse, till e'en such you do choose
    As encourage our own manufactory.

To the Ladies
1769

[*In 1768, Bostonians resolved that they would not import any tea, glass, paper, or other commodities commonly brought from Great Britain, until the act imposing duties upon all such articles was repealed. This anonymous poetical appeal to the ladies of the country to lend a "helping hand" for the furtherance of that resolution appeared in the* Boston News Letter.]

Young ladies in town, and those that live round,
    Let a friend at this season advise you;
Since money's so scarce, and times growing worse,
    Strange things may soon hap and surprise you.

First, then, throw aside your topknots of pride;
    Wear none but your own country linen;
Of economy boast, let your pride be the most
    To show clothes of your own make and spinning.

132

What if homespun they say is not quite so gay
    As brocades, yet be not in a passion,
For when once it is known this is much worn in town,
    One and all will cry out—'Tis the fashion!

And, as one, all agree, that you'll not married be
    To such as will wear London factory,
But at first sight refuse, tell 'em such you will choose
    As encourage our own manufactory.

No more ribbons wear, nor in rich silks appear;
    Love your country much better than fine things;
Begin without passion, 'twill soon be the fashion
    To grace your smooth locks with a twine string.

Our Women
1780

[*These lines were addressed to the ladies of Pennsylvania and New Jersey, who showed their patriotism through generous subscriptions to the suffering soldiers of the American army. The author is unknown.*]

All hail! superior sex, exalted fair,
Mirrors of virtue, Heaven's peculiar care;
Form'd to enspirit and enoble man
The immortal finish of Creation's plan!

Accept the tribute of our warmest praise
The soldier's blessing and the patriot's bays!
For fame's first plaudit we no more contest
Constrain'd to own it decks the female breast.
While partial prejudice is quite disarm'd,
And e'en pale envy with encomiums charm'd,
Freedom no more shall droop her languid head,
Nor dream supine on sloth's lethargic bed.

No more sit weeping o'er the veteran band,
Those virtuous, brave protectors of her land;
Who, nobly daring, stem despotic sway,
And live the patriot wonders of the day.

For lo! these sons her glorious work renew,
Cheer'd by such gifts, and smiles, and pray'rs from
      you!
More precious treasure in the soldier's eye
Than all the wealth Potosi's mines supply.

    . . . .

The Old Man's Song
1778

[This is part of a song lauding the patriotism and courage of American women during the Revolution.]

"Boy, fill me a bumper! as long as I live,
The patriot fair for my toast must I give:
Here's a health to the sex of every degree—
Where sweetness and beauty with firmness agree.

"No more will I babble of times that are past,
My wish is, the present forever may last;
Already I see sulky George in despair—
Should he vanquish the men—to vanquish the fair!

"Of Greeks and of Romans enough has been said,
To Codrus and Brutus full tribute been paid:
O'er musty old heroes no longer I'll dream—
Living beauty and virtue enliven my theme.

"Fill a bumper again, boy, and let it go round,
For the waters of youth in claret are found;
The younkers shall know, I've the courage to dare
Drink as deep as the best to the patriot fair."

The years 1775 and 1776 ushered in an abundance of spirited ballads of liberty and independence.

Liberty Tree
by
Thomas Paine

[Published in the Pennsylvania Magazine, 1775]

In a chariot of light from the regions of day,
   The Goddess of Liberty came;
Ten thousand celestials directed the way,
   And hither conducted the dame.
A fair budding branch from the gardens above,
   Where millions with millions agree,
She brought in her hand as a pledge of her love,
   And the plant she named *Liberty Tree.*

The celestial exotic struck deep in the ground,
   Like a native it flourished and bore;
The fame of its fruit drew the nations around,
   To seek out this peaceable shore.

Unmindful of names or distinctions they came,
  For freemen like brothers agree;
With one spirit endued, they one friendship pursued,
  And their temple was *Liberty Tree.*

Beneath this fair tree, like the patriarchs of old,
  Their bread in contentment they ate
Unvexed with the troubles of silver and gold,
  The cares of the grand and the great.
With timber and tar they Old England supplied,
  And supported her power on the sea;
Her battles they fought, without getting a groat,
  For the honor of *Liberty Tree.*

But hear, O ye swains, 'tis a tale most profane,
  How all the tyrannical powers,
Kings, Commons and Lords, are uniting amain,
  To cut down this guardian of ours;
From the east to the west blow the trumpet to arms,
  Through the land let the sound of it flee,
Let the far and the near, all unite with a cheer,
  In defence of our *Liberty Tree.*

The Pennsylvania Song
1775

[*This sparkling ballad by an unknown author appeared originally in the "Poet's Corner"
of Dunlap's* Packet, *as the "Pennsylvania March," to be sung to the tune of the Scottish song,
"I winna marry any lad, but Sandy o'er the lea."*]

We are the troop that ne'er will stoop,
  To wretched slavery,
Nor shall our seed, by our base deed
  Despisèd vassals be;
Freedom we will bequeathe to them,
  Or we will bravely die;
Our greatest foe, ere long shall know,
  How much did Sandwich lie.
    And all the world shall know,
      Americans are free;
    Nor slaves nor cowards we will prove,
      Great Britain soon shall see.

We'll not give up our birthright,
  Our foes shall find us men;
As good as they, in any shape,
  The British troops shall ken.
Huzza! brave boys, we'll beat them
  On any hostile plain;

For freedom, wives, and children dear,
  The battle we'll maintain.

What! can those British tyrants think,
  Our fathers cross'd the main,
And savage foes, and dangers met,
  To be enslav'd by them?
If so, they are mistaken,
  For we will rather die;
And since they have become our foes,
  Their forces we defy.
    And all the world shall know,
      Americans are free,
    Nor slaves nor cowards we will prove,
      Great Britain soon shall see.*

Liberty's Call
1775

[*This ballad is said to have been written by Jere. Sargent of Philadelphia, of whom little is known, and also by Francis Hopkinson, the author of "The Battle of the Kegs." But it is most probable it came from the pen of John Mason, of the* Pennsylvania Packet, *the newspaper in which it first appeared.*]

High on the banks of Delaware,
  Fair Liberty she stood;
And waving with her lovely hand,
  Cried, "Still, thou roaring flood.

Be still ye winds, be still ye seas,
  Let only zephyrs play!"
Just as she spoke, they all obeyed;
  And thus the maid did say:

"Welcome my friends, from every land
  Where freedom doth not reign;
Oh! hither fly from every clime,
  Sweet liberty to gain.

"Mark Londonderry's brave defence
  'Gainst tyranny that swayed ;
Americans, the example's great!
  Like them, be not dismayed.

"Expect not that on downy beds,
  This boon you can secure;
At perils smile, rouse up your souls!
  War's dangers to endure.

*Omitted from songs with music since sheet music is unobtainable

On Independence
1776

[*The author of this poem,* JOHNATHAN MITCHELL SEWALL, *was born in 1749. He studied law and in 1774 was Register of Probate for Grafton County, New Hampshire. Later he moved to Portsmouth, where he died March 29, 1808.*]

Come all you brave soldiers, both valiant and free,
It's for Independence we all now agree;
Let us gird on our swords, and prepare to defend,
Our liberty, property, ourselves and our friends.
In a cause that's so righteous, come let us agree,
And from hostile invaders set America free,
The cause is so glorious we need not to fear,
But from merciless tyrants we'll set ourselves clear.

  · · · · · · · · · · ·

George the Third, of Great Britain, no more shall he
    reign,
With unlimited sway o'er these free States again,
Lord North, nor old Bute, nor none of their clan,
Shall ever be honor'd by an American.

May Heaven's blessings descend on our United States,
And grant that the union may never abate;
May love, peace, and harmony, ever be found,
For to go hand in hand America round.

  · · · · · · · · · · ·

Independence
1776

[*In 1774 this song appeared in the* Freeman's Journal, *about one month prior to the Declaration of Independence, as a "Parody on an ode published in the Town and Country Magazine. The loyal papers of the time speak of it as a specimen of "high-born rebel melody."*]

Freemen! if you pant for glory,
If you sigh to live in story,
   If you burn with patriot zeal;
Seize this bright auspicious hour,
Chase those venal tools of power,
   Who subvert the public weal.

Huzza! Huzza! Huzza!
See Freedom her banner display,
Whilst glory and virtue your bosoms inspire,
Corruption's proud slaves shall with anguish retire.

  · · · · · · · · · · ·

See, their glorious path pursuing,
All Britannia's troops subduing,
   Patriots whom no threats restrain.
Lawless tyrants all confounding,
Future times their praise resounding,
   Shall their triumphs long maintain.

The Patriots became more zealous. The ladies became dead serious about the war and enlistment.

By "A Lady o' Pennsylvania"

[*Early in 1774 inhabitants of Middlesex County, Virginia, made some resolutions contradictory to the general sentiment of that colony. A nameless female was inspired to pen these lines.*]

To manhood he makes a vain pretence,
Who wants both manly force and sense;
'Tis but the form not the matter,
According to the schoolmen's clatter!
From such a creature, Heaven defend her!
Each lady cries, no neuter gender!
But when a number of such creatures,
With woman's hearts and manly features,
Their country's generous schemes perplex,
I own I hate this Middle-sex.

Shortage of ammunition forced the Americans to retreat at Bunker Hill, but the outcome of the battle gave the Patriots a new sense of self-reliance and courage. And inspired poems of a serious vein.

*An Ode
on the Battle of Bunker's-Hill*

[HUGH HENRY BRACKENRIDGE, *author of this ode, was born in Scotland in 1748. His family moved to America and settled in Pennsylvania, where he was reared. At eighteen he went to the college of New Jersey where he taught classes in order to pay for his studies. He became very friendly with a classmate, the poet Philip Freneau, with whom he wrote a dramatic piece,* The Rising Glory of America. *After his graduation he tutored in Maryland. Like other playwrights he was deeply moved by the battle of Bunker Hill and wrote the play* The Battle of Bunker's-Hill *as a dramatic vehicle for his pupils. After his play was published in 1776 he left the teaching field to edit the* United States Magazine. *The following year he enlisted as Chaplain in the Continental Army. He wrote several other dramas, including the tragedy* The Death of General Montgomery at the Siege of Quebec. *This ode was "Sung and Acted by a Soldier in a Military Habit, with his Firelock, etc." Brackenridge died in 1816.*]

You bold warriors, who resemble
    Flames upon the distant hill;
At whose view the heroes tremble,
    Fighting with unequal skill.
Loud-sounding drums, now with hoarse murmurs,
    Rouse the spirit up to war;
Fear not, fear not, though their numbers
    Much to ours superior are.
Hear brave Warren, bold commanding:
    "Gallant souls and veterans brave,
See the enemy just landing
    From the navy-covered wave.
Close the wings—advance the centre—
    Engineers point well your guns—
Clap the matches—let the rent air
    Bellow to Britannia's sons."

Now, think you see three thousand moving,
    Up the brow of Bunker's hill;
Many a gallant veteran shoving
    Cowards on, against their will.
The curling volumes all behind them,
    Dusky clouds of smoke arise;
Our cannon-balls, brave boys, shall find them,
    At each shot a hero dies.
Once more, Warren, 'midst this terror,
    "Charge, brave soldiers, charge again!
Many an expert veteran warrior
    Of the enemy is slain.
Level well your charged pieces,
    In direction to the town;
They shake, they shake, their lightning ceases;
    That shot brought six standards down."
Maids in virgin beauty blooming,
On Britannia's sea-girt isle,
Say no more your swains are coming,
    Or with songs the day beguile,
For sleeping found in death's embraces,
    On their clay-cold beds they lie;
Death, grim death, alas, defaces
    Youth and pleasure, which must die.
"March the right wing, Gardiner, yonder;
    The hero spirit lives in thunder;
Take the assailing foe in flank,
    Close there, sergeants, close that rank.
The conflict now doth loudly call on
    Highest proof of martial skill;
Heroes shall sing of them, who fall on
    The slippery brow of Bunker's Hill."

Midnight Musings: or A Trip to Boston, 1775
by
Philip Freneau

[PHILIP FRENEAU, *a native of the city of New York, was born on January 2, 1752, and died December 18, 1832. He is regarded as the most popular poet of the revolution. The greater part of his work does not come under the class of songs or ballads.*

The surrounding of Boston with military troops on land and privateers at sea began to have a serious effect upon the officers, troops, and people in the city. They had an abundance of salt provision, but, being unaccustomed to such diet, many fell sick. This satire was first published as "A Voyage to Boston." The scene was laid in the quarters of General Gage the night after the battle of Bunker Hill, where Lord Percy and General Gage commiserated about the scanty diet.]

Lord Percy seem'd to snore—O conscious Muse,
This ill-timed snoring to the Peer excuse,
Tir'd was the Hero of his toilsome day,
Full fifteen miles he fled,—a tedious way—
How should he then the dews of Somnus shun,
Perhaps not us'd to walk, much less to run.

. . . .

Three weeks, ye gods! nay, three long years it seems
Since roast beef I have touched, except in dreams.
In sleep, choice dishes to my view repair;
Waking, I gape, and champ the empty air.
Say, is it just that I, who rule these bands,
Should live on husks, like rakes in foreign lands?
Come, let us plan some project ere we sleep,
And drink destruction to the rebel sheep.
On neighboring isles uncounted cattle stray;
Fat beeves and swine—an ill-defended prey—
These are fit 'visions for my noonday dish;
These, if my soldiers act as I could wish,
In one short week would glad your maws and mine;
On mutton we will sup—on roast beef dine."

The Epistle to the Troops in Boston
1775

[*There were four different editions of this ballad, published as broadsides, a short time after its first appearance in the* Pennsylvania Magazine. *The first broadside was printed in May, 1775, and differs slightly in language from the version in the periodical. It is said to have been written by a Yankee-Irishman.*]

By my faith, but I think ye're all makers of bulls,
With your brains in your breeches, your —— in your
    skulls,
Get home with your muskets, and put up your swords,

140

And look in your books for the meaning of words.
You see now, my honies, how much your mistaken,
For Concord by discord can never be beaten.

How brave ye went out with your muskets all bright,
And thought to be-frighten the folks with the sight;
But when you got there how they powder'd your pums,
And all the way home how they pepper'd your ——,
And is it not, honeys, a comical crack,
To be proud in the face, and be shot in the back.

. . . .

How come ye to think, now, they did not know how,
To be after their firelocks as smartly as you?
Why, you see now, my honies, 'tis nothing at all,
But to pull at the trigger, and pop goes the ball.

And what have you got now with all your designing,
But a town without victuals to sit down and dine in;
And to look on the ground like a parcel of noodles,
And sing, how the Yankees have beaten the Doodles.
I'm sure if you're wise you'll make peace for a dinner,
For fighting and fasting will soon make ye thinner.

The Quarrel with America Fairly Stated

[*This poem appeared in Anderson's* Constitutional Gazette, *published in New York, 1775. This paper was an opponent of Rivington's (Tory)* Gazette *published in the same city.*]

Rudely forced to drink tea, Massachusetts in anger
Spills the tea on John Bull—John falls on to bang her;
Massachusetts, enraged, calls her neighbors to aid,
And gives Master John a severe bastinade
Now, good men of the law! pray, who is in fault,
The one who begun, or resents the assult?

. . . .

See the steely points, bright gleaming
    In the sun's fierce dazzling ray;
Groans arising, life-blood streaming
    Purple o'er the face of day.
The field is covered with the dying,
    Freemen mixed with tyrants lie,
The living with each other vying
    Raise the shout of battle high.
Now brave Putnam, aged soldier:
    "Come, my veterans, we must yield;

More equal matched, we'll yet charge bolder,
    For the present quit the field.
The God of battles shall revisit
    On their heads each soul that dies;
Take courage, boys, we yet sha'n't miss it,
    From a thousand victories."

A Military Song
by the
Army:
On General Washington's victorious entry
into the Town of Boston

[*Excerpts from Hugh Henry Brackenridge's drama* Bunker's Hill]

I.
Sons of valour, taste the glories,
    Of Celestial LIBERTY,
Sing a Triumph o'er the Tories
    Let the pulse of joy beat high.
II.
Heaven this day hath foil'd the many
    Fallacies of GEORGE their King,
Let the echo reach Britan'y
    Bid her mountain summits ring.
III.
See yon Navy swell the bosom,
    Of the late enraged sea,
Where e'er they go we shall oppose them,
    Sons of valour must be free.
IV.
Should they touch at fair RHOPE-ISLAND,
    There to combat with the brave,
Driven, from each hill, and high-land,
    They shall plough the purple wave.

. . . .

VI.
To CAROLINA or to GEORG'Y
    Should they next advance their fame,
This land of heroes shall disgorge the
    Sons of tyranny and shame.

. . . .

XII.
Like Satan banished from HEAVEN,
    Never see the smiling shore,
From this land so happy, driven,
    Never stain its bosom more.
The End.

Loyal York
1775

[*In January 1775, William Franklin, the governor of the colony of New Jersey, warned the legislature not to sanction certain proceedings connected with the dispute existing between the mother country and the colonies, assuring them that all their grievances would be redressed on petition. Lieutenant-Governor Colden of New York followed his example, and the majority of the New York assembly agreed not to send delegates to the Congress that was to assemble in May of that year. This was a triumph for the Loyalists, and the cause of great rejoicing. The following song appeared a short time after the event in the* Gazetteer *at New York, and has been attributed to Rivington, the editor of that Loyalist paper, but without any authority.*]

And so, my good master, I find 'tis no joke,
For York has stepp'd forward, and thrown off the yoke
Of Congress, committees, and even King Sears,
Who shows you good nature, by showing his ears.

I trembled lest York should have join'd the mad freak,
And formed a part of the damnable sneak;
The fever abated, see order arise,
With ag'd constitutional tears in her eyes.

Having summon'd her sons, who too wantonly stray'd,
And calling her fair sister Grace to her aid,
The youth she address'd, in such accents of love,
As coming from mothers, ought always to move.

Says she, "My dear children, ah! why should ye roam,
In quest of rude discord, and leave me at home?
Your godfather Monarchy, bleeds at the heart,
To think that his sons should from virtue depart.

"Consider how long we have cherish'd, protected,
How much we've indulg'd, and how little corrected,
How oft we're provok'd, and our councils tormented;
What insults forgiven, what bloodshed prevented.

"Behold your good brother, who rules in the north,
Examine his conduct and copy his worth:
Observe how Apollo presides, and you'll find,
How lovely are mercy and power combin'd.

"His task, though severe, he discharges with ease,
And studies, like us, to preserve and to please;
Oh! think how he feels, between brother and brother,
When he's sent to reconcile one to the other.

"Then cease, I beseech you, nor longer provoke
The hand, which so tenderly wards off the stroke.

Such counsel as this was enough, one would think,
To save them from ruin, though just on the brink.

"But would you believe, a committee they'd choose,
Consisting of three, who had nothing to lose?
One was a cock of the first game,
Who hand over hand was determin'd on fame.

"The second A-dam dog who lives upon strife,
And knows nought but hemp can lead him a worse
     life:
The third was a Cooper, good Lord, long preserve him,
Or, as I want rhyme, may his customers starve him!

"Together they went on a grand consultation,
To prove a republic was good for the nation,
And to show the old dame, it was easily prov'd,
Pronounced, by four words, all objections remov'd.

"Inestimable rights, infernal chains,"
A sleeping potion for a Briton's brains.—
The aged matron silently withdrew,
Wept for her sons, and left them, Gage! to you.

The Times
1776

[*There were a number of songs written under this title during the Revolutionary War. This spirited one appeared on a broadside in 1776. Later, it appeared in a music sheet adapted to the "Tune of the sweeper:—Though I sweep to and fro" for which despite careful researching no sheet music was found.*]

My muse, now thy aid and assistance we claim,
Whilst freedom, dear freedom, affords us a theme,
Invok'd, be propitious, nor madly forbear,
When a theme that's so sacred should ring far and near.
    Oh! let freedom, and friendship, for ever remain,
    Nor that rascal draw breath, who would forge us a
        chain.

As our fathers have fought, and our grandfathers bled,
And many a hero now sleeps with the dead;
Let us nobly defend, what they bravely maintain'd,
Nor suffer our sons to be fetter'd and chain'd.

        .   .   .   .

Though our foes may look on, and our friends may
        admire,
How a BUTE or a NORTH, should set nations on fire,

Yet Satan, when suffer'd his madness to vent,
In meanest of mansions sure pitches his tent.

Shall freedom, that blessing sent down from above,
A manifest mark of God's wonderful love,
Be left at his will, who delights to annoy,
Whose pleasure is nought but to kill and destroy?

.   .   .   .

May our King be as wise as we mortals expect;
Each rascal from council then boldly eject;
May his life be as good, and his reign be as great,
As ever was Solomon's wonderful state.

.   .   .   .

Let singular blessings America crown;
May the Congress be blest with immortal renown;
Each colony live in true sisterly peace,
Whilst harmony, honor, and riches increase.
   Oh! let freedom and friendship for ever remain,
   Nor that rascal draw breath, who would forge us a
   chain.*

.   .   .   .

[*In a version of this song published in 1777, the following stanza was added:*]

The times, it seems, are altered quite,
The scales are cracked, the sword is broke,
Right is now wrong, and wrong is right.
And justice is a standing joke.

By '76 battle cries and war songs erupted as an increasing number of men were mustered into the Continental Army. Their mood reflects the mood of the people.

War Song

[*This song is believed to have been published in 1776. Frank Moore, in his* Ballads and Songs of the Revolution, *had a music sheet containing it and* The Liberty Song *with the impress showing it was printed by Benjamin Dearborn in that year.*]

Hark, hark, the sound of war is heard,
   And we must all attend;
Take up our arms and go with speed,
   Our country to defend.

Our parent state has turned our foe,
   Which fills our land with pain;
Her gallant ships, manned out for war,
   Come thundering o'er the main.

*Omitted from songs with music since sheet music is unobtainable

145

There's Carleton, Howe, and Clinton too.
    And many thousands more,
May cross the sea, but all in vain,
    Our rights we'll ne'er give o'er.

Our pleasant homes they do invade,
    Our property devour;
And all because we won't submit
    To their despotic power.

Then let us go against our foe,
    We'd better die than yield;
We and our sons are all undone,
    If Britain wins the field.

. . . .

As George III's lackeys bowed out of Boston, George Washington bowed in.

A Military Song
1776

[*This stanza from a song of 48 lines, by an anonymous writer, was entitled "A Military Song, by the Army, on General Washington's victorious entry into the town of Boston."*]

War, fierce war, shall break their forces;
    Nerves of Tory men shall fail;
Seeing Howe, with alter'd courses,
    Bending to the Western gale.
Thus from every bay of ocean
    Flying back with sails unfurl'd,
Toss'd with ever-troubled motion,
    They shall quit this smiling world.

Burrowing Yankees
1776

[*Four different editions of this song were published on broadsides during the two years following its first appearance in the* Halifax Journal *shortly after the evacuation of Boston. The newspapers, attached to the cause of the patriots, generally republished as "a piece of tory gasconading."*]

Ye Yankees who, mole-like still throw up the earth,
And like them, to your follies are blind from your birth;
Attempt not to hold British troops at defiance,
True Britons, with whom you pretend an alliance.

Mistake not; such blood ne'er run in your veins,
'Tis no more than the dregs, the lees, or the drains:

Ye affect to talk big of your hourly attacks;
Come on! and I'll warrant, we'll soon see your backs.

Such threats of bravadoes serve only to warm
The true British hearts, you ne'er can alarm;
The Lion once rous'd, will strike such a terror,
Shall show you, poor fools, your presumption and error.

And the time will soon come when your whole rebel race
Will be drove from the lands, nor dare show your face:
Here's a health to great *George,* may he fully determine,
To root from the earth all such insolent vermin.

Burgoyne's Proclamation
1777

[*On the 4th of July, 1777, General Burgoyne issued a proclamation from his camp near Ticonderoga, which he hoped would spread terror among the Americans. But it was so pompous and bombastic that, instead of producing the desired effect, it became the subject of ridicule and derision. This poem is alleged to have been written by Francis Hopkinson.*]

By John Burgoyne, and Burgoyne, John, Esq.,
And grac'd with titles still more higher,
For I'm Lieutenant-general, too,
Of George's troops both red and blue,
On this extensive continent;
And of Queen Charlotte's regiment
Of light dragoons the Colonel;
And Governor eke of Castle Wil—
And furthermore, when I am there,
In House of Commons I appear,
[Hoping ere long to be a Peer.]
Being a member of that virtuous band
Who always vote at North's command;
Directing too the fleet and troops
From Canada as thick as hops;
And all my titles to display,
I'll end with thrice et cetera.

    . . . .

But now inspired with patriot love
I come th' oppression to remove;
To free you from the heavy clog
Of every tyrant demagogue.
Who for the most romantic story,
Claps into limbo loyal Tory,
All hurly burly, hot and hasty,
Without a writ to hold him fast by;
Nor suffers any living creature,
[Led by the dictates of his nature,]

147

To fight in green for Britain's cause,
Or aid us to restore her laws;

.   .   .   .

I swear by George, and by St. Paul
I will exterminate you all.
Subscrib'd with my manual sign
To test these presents, John Burgoyne.

In days of gloom Hopkinson's songs and ballads raised the spirits of the soldiers.

Camp Ballad
1777
by
Francis Hopkinson

[*In the critical year 1777 this popular ode of Hopkinson's stirred the hearts of his countrymen.*]

Make room, oh! ye kingdoms in hist'ry renowned,—
Whose arms have in battle with glory been crowned,—
Make room for America,—another great nation
Arising to claim in your council a station.

.   .   .   .

With glory immortal she here sits enthroned,
Nor fears the vain vengeance of Britain disowned;
Whilst Washington guards her, with heroes surrounded,
Her foes shall with shameful defeat be confounded.

To arms, then, to arms!—'t is fair freedom invites us;
The trumpet, shrill sounding, to battle excites us;
The banners of virtue unfurled shall wave o'er us,
Our heroes lead on, and the foe fly before us.

On Heaven and Washington placing reliance,
We'll meet the bold Briton, and bid him defiance;
Our cause we'll support, for 't is just and 't is glorious—
When men fight for freedom, they must be victorious.

Sweet was the taste of glory in New Jersey.

Battle of Trenton

[*The success of the Americans at Trenton and Princeton brought forth numerous songs, odes, epigrams and pasquinades commemorating the battle. The author of this poem is unknown. It is believed to have been modeled on the Earl of Dorset's lyric "Fire of Love," which was very popular at the time of the Revolution.*]

148

On Christmas-day in seventy-six,
Our ragged troops, with bayonets fixed,
  For Trenton marched away.
The Delaware see! the boats below!
The light obscured by hail and snow!
  But no signs of dismay.

Our object was the Hessian band,
That dared invade fair freedom's land,
  And quarter in that place.
Great Washington he led us on,
Whose streaming flag, in storm or sun,
  Had never known disgrace.

In silent march we passed the night,
Each soldier panting for the fight,
  Though quite benumbed with frost.
Greene on the left at six began,
The right was led by Sullivan
  Who ne'er a moment lost.

Their pickets stormed, the alarm was spread,
That rebels risen from the dead
  Were marching into town.
Some scampered here, some scampered there,
And some for action did prepare;
  But soon their arms laid down.

Twelve hundred servile miscreants,
With all their colors, guns, and tents,
  Were trophies of the day.
The frolic o'er, the bright canteen,
In centre, front, and rear was seen
  Driving fatigue away.

Now, brothers of the patriot bands,
Let's sing deliverance from the hands
  Of arbitrary sway.
And as our life is but a span,
Let's touch the tankard while we can,
  In memory of that day.

[*On the Hessian standards taken at Trenton were the words* Nescit Pericula, *"He knows no danger," which were hardly appropriate in the battle where the standards were surrendered.* The New Hampshire Gazette *came up with the following epigram.*]

The man who submits without striking a blow,
May be said, in a sense, no danger to know:
I pray then, what harm, but the humble submission,
At Trenton was done by the standard of Hessians?

149

The early failures of British generals were grist for the mill. Burgoyne had more than his share of brickbats.

The Fate of John Burgoyne

[*This ballad, written in 1777, starts out by telling of the hero's lively departure from London to conquer America.*]

When Jack the king's commander
  Was going to his duty,
Through all the crowd he smiled and bowed
  To every blooming beauty.

The city rung with feats he'd done
  In Portugal and Flanders,
And all the town thought he'd be crowned
  The first of Alexanders.

To Hampton Court he first repairs
  To kiss great George's hand, sirs;
Then to harangue on state affairs
  Before he left the land, sirs.

The "Lower House" sat mute as mouse
  To hear his grand oration;
And "all the peers," with loudest cheers,
  Proclaimed him to the nation.

Then off he went to Canada,
  Next to Ticonderoga,
And quitting those away he goes
  Straightway to Saratoga.

With great parade his march he made
  To gain his wished-for station,
While far and wide his minions hied
  To spread his "Proclamation."

To such as stayed he offers made
  Of "pardon on submission;
But savage bands should waste the lands
  Of all in opposition."

The Continental Army had its ups and downs (mostly downs) until 1777 at Saratoga, when, to everyone's surprise, Burgoyne was overthrown.

Burgoyne's Overthrow at Saratoga
1777

[This poem was first published in the Iris *in June, 1841; the original manuscript was then in the possession of George H. Moore, an editor of that periodical. It is a résumé of the losses of the British army during the northern campaign which terminated at Saratoga. The results are given in round numbers.]*

Here followeth the direful fate
Of Burgoyne and his army great,
Who so proudly did display
The terrors of despotic sway.
His power, and pride, and many threats,
Have been brought low by fort'nate Gates,
To bend to the United States.
British prisoners by Convention, . . . 2442
Foreigners—by Contra-vention, . . . 2198
Tories sent across the Lake, . . . 1100
Burgoyne and suite, in state, . . . 12
Sick and wounded, bruised and pounded, ⎫
Ne'er so much before confounded, ⎬ 528
Prisoners of war before Convention, . . 400
Deserters come with kind intention, . . 300
They lost at Bennington's great battle, ⎫
Where glorious Starke's arms did rattle, ⎬ 1220
Killed in September and October, . . . 600
Ta'en by brave Brown, some drunk, some sober, 413
Slain by high-famed Herkerman, ⎫
On both flanks, on rear and van, ⎬ 300
Indians, suttlers, and drovers, ⎫
Enough to crowd large plains all over, ⎪
And those whom grim Death did prevent ⎪
From fighting against our continent; ⎬ 4413
And also those who stole away, ⎪
Lest down their arms they should lay, ⎪
Abhorring that obnoxious day; ⎭
The whole make fourteen thousand men, ⎫
Who may not with us fight again, ⎬ 14,000
This is a pretty just account
Of Burgoyne's legions whole amount,
Who came across the Northern Lakes
To desolate our happy States.
Their brass cannons we have got all—
Fifty-six—both great and small;
And ten thousand stand of arms,
To prevent all future harms;
Stores and implements complete,
Of workmanship exceeding neat;

Covered wagons in great plenty,
And proper harness, no way scanty.
Among our prisoners there are
Six Generals, of fame most rare;
Six members of their Parliament—
Reluctantly they seem content;
Three British Lords, and Lord Bellcaras,
Who came, our country free to harass.
Two Baronets of high extraction,
Were sorely wounded in the action.

"On Gen. Burgoyne's Defeat"

[This song is from the Rare Book Room of the Library of Congress. It was to be sung to the tune of "Jack, a brisk young drummer," but the sheet music has not yet been uncovered.]

As Jack, the king's commander,
　　Was going to his duty,
Thro' all the croud he smil'd and bow'd
　　To ev'ry blooming beauty;

The city rung of feats he'd done,
　　In Portugal and Flanders,
And all the town thought he'd be crown'd
　　The first of Alexanders.

To Hompton-court he first repair'd
　　To kiss great George's hand, sir;
Then to harangue on state affairs,
　　Before he left the land, sir;

The lower house sat mute as mouse,
　　To hear his grand oration;
And all the peers, with loudest cheers,
　　Proclaim'd him thro' the nation.

Then strait he went to Canada,
　　Next to Ticonderoga;
And passing those, away he goes
　　Straight way to Saratoga,

With grand parade his march he made,
　　To gain his wish'd for station;
Whilst far and wide his minions try'd
　　To spread his proclamation.

To such as staid, he offers made
　　Of pardon on submission;
But savage band should waste the land
　　Of all in opposition:

But ah, the cruel fate of war,
   This boasted son of Britain,
When mounting his triumphal car,
   With sudden fear was smitten.

The sons of freedom gather'd round,
   His hostile band confounded,
And when they'd fain have turn'd their backs,
   They found themselves surrounded.

In vain they fought, in vain they fled,
   Their chief, humane and tender,
To save the rest, he thought it best
   His forces to surrender.

Brave St. Clair, when he first retir'd,
   Knew what the fates portended,
And Arnold, with heroic Gates,
   His conduct have defended.

Thus may America's brave sons
   With honor be rewarded;
And be the fate of all her foes
   The fame as here recorded.

Francis Hopkinson comes up with some of his satirical doggerel.

Burgoyne

[*From manuscript volumes owned by Mrs. Florence Scovel Shinn, a descendant of Hopkinson. Printed in* Heralds of American Literature.]

Burgoyne with thousand came
In hopes of Wealth and Fame
   What hath he done?
At Saratoga he
Had the Disgrace to see
Each soldier manfully
   Lay down his Gun.

The defeat of Burgoyne caused uneasiness and alarm in England. In 1778 Parliament tried to pull a fast one but the Americans blocked it.

The Gamester
1778

[*Not long after, Parliament sent commissioners to the Continental Congress, with proposals for a mutual adjustment of the existing difficulties. The terms were conciliatory, and it was hoped they might sway the colonists against their leaders, as many were disheartened and tired of the war. Fearing such an event, Congress immediately published an address, wherein they fully exposed the trap laid by the royal commissioners. At the same time, they presented the Patriots with the bright prospects of success in winning their liberty and independence. This address had the desired effect: the people resolved not to be deceived. The following ballad appeared before the royal commissioners returned to England, in a double-columned sheet, adapted to the tune, "A late worthy old Lion."*]

West of the old Atlantic, firm Liberty stands!
Hov'ring Fame just alighted, supported by bands
Of natives free born, who loud echoing sing,
"We'll support our just rights 'gainst tyrannic kings!"
        Caral-laddy—caral-laddy, &c.

George the Third she disowns and his proud lordly cheats,
His murdering legions and half-famish'd fleets;
To the Jerseys sneak'd off, with fear quite dismay'd,
Although they much boasted, that fighting's their trade.

Our just rights to assert, hath the Congress oft tried,
Whose wisdom and strength our opponents deride,
And still madly in rage their weak thunders are hurl'd,
To bring us on our knees and to bully the world.

Too haughty to yield, yet too weak to withstand,
They skulk to their ships and leave us the firm land;
In dread lest they share what Jack Burgoyne did feel,
And the game be quite lost, as poor Jack had lost deal.

Jack, thinking of cribbage, all fours, or of put,
With a dexterous hand, he did shuffle and cut,
And when likely to lose—like a sharper they say—
Did attempt to renege—I mean, run away.

But watch'd so closely, he could not play booty,
Yet to cheat he fain would, for George—'twas his duty;
A great bet depending on that single game;
Dominion and honor—destruction and shame.

Examin'd with care his most critical hand,
At a loss, if better to beg or to stand,
His tricks reckon'd up; for all sharpers can jangle;
Then kick'd up a dust, for his favorite wrangle.

'Twas diamond cut diamond, spades were of no use,
But to dig up the way for surrender and truce;
For he dreaded the hand that dealt out such thumps;
As the hearts were run out, and clubs were then trumps.

Thus he met with the rubbers, as the game it turn'd out,
Poor Jack, although beat, made a damnable rout,
Complain'd he was cheated, and pompously talks;
Quit the game with a curse, while he rubb'd out the chalks.

   · · · · · · · ·

The haughty great George then to peace is now prone;
A bully when matched soon can alter his tone;
'Tis the act of a Briton to bluster and threaten;
Hangs his tail like a spaniel, when handsomely beaten.

Charge your glasses lip high, to brave Washington sing,
To the union so glorious the whole world shall ring;
May their councils in wisdom and valor unite,
And the men ne'er be wrong, who yet so far are right.

   · · · · · · · ·

To Gates and to Arnold, with bumpers we'll join,
And to all our brave troops who took gambling Burgoyne.
May their luck still increase, as they've turn'd up one Jack,
To cut and turn up all the knaves in the pack.

The Tories lyricize their invincibility, sneer at the rebellion, and mock the low origin and vulgar occupations of the Patriots. Continental troops ignored the sneers. . . .

A Fable
[Rivington's Royal Gazette, *1778*]

Rejoice, Americans, rejoice!
Praise ye the Lord with heart and voice!
The treaty's signed with faithful France,
And now, like Frenchmen, sing and dance!

But when your joy gives way to reason,
And friendly hints are not deemed treason,
Let me, as well as I am able,
Present your Congress with a fable.

Tired out with happiness, the frogs
Sedition croaked through all their bogs;
And thus to Jove the restless race,
Made out their melancholy case.

"Famed, as we are, for faith and prayer,
We merit sure peculiar care;
But can we think great good was meant us,
When logs for Governors were sent us?

"Which numbers crushed they fell upon,
And caused great fear,—till one by one,
As courage came, we boldly faced 'em,
Then leaped upon 'em, and disgraced 'em!

"Great Jove," they croaked, "no longer fool us,
None but ourselves are fit to rule us;
We are too large, too free a nation,
To be encumbered with taxation!

We pray for peace, but wish confusion,
Then right or wrong, a—revolution!
Our hearts can never bend to obey;
Therefore no king—and more we'll pray.

Jove smiled, and to their fate resigned
The restless, thankless, rebel kind;
Left to themselves, they went to work,
First signed a treaty with king Stork.

. . . .

The Stork grew hungry, longed for fish;
The monarch could not have his wish;
In rage he to the marshes flies,
And makes a meal of his allies.

Then grew so fond of well-fed frogs,
He made a larder of the bogs!
Say, Yankees, don't you feel compunction,
At your unnatural rash conjunction?

. . . .

The Rebels
1778

[*A Captain Smyth, an officer in Simcoe's Queen's Rangers, was the author of this bold and loyal song. Many of his compositions were published during the war. The present one appeared first in the* Pennsylvania Ledger *as "a new song, to the old tune of Black Joke," and subsequently in a ballad sheet, under its present title.*]

Ye brave, honest subjects, who dare to be loyal,
And have stood the brunt of every trial,
  Of hunting-shirts, and rifle-guns:
Come listen awhile, and I'll sing you a song;
I'll show you, those Yankees are all in the wrong,
Who, with blustering look and most awkward gait,
'Gainst their lawful sovereign dare for to prate,
  With their hunting-shirts, and rifle-guns.

The arch-rebels, barefooted tatterdemalions,
In baseness exceed all other rebellions,
  With their hunting-shirts, and rifle-guns.
To rend the empire, the most infamous lies,
Their mock-patriot Congress, do always devise;
Independence, like the first of rebels, they claim,
But their plots will be damn'd in the annals of fame,
  With their hunting-shirts, and rifle-guns.

Forgetting the mercies of Great Britain's king,
Who saved their forefathers' necks from the string;
   With their hunting-shirts, and rifle guns.
They renounce allegiance and take up their arms,
Assemble together like hornets in swarms,
So dirty their backs, and so wretched their show,
That carrion-crow follows wherever they go,
   With their hunting-shirts, and rifle-guns.
     . . . .

For one lawful ruler, many tyrants we've got,
Who force young and old to their wars, to be shot,
   With their hunting-shirts, and rifle-guns.
Our good king, God speed him! never used men so,
We then could speak, act, and like freemen could go;
But committees enslave us, our Liberty's gone,
Our trade and church murder'd; our country's undone,
   By hunting-shirts, and rifle-guns.
     . . . .

Come take up your glasses, each true loyal heart,
And may every rebel meet his due desert,
   With his hunting-shirt, and rifle-gun.
May Congress, Conventions, those damn'd inquisitions,
Be fed with hot sulphur, from Lucifer's kitchens,
May commerce and peace again be restored,
And Americans own their true sovereign lord.
   Then oblivion to shirts, and rifle-guns.
     God save the King.

The Etiquette
1779

[*The writer of this derisive English ballad is unknown. "The Etiquette" first appeared in the* London Magazine *in 1778. The many editions of it that appeared during the last year of the Revolution established its popularity.*]

What though America doth pour
Her millions to Britannia's store,
Quoth Grenville, that won't do—for yet,
Taxation is the etiquette.

The tea destroy'd, the offer made
That all the loss should be repaid—
North asks not justice, nor the debt,
But he must have the etiquette.

He'd stop their port—annul their laws—
"Hear us," cried Franklin, "for our cause!"
To hear th' accus'd, the senate met,
Decreed 'twas not the etiquette.

At Bunker's Hill the cause was tried,
The earth with British blood was dyed;
Our army, though 'twas soundly beat,
We hear, bore off the etiquette.

The bond dissolv'd, the people rose,
Their rulers from themselves they chose;
Their Congress then at naught was set—
Its name was not the etiquette.

. . . .

The Yankees at Long Island found
That they were nearly run aground;
Howe let them 'scape when so beset—
He will explain the etiquette.

His aide-de-camps to Britain boast
Of battles—Yankee never lost;
But they are won in the Gazette—
That saves the nation's etiquette.

Clinton his injur'd honor saw,
Swore he'd be tried by martial law,
And kick Germaine whene'er they met—
A ribbon sav'd that etiquette.

Of Saratoga's dreadful plain—
An army ruin'd; why complain?
To pile their arms as they were let,
Sure they came off with etiquette!

Cries Burgoyne, "They may be reliev'd,
That army still may be retriev'd,
To see the king if I be let;"
"No, sir! 'tis not the etiquette."

God save the king! and should he choose
His people's confidence to lose,
What matters it? they'll not forget
To serve him still—through etiquette.

Royalty was not exempt from versified ridicule. In fact, if there had been an unpopularity contest in America, George might have won.

George the Third's Soliloquy
1779
by
Philip Freneau

[*This specimen of Freneau's writings was first published in the* United States Magazine, *and afterwards, with some changes by the poet, appeared in the various editions of his poems.*]

Oh! blast this Congress, blast each upstart State,
On whose commands ten thousand warriors wait;
From various climes that dire assembly came,
True to their trust, yet hostile to my fame.
'Tis these, ah! these have ruin'd half my sway,
Disgrac'd my arms, and lead my realm astray.

France aids them now; I play a desperate game,
And sunburnt Spain they say will do the same;
My armies vanquish'd, and my heroes fled,
My people murmuring, and my commerce dead.
My shatter'd navy, pelted, bruis'd, and clubb'd,
By Dutchmen bullied, and by Frenchmen drubb'd.

My name abhorr'd, my nation in disgrace,
What should I do in such a mournful case?
My hopes and joys are vanish'd, with my coin,
My ruined army, and my lost Burgoyne!
What shall I do, confess my labors vain,
Or whet my tusks, and to the charge again?
. . . .

Yet rogues and savage tribes I must employ,
And what I cannot conquer, will destroy.
Is there a robber close in Newgate hemm'd?
Is there a cut-throat fetter'd and condemn'd?
Haste, loyal slaves, to George's standard come,
Attend his lectures when you hear the drum.
. . . .

"Come labor and sing," warbled Sir Henry Clinton, but at this point few loyalists harkened.

Sir Henry Clinton's Invitation to the Refugees
1779
by
Philip Freneau

Come, gentlemen tories, firm, loyal, and true,
Here are axes and shovels, and something to do!
For the sake of our King,

> Come labor and sing.
> You left all you had for his honor and glory,
> And he will remember the suffering tory.
> > We have, it is true,
> > Some small work to do;
> But here's for your pay, twelve coppers a day,
> And never regard what the rebels may say,
> But throw off your jerkins and labor away.
>
> . . . .
>
> Attend at the call of the fifer and drummer,
> The French and the rebels are coming next summer,
> > And the forts we must build
> > Though tories are killed.
> Take courage, my jockies, and work for your king,
> For if you are taken, no doubt you will swing.
> > If York we can hold,
> > I'll have you enroll'd;
> And after you're dead, your names shall be read,
> As who for their monarch both labor'd and bled,
> And ventur'd their necks for their beef and their bread.
> 'Tis an honor to serve the bravest of nations,
> And be left to be hang'd in their capitulations.
> > Then scour up your mortars,
> > And stand to your quarters,
> 'Tis nonsense for tories in battle to run,
> They never need fear sword, halberd, or gun;
> > Their hearts should not fail 'em,
> > No balls will assail 'em;
> Forget your disgraces, and shorten your faces,
> For 'tis true as the gospel, believe it or not,
> Who are born to be hang'd, will never be shot.

In one home John Adams found a picture of the king standing upside down on the floor, facing the wall, with a lyrical inscription attached.

> Behold the man who had it in his power,
> To make a kingdom tremble and adore.
> Intoxicate with folly, see his head
> Placed where the meanest of his subjects tread.
> Like Lucifer, the giddy tyrant fell:
> He lifts his heels to Heaven, but points his head to
> > Hell.

General Wayne stormed the British fort at Stony Point in July 1779.

"On Gen. Wayne's taking Stoney Point"

[*This song from the Rare Book Room of the Library of Congress was written after the brilliant action taken by General Wayne. The music for it, "One night as Ned stept into bed," is not available at this time.*]

July they say, the fifteenth day,
    In glittering arms arrayed,
That gen'ral Wayne and his brave men
    The British lines essayed;
Just twelve at night, if I am right,
    And honestly informed,
Both wings at once they did advance,
    And Stoney Point they stormed.

    With ascents steep, morasses deep,
This boasted place abounded,
Strong abettees, of forked trees,
    Were doubly plac'd around it;
"In this strong place the rebel race
"Us never dare come nigh, sir,
"Great Washington, and all his train,
"I Johnson do defy, sir,"

    But mark the fate of Johnson's hate,
How quickly he was humbled,
When light'ning like, bold WAYNE did strike,
    His pride and glory tumbled:
See FLEURY brave the standard wave,
    Which strongly was defended,
And from his foes, 'midst of their blows,
    Most gallantly did rend it.

    Let STEWART'S name in books of fame
For ever be recorded,
Through show'rs of balls he scaled their walls,
    And danger disregarded;
O'er stones and rocks heroic KNOX
To charge the foe he pushed,
In gallant fight, with eagle's flight,
    O'er their strong ramparts rushed.

    And GIBSONS, gay as chearful May,
His duty well discharged,
He dealt his foes such deadly blows,
That left their walls unguarded.

161

May war's alarms still rouse to arms
The gallant sons of brav'ry,
Who dare withstand a tyrant's band,
And crush infernal slav'ry.*

War

[*This song appeared in* Stafford's Almanac *for 1780, printed by Thomas and Samuel Green at New Haven, Connecticut.*]

I.
I hear the drum beat with the impulse that warns
The soldier's brave heart, for the sound is, "To arms!"
I leave thee, my Nelly, and all the soft tales
Of love in the mountains, or love in the vales.
For war is the scene where true glory is won,
And valour the virtue that clothes with renown.
II.
It delights me to rove where the thunders remain,
And war's liquid thunders disport on the plain.
The lightenings that play, and the thunders that roll,
With lofty conception enrapture the soul,
The cause which we fight for let no man disown,
For we fight for a cause that will clothe with renown.
III.
When the cannon discharges her swift-flying ball,
The air may be cut and the hero may fall;
But the maids shall lament when they hear of the news,
And the heavens shall weep with their soft falling dews.
The ages to come shall convey his fame down
And the world shall surround him with eternal renown.
IV.
Then let us to arms and encounter the foe—
'Tis to bright-beaming glory and conquest we go;
We shall drive them from hill and from vale and from plain,
To measure the ocean and sail back again,
The General who commands is the brave Washington;
With him we shall vanquish and rise to renown.

King's Mountain
1780

[*The victory of the Patriots over the forces of Ferguson and his Tory command at King's Mountain, South Carolina, was the subject of many ballads. The following was written a short time after the action and published on a small sheet the following year, 1781.*]

'Twas on a pleasant mountain
The Tory heathens lay;

*Omitted from songs with music since sheet music is unobtainable

162

With a doughty major at their head,
    One Ferguson they say.

Cornwallis had detach'd him,
    A thieving for to go,
And catch the Carolina men,
    Or bring the rebels low.

The scamp had rang'd the country
    In search of royal aid,
And with his owls, perched on high,
    He taught them all his trade.

But ah! that fatal morning,
    When Shelby brave drew near!
'Tis certainly a warning
    That ministers should hear.

And Campbell, and Cleveland,
    And Colonel Sevier,
Each with a band of gallant men,
    To Ferguson appear.

Just as the sun was setting
    Behind the western hills,
Just then our trusty rifles sent
    A dose of leaden pills.

    .   .   .   .

I would not tell the number
    Of Tories slain that day,
But surely it is certain
    That none did run away.

For all that were a living,
    Were happy to give up;
So let us make thanksgiving,
    And pass the bright tin-cup.

To all the brave regiments,
    Let's toast 'em for their health,
And may our good country
    Have quietude and wealth.

Even the British were forced to take a crack at their military high command.

Our Commanders

Gage nothing did, and went to pot;
Howe lost one town, another got;

Guy nothing lost, and nothing won;
Dunmore was homewards forced to run;
Clinton was beat and got a garter,
And bouncing Burgoyne catch'd a tartar;
Thus all we gain for millions spent
Is to be laughed at, and repent.

An English gentleman of Chester expressed his opinion of Lord North.

Lord North's Recantation
A song
1778

[*"Lord North's Recantation" first appeared in the* London Evening Post. *Many news-papers published it in 1779.*]

When North first began,
With his taxation plan,
The Colonies all to supplant;
To Britain's true cause,
And her liberty, laws,
O, how did he scorn to recant.

Oh! how did he boast,
Of his pow'r and his host,
Alternately swagger and cant;
Of freedom so dear,
Not a word would he hear,
Nor believe he'd be forc'd to recant.

. . . .

He armies sent o'er
To America's shore,
New government there to transplant;
But every campaign
Prov'd his force to be vain,
Yet still he refus'd to recant.

. . . .

With his brother Burgoyne,
He's forc'd now to join,
And a treaty of peace for to want;
Says he ne'er will fight,
But will give up his right
To taxation, and freely recant.

With the great General Howe,
He'd be very glad now,
He ne'er had engag'd in the jaunt;
And ev'ry proud Scot,
In the devilish plot,
With his lordship, are forc'd to recant.

164

Old England alas!
They have brought to such pass,
Too late are proposals extant;
America's lost,
Our glory at most
Is only that—tyrants recant.

The Congress

[*Tory writers spoke in derogatory terms of the men who brought on and conducted the Revolution. They looked down upon these patriots and referred to them as positively bad men, insincere and selfish men, political hypocrites, knaves who were misleading the people. They took delight in verbally attacking the Continental Congress. This ballad of that name, meant to be sung to the tune of "Nancy Dawson," was written in the spring of 1776 and first printed in Towne's* Evening Post *that year. It became very popular among the Loyalists because of the "comprehensiveness and alacrity" of its curses on members of what they called the sham-legislature. In this ballad the Loyalist sums up his feelings about the lack of social standing of the majority of the patriots.*]*

Ye Tories all rejoice and sing
Success to George our gracious king;
The faithful subjects tribute bring
And execrate the Congress.

These hardy knaves and stupid fools,
Some apish and pragmatic mules,
Some servile acquiescing tools,—
These, these compose the Congress.

When Jove resolved to send a curse,
And all the woes of life rehearse,—
Not plague, not famine, but much worse,—
He cursed us with a Congress.

. . . .

With freemen's rights they wanton play;
At their command, we fast and pray;
With worthless paper they us pay;
A fine device of Congress.

With poverty and dire distress,
With standing armies us oppress;
Whole troops to Pluto swiftly press,
As victims to the Congress.

Time-serving priests to zealots preach,
Who king and parliament impeach;
Seditious lessons to us teach
At the command of Congress.

. . . .

*Omitted from songs with music since sheet music is unobtainable

The world's amazed to see the pest
The tranquil land with wars infest;
Britannia puts them to the test,
      And tries the strength of Congress.

O goddess, hear our hearty prayers!
Confound the villains by the cars;
Disperse the plebeians—try the peers,
      And execute the Congress.

See, see, our hope begins to dawn;
Bold Carleton scours the northern lawn;
The sons of faction sigh forlorn;
      Dejected is the Congress.

Clinton, Burgoyne, and gallant Howe,
Will soon reward our conduct true,
And to each traitor give his due;
      Perdition waits the Congress.

See noble Dunmore keeps his post;
Maraudes and ravages the coast;
Despises Lee and all his host,
      That hair-brain tool of Congress.

There's Washington and all his men—
Where Howe had one, the goose had ten—
Marched up the hill, and down again,
      And sent returns to Congress.

Prepare, prepare, my friends prepare,
For scenes of blood, the field of war;
To royal standard we'll repair,
      And curse the haughty Congress.

Huzza! Huzza! we thrice huzza!
Return peace, harmony, and law!
Restore such times as once we saw
      And bid adieu to Congress.

Jonathan Odell was considered the most "powerful and unrelenting tory satirist."

The Old Year and the New: A Prophecy
by
Jonathan Odell

[JONATHAN ODELL *was born at Newark, New Jersey, September 25, 1737. After his graduation from the College of New Jersey in 1754 he studied to be a doctor and became a surgeon in the British army. After a few years he went to England to study for the ministry.*

He returned to the United States, where he soon assumed duties as a parish priest, missionary, and physician.

In 1777 he went to live within the British lines and became an impassioned observer of the war. He believed firmly in the ultimate triumph of the British.]

What though last year be past and gone,
    Why should we grieve or mourn about it?
As good a year is now begun,
    And better, too—let no one doubt it.

'Tis New Year's morn; why should we part?
    Why not enjoy what heaven has sent us?
Let wine expand the social heart,
    Let friends, and mirth, and wine content us.

War's rude alarms disturbed last year;
    Our country bled and wept around us;
But this each honest heart shall cheer,
    And peace and plenty shall surround us . . .

Last year rebellion proudly stood,
    Elate, in her meridian glory;
But this shall quench her pride in blood;
    George will avenge each martyrd Tory . . .

Then bring us wine, full bumpers bring;
    Hail this New Year in joyful chorus;
God bless great George our Gracious King
    And crush rebellion down before us!

During all this Gibbon's writing hand was stilled.

[*Edward Gibbon, author of* Decline and Fall of the Roman Empire, *was very much inclined to take the side of the Americans. This poem was allegedly written by Charles Fox and printed in England.*]

King George, in a fright, lest Gibbon should write
    The story of Britain's disgrace,
Thought no means more sure his pen to secure
    Than to give the historian a place.
But his caution is vain, 'tis the curse of his reign
    That his projects should never succeed
Though he write not a line, yet a cause of decline
    In the author's example we read.

Feelings were strong, emotions deep. The abhorrence of the American people for the traitor Benedict Arnold was reflected in ballads and poems as well as in cartoons.

To the Traitor Arnold

[*This poem was published in* The Pennsylvania Packet *for October 24, 1780.*]

Arnold! thy name, as heretofore,
Shall now be Benedict no more;
Since, instigated by the devil,
Thy ways are turned from good to evil.
'T is fit we brand thee with a name
To suit thy infamy and shame;
And since of treason thou 'rt convicted,
Thy name should now be Maledict-ed.

. . . .

And odious for the blackest crimes,
Arnold shall stink to latest times."

[*In the same issue of the* Packet *an epigram appeared on the visible result of the bargain between Arnold and Sir Henry Clinton:*]

'T was Arnold's post Sir Harry sought,
Arnold ne'er entered in his thought.
How ends the bargain? Let us see,—
The fort is safe as safe can be:
His favorite perforce must die;
His view's laid bare to every eye;
His money's gone—and lo! he gains
One scoundrel more for all his pains.
André was generous, true, and brave,
And in his room he buys a knave.
'T is sure ordained that Arnold cheats
All those, of course, with whom he treats.
Now let the devil suspect a bite—
Or Arnold cheats him of his right.

Thereafter Arnold's name was linked with Satan.

[*The following verses appeared in the* New Jersey Gazette *for November 1, 1780, supposedly describing an "affectionate" conversation between the two distinguished persons.*]

Quoth Satan to Arnold: 'My worthy good fellow,
I love you much better than ever I did;
You live like a prince, with Hal may get mellow,—
But mind that you both do just what I bid.'

Quoth Arnold to Satan: 'My friend, do not doubt me!
  I will strictly adhere to all your great views;
To you I'm devoted, with all things about me—
  You'll permit me, I hope, to die in my shoes.'

By way of contrast the Patriots had earlier mourned the tragic death of the man who became a spy to help his country

Nathan Hale
1776

[*After the retreat of his army from Long Island in 1776, George Washington was eager to learn about the future plans of the royal forces. For this dangerous assignment he sought an officer who would be willing to go to the enemy's camp to get the information. Dedicated to the cause of the Americans, Nathan Hale, a captain in Colonel Knowlton's regiment, agreed to take on the assignment and penetrated the British lines in disguise. He got the desired information but on his way back to the American encampment he was apprehended and brought before Lord Howe. After being questioned, he admitted that he was a spy. Howe immediately gave an order to the provost marshall, and Captain Hale was executed early the following day. He was treated in a cruel and callous fashion, denied the attendance of a clergyman, and refused a Bible. Letters which he wrote to his mother and friends before the execution were destroyed on the ground that "the rebels should not know they had a man in their army who could die with such firmness." The* Freeman's Journal, *February 18, 1777, printed these verses.*]

The breezes went steadily thro' the tall pines,
  A saying "oh! hu-ush!" a saying "oh! hu-ush!"
As stilly stole by a bold legion of horse,
  For Hale in the bush, for Hale in the bush.

"Keep still!" said the thrush as she nestled her young,
  In a nest by the road; in a nest by the road.
"For the tyrants are near, and with them appear,
  What bodes us no good, what bodes us no good."

The brave captain heard it, and thought of his home,
  In a cot by the brook; in a cot by the brook.
With mother and sister and memories dear,
  He so gaily forsook; he so gaily forsook.

Cooling shades of the night were coming apace,
  The tattoo had beat; the tattoo had beat.
The noble one sprang from his dark lurking place,
  To make his retreat; to make his retreat.

He warily trod on the dry rustling leaves,
  As he pass'd thro' the wood; as he pass'd thro' the
    wood;

And silently gain'd his rude launch on the shore,
  As she play'd with the flood; as she played with the
    flood.

The guards of the camp, on that dark, dreary night,
  Had a murderous will; had a murderous will.
They took him and bore him afar from the shore,
  To a hut on the hill; to a hut on the hill.
    .   .   .   .

The brave fellow told them, no thing he restrain'd,
  The cruel gen'ral; the cruel gen'ral.
His errand from camp, of the ends to be gain'd,
  And said that was all; and said that was all.

They took him and bound him and bore him away,
  Down the hill's grassy side; down the hill's grassy
    side.
'Twas there the base hirelings, in royal array,
  His cause did deride; his cause did deride.

Five minutes were given, short moments, no more,
  For him to repent; for him to repent;
He pray'd for his mother, he ask'd not another,
  To Heaven he went; to Heaven he went.
    .   .   .   .

A Venison Dinner at Mr. Bunyan's
by
John Stansbury

[JOHN STANSBURY *was born in London in 1740. He came to America in 1767 and went into business in Philadelphia. He wrote songs with ease and sang with vivacity in a melodious voice. He was extremely popular socially and was welcomed wherever he went not only for his intelligence and fine manner but for his cheerful, lively disposition. Stansbury was considered without a rival as a writer of festive political songs and humorous rather than vitriolic satire in verse. When the British army retired from Philadelphia in the spring of 1778, Stansbury left with it, and until the close of the war remained with British lines at New York. This lively song was written in New York in 1781 when Washington's headquarters were still in the Highlands (as the West Point area was known) on the Hudson River. This was, as Moses Tyler writes, before that impenitent rebel had developed to the enemy his purpose of marching toward Virginia for an interview with Cornwallis.*]

Friends, push round the bottle, and let us be drinking,
While Washington up in his mountains is slinking:
Good faith, if he's wise he'll not leave them behind him,
For he knows he's safe nowheres where Britons can find him.
When he and Fayette talk of taking this city,
Their vaunting moves only our mirth and our pity.

But, though near our lines they're too cautious to tarry,
What courage they shew when a hen-roost they harry!
Who can wonder that poultry and oxen and swine
Seek shelter in York from such valor divine,—
While Washington's jaws and the Frenchman's are aching
The spoil they have lost, to be boiling and baking.

Let Clinton and Arnold bring both to subjection,
And send us more geese here to seek our protection.
Their flesh and their feathers shall meet a kind greeting;
A fat rebel turkey is excellent eating,
A lamb fat as butter, and white as a chicken—
These sorts of tame rebels are excellent pickin'.

  . . . .

Then cheer up, my lads! if the prospect grows rougher,
Remember from whence and for whom 't is you suffer:–
From men whom mild laws and too happy condition
Have puffed up with pride and inflamed with sedition;
For George, whose reluctance to punish offenders
Has strengthened the hands of these upstart pretenders.

The surrender of the royal army at Yorktown inspired several songsters.

The Prophecy
1782
by
Philip Freneau

[*By this time it was obvious to everyone that the Americans were not to be conquered.*]

When a certain great king, whose initial is G,
Shall force stamps upon paper, and folks to drink
    tea;
When these folks burn his tea and stampt paper
    like stubble,
You may guess that this king is then coming to
    trouble.
But when a petition he treads under his feet,
And sends over the ocean an army and fleet;
When that army, half-starved and frantic with rage,
Shall be cooped up with a leader whose name
    rhymes with cage;
When that leader goes home dejected and sad,
You may then be assured that the king's prospects
    are bad.
But when B and C with their armies are taken,
This king will do well if he saves his own bacon.
In the year seventeen hundred and eighty and two
A stroke he shall get that will make him look blue;
In the years eighty-three, eighty-four, eighty-five
You hardly shall know that the king is alive;
In the year eighty-six the affair will be over.
And he shall eat turnips that grow in Hanover.
The face of the Lion shall then become pale,
He shall yield fifteen teeth and be sheared of his
    tail.
O king, my dear king, you shall be very sore;
The Stars and the Lily shall run you on shore,
And your Lion shall growl—but never bite more!

*The King's Speech, Recommending Peace with
the United States
1783
by
Philip Freneau*

[*This poem expresses Freneau's "ban and malediction" written in "the ruthlessness of unforgiving hate" on King George of England and his people.*]

Grown sick of war, and war's alarms,
　Good George has changed his note at last—
Conquest and Death have lost their charms;
　He and his nation stand aghast
To see what horrid lengths they've gone,
And what a brink they stand upon.

· · · · · · · · · ·

Let jarring powers make war or peace,
　Monster!—no peace shall greet thy breast:
Our murdered friends shall never cease
　To hover round and break thy rest!
The Furies shall thy bosom tear,
Remorse, Distraction, and Despair,
And Hell with all its fiends, be there!

· · · · · · · · · ·

Genius! that first our race designed,
　To other kings impart
The finer feelings of the mind,
　The virtues of the heart!
When'er the honors of a throne
　Fall to the bloody and the base,
Like Britain's monster, pull them down!—
　Like his, be their disgrace!
Hibernia, seize each native right!
　Neptune, exclude him from the main;
Like her that sunk with all her freight,
The 'Royal George,' take all his fleet,
　And never let them rise again;
Confine him to his gloomy isle,
　Let Scotland rule her half;
Spare him to curse his fate awhile,
　And Whitehead—thou to write his epitaph!

M'FINGAL:

A MODERN

EPIC POEM.

CANTO FIRST,

OR

THE TOWN-MEETING.

By John Trumbull. of Conn.

PHILADELPHIA:

Printed and Sold by WILLIAM and THOMAS BRAD-
FORD, at the London Coffee-House, 1775.

Title page of Trumbull's M'Fingal. *Courtesy of The New-York Historical Society, New York City.*

Connecticut-born JOHN TRUMBULL was an American lawyer and poet. He became a judge, first of the Connecticut Superior Court and later of the Supreme Court of Errors. His great contribution to the witty, satirical, poetical outpourings of the period was his mock epic in four cantos about the Tory rascal, Squire M'Fingal. Trumbull wrote the first canto in January of 1776. In 1781 he divided it into two parts and added two more cantos. The first printing of the epic was embellished with nine engravings designed and executed by E. Tisdale.

The protagonist of the epic was Squire M'Fingal, a Scottish-American living in a provincial town in Massachusetts, who strongly believed in absolute submission to Parliament. M'Fingal, a windy orator, looked upon himself as somewhat of a prophet and was given to sounding off in thunderous tones about what would happen if the Americans did not mend their ways.

Squire M'Fingal's chief rival in town was a Patriot named Honorius (believed to be a portrait of John Adams). A town meeting was held in which Honorius delivered a fiery harangue to the citizens. In the midst of the speech the Squire came in, not concealing his annoyance, and took a seat near the orator. Honorious continued his loud-voiced discourse. Finally, in his wrath, he turned on the Squire himself, accusing him of being the leader of a party composed of men who toadied to Satan.

M'Fingal could stand no more. Rising in anger, he made a few preliminary remarks and then entered as usual into a hair-raising prophecy. The new-fangled notions of Honorious and the other Patriots would never win out. The so-called Patriots would become "hewers of wood and drawers of water."

"The vulgar knaves," orated M'Fingal, "would do more good preserved as slaves."

Affairs now became decidedly exciting. Honorious, in replying to the Squire's speech, was interrupted by some Tory rowdies. It looked as though the meeting would end in a free-for-all fight, but luckily a loud disturbance outside caught the people's attention and the meeting adjourned. Here the original M'Fingal story ends.

In the third canto Squire M'Fingal got his come-uppence. The Patriots had erected a Liberty Pole at the top of which the Stars and Stripes waved "defiantly for all to see." The sight of it was too much for the Scotchman's blood. Summoning a few Tory friends to his aid, he sought to cut down the "unseemly" staff. A fight between Tories and Patriots followed. The Scotchman's friends fled, and M'Fingal tried to get away, but it was too late. At this dread "Crisis" the Patriots fell on him and bound him. He was led prisoner to the pole and the rope from the flagstaff was tied around his waist. Then, using the rope as a pully,

> They swung him like a keg of ale,
> Till to the pinnacle in height
> He vaulted, like a balloon or kite.

The Squire's Tory heart fluttered wildly. In "bawling voice" he repented for the moment of his Tory wrong-doings and promised to be a good boy if they would only let him go.

The Patriots lowered their victim to the ground. A court was hastily formed, and a decision as hastily reached.

> That first the mob a slip not single
> Tie round the neck of said M'Fingal,
> And in due form do tar him next,
> And feather as the law directs;

175

At the end of this Canto M'Fingal managed to escape, and hurried home—still in his tar and plumage. He hid in a turnip bin in the cellar and from this lowly station delivered a farewell address to the remnants of his terrified followers. Hopeless and fed up with Whigs and liberty, he went to Boston.

M'FINGAL

CANTO FIRST

THE TOWN MEETING, A.M.

When Yankies, skill'd in martial rule,
First put the British troops to school;
Instructed them in warlike trade,
And new manœuvres of parade;
The true war-dance of Yankey-reels,
And *manual exercise* of heels;
Made them give up, like saints complete,
The arm of flesh, and trust the feet,
Aad work, like Christians undissembling,
Salvation out by fear and trembling;
Taught Percy fashionable races,
And modern modes of Chevy-Chaces:

From Boston, in his best array,
Great 'Squire M'Fingal took his way,
And, grac'd with ensigns of renown,
Steer'd homeward to his native town.
  His high descent our heralds trace
To Ossian's fam'd Fingalian race;
For though their name some part may lack,
Old Fingal spelt it with a Mac;
Which great M'Pherson, with submission,
We hope will add the next edition.
  His fathers flourish'd in the Highlands
Of Scotia's fog-benighted islands;
Whence gain'd our 'Squire two gifts by right,
Rebellion and the Second-sight.
Of these the first, in ancient days,
Had gain'd the noblest palms of praise,
'Gainst Kings stood forth, and many a crown'd head
With terror of its might confounded;
Till rose a King with potent charm
His foes by goodness to disarm;
Whom ev'ry Scot and Jacobite
Straight fell in love with—at first sight;
Whose gracious speech, with aid of pensions,
Hush'd down all murmurs of dissensions,
And with the sound of potent metal,
Brought all their blust'ring swarms to settle;
Who rain'd his ministerial mannas,

Till loud Sedition sung Hosannas;
The good Lords-Bishops and the Kirk
United in the public work;

Rebellion from the northern regions,
With Bute and Mansfield swore allegiance,
And all combin'd to raze, as nuisance,
Of church and state, the constitutions;
Pull down the empire, on whose ruins
They meant to edify their new ones;
Enslave the Amer'can wildernesses,
And tear the provinces in pieces.
For these our 'Squire, among the valiant'st,
Employ'd his time and tools and talents;
And in their cause, with manly zeal,
Us'd his first virtue to rebel;
And found this new rebellion pleasing
As his old king-destroying treason.
  Nor less avail'd his optic sleight,
And Scottish gift of second-sight.
No ancient sybil, fam'd in rhyme,
Saw deeper in the womb of time;

   . . . .

So gain'd our 'Squire his fame by seeing
Such things as never would have being.
Whence he for oracles was grown
The very tripod of his town.
Gazettes no sooner rose a lie in,
But straight he fell to prophesying;
Made dreadful slaughter in his course,
O'erthrew provincials, foot and horse;
Brought armies o'er by sudden pressings,
Of Hanoverians, Swiss, and Hessians;
Feasted with blood his Scottish clan,
And hang'd all rebels to a man;
Divided their estates and pelf,
And took a goodly share himself.
All this with spirit energetic,
He did by second-sight prophetic.
  Thus stor'd with intellectual riches,
Skill'd was our 'Squire in making speeches,
Where strength of brains united centres
With strength of lungs surpassing Stentor's.
But as some muskets so contrive it,
As oft to miss the mark they drive at,
And though well aim'd at duck or plover,
Bear wide and kick their owners over:
So far'd our 'Squire, whose reas'ning toil
Would often on himself recoil,

   . . . .

177

Yet at town meetings ev'ry chief
Pinn'd faith on great M'Fingal's sleeve,
And, as he motioned all by rote
Rāis'd sympathetic hands to vote.
  The town, our Hero's scene of action,
Had long been torn by feuds of faction;
And as each party's strength prevails,
It turn'd up diff'rent heads or tails;
With constant rattling, in a trice
Show'd various sides, as oft as dice:
As that fam'd weaver, wife t' Ulysses,
By night each day's-work pick'd in pieces;
And though she stoutly did bestir her,
Its finishing was ne'er the nearer:
So did this town, with stedfast zeal,
Weave cobwebs for the public weal,
Which when completed, or before,
A second vote in pieces tore.
They met, made speeches full long-winded,
Resolv'd, protested, and rescinded;
Addresses sign'd, then chose Committees,
To stop all drinking of Bohea-teas;
With winds of doctrine veer'd about,
And turn'd all Whig-Committees out.
Meanwhile our Hero, as their head,
In pomp the tory faction led,
Still following, as the 'Squire should please,
Successive on, like files of geese.
  And now the town was summon'd, greeting,
To grand parading of town-meeting;

  .   .   .   .

  With daring zeal and courage blest,
Honorius first the crowd address'd;
When now our 'Squire, returning late,
Arriv'd to aid the grand debate,
With strange sour faces sat him down,
While thus the orator went on:
  "—For ages blest, thus Britain rose,
The terror of encircling foes;·
Her heroes rul'd the bloody plain;
Her conqu'ring standard aw'd the main;
The diff'rent palms her triumphs grace,
Of arms in war, of arts in peace:
Unharass'd by maternal care,
Each rising province flourish'd fair;
Whose various wealth with lib'ral hand,
By far o'erpaid the parent land.
But though so bright her sun might shine,
'Twas quickly hasting to decline,

With feeble rays, too weak t' assuage
The damps, that chill the eve of age.
　"For states, like men, are doom'd as well
Th' infirmities of age to feel;

．　．　．　．　．　．　．　．　．

　"Thus now, while hoary years prevail,
Good Mother Britain seem'd to fail;
Her back bent, crippled with the weight
Of age and debts, and cares of state:
For debts she ow'd and those so large
That twice her wealth could not discharge;
And now 'twas thought, so high they'd grown,
She'd break, and come upon the town;
Her arms, of nations once the dread,
She scarce could lift above her head;
Her deafen'd ears ('twas all their hope)
The final trump perhaps might ope,
So long they'd been in stupid mood,
Shut to the hearing of all good;

．　．　．　．　．　．　．　．

So Britain, 'midst her airs so flighty,
Now took a whim to be almighty;
Urg'd on to desp'rate heights of frenzy,
Affirm'd her own Omnipotency;
Would rather ruin all her race,
Than 'bate supremacy an ace;
Assum'd all rights divine, as grown
The church's head, like good pope Joan;
Swore all the world should bow and skip
To her almighty Goodyship;
　"Thus, spite of pray'rs her schemes pursuing,
She still went on to work our ruin;
Annull'd our charters of releases,
And tore our title-deeds in pieces;
Then sign'd her warrants of ejection,
And gallows rais'd to stretch our necks on:
And on these errands sent in rage,
Her bailiff, and her hangman, Gage,
And at his heels, like dogs to bait us,
Dispatch'd her *Posse Comitatus*.
　"No state e'er chose a fitter person
To carry such a silly farce on.
As heathen gods in ancient days
Receiv'd at second hand their praise,
Stood imag'd forth in stones and stocks,
And deified in barbers' blocks;
So Gage was chose to represent
Th' omnipotence of Parl'ment.
And as old heroes gain'd, by shifts,

From gods (as poets tell) their gifts;
Our gen'ral, as his actions show,
Gain'd like assistance from below,
By Satan graced with full supplies,
From all his magazine of lies:
Yet could his practice ne'er impart
The wit, to tell a lie with art:
Those lies alone are formidable,
Where artful truth is mix'd with fable;
But Gage has bungled oft so vilely,
No soul could credit lies so silly;
Outwent all faith, and stretch'd beyond
Credulity's extremest end.

 . . . .

Nor e'er could Gage, by craft or prowess,
Have done a whit more mischief to us,
Since he began th' unnatural war,
The work his masters sent him for.
 "And are there in this free-born land,
Among ourselves, a venal band,
A dastard race, who long have sold
Their souls and consciences for gold;
Who wish to stab their country's vitals,
If they might heir surviving titles:
With joy behold our mischief brewing,
Insult and triumph in our ruin?
Priests, who, if Satan should sit down
To make a Bible of his own,
Would gladly for the sake of mitres,
Turn his inspir'd and sacred writers;
Lawyers, who, should he wish to prove
His title t' his old seat above,
Would, if his cause he'd give 'em fees in,
Bring writs of *Entry sur disseisin,*
Plead for him boldly at the session,
And hope to put him in possession;
Merchants, who, for his kindly aid,
Would make him partner in their trade,
Hang out their signs with goodly show,
Inscrib'd with *"Beelzebub and Co."*

 . . . .

 As thus he spake, our 'Squire M'Fingal
Gave to his partisans a signal.
Not quicker roll'd the waves to land,
When Moses wav'd his potent wand,
Nor with more uproar, than the Tories
Sat up a gen'ral rout in chorus;
Laugh'd, hiss'd, hemm'd, murmur'd, groan'd, and
  jeer'd:
Honorius now could scarce be heard.

. . . .

Quoth he, "Tis wond'rous what strange stuff
Your Whigs' heads are compounded of;
Which force of logic cannot pierce,
Nor sylogistic *carte & tierce,*
Nor weight of scripture or of reason
Suffice to make the least impression.
Nor heeding what ye rais'd contest on,
Ye prate, and beg or steal the question;
And when your boasted arguings fail,
Straight leave all reas'ning off, to rail.
Have not our High-Church Clergy made it
Appear from scriptures, which ye credit,
That *right divine* from heaven was lent
To kings, that is, the Parliament,
Their subjects to oppress and teaze,
And serve the Devil when they please?
Did they not write, and pray, and preach,
And torture all the parts of speech;
About Rebellion make a pother,
From one end of the land to th'other?
And yet gain'd fewer pros'lyte Whigs,
Than old St. Anth'ny 'mongst the pigs;
And chang'd not half so many vicious
As Austin, when he preach'd to fishes;
Who throng'd to hear, the legend tells,
Were edified and wagg'd their tails;
But scarce you'd prove it, if you tried,
That e'er one whig was edified.

. . . .

Had I the Poet's brazen lungs,
As sound-board to his hundred tongues,
I could not half the scribblers muster
That swarm'd round Rivington in cluster;
Assemblies, Councilmen, forsooth;
Brush, Cooper, Wilkins, Chandler, Booth;
Yet all their arguments and sap'ence
You did not value at three half-pence.
Did not our Massachusettensis
For your conviction strain his senses?
Scrawl every moment he could spare,
From cards and barbers and the fair;
Show clear as sun in noon-day heavens,
You did not feel a single grievance;
Demonstrate all your opposition
Sprung from the eggs of foul sedition;
Swear he had seen the nest she laid in,
And knew how long she had been sitting;
Could tell exact what strength of heat is

181

Requir'd to hatch her out Committees;
What shapes they take, and how much longer's
The space before they grow t' a Congress?
New white-wash'd Hutchinson, and varnish'd
Our Gage, who'd got a little tarnish'd;
Made 'em new masks in time, no doubt,
For Hutchinson's was quite worn out;
And while he muddled all his head,
You did not heed a word he said.
Did not our grave Judge Sewall hit
The summit of Newspaper wit?
Fill'd every leaf of every paper,
Of Mills, and Hicks, and Mother Draper;
Drew proclamations, works of toil,
In true sublime, of scare crow-stile;
Wrote farces too, 'gainst Sons of Freedom,
All for your good, and none would read 'em;
Denounc'd damnation on their frenzy,
Who died in Whig impenitency;
Affirm'd that Heav'n would lend us aid,
As all our Tory writers said;
And calculated so its kindness,
He told the moment when it join'd us."

"'Twas then belike," Honorius cried,
"When you the public fast defied,
Refus'd to Heav'n to raise a prayer,
Because you'd no connexions there:
And since, with rev'rend hearts and faces,
To Governors you'd made addresses,
In them who made you Tories seeing
You liv'd and mov'd, and had your being,
Your humble vows you would not breathe
To Pow'rs you'd no acquaintance with."

"As for your fasts," replied our 'Squire,
"What circumstance could fasts require?
We kept them not, but 'twas no crime;
We held them merely loss of time:
For what advantage firm and lasting,
Pray, did you ever get by fasting?
And what the gains that can arise
From vows and off'rings to the skies?
Will Heav'n reward with posts and fees,
Or send us Tea, as Consignees,
Give pensions, sal'ries, places, bribes,
Or choose us judges, clerks, or scribes;
Has it commissions in its gift,
Or cash to serve us at a lift?
Are acts of Parliament there made,
To carry on the Placeman's trade?
Or has it pass'd a single bill
To let us plunder whom we will?

M'FINGAL
CANTO THIRD
THE TORY'S DAY OF JUDGMENT

The story of M'Fingal is of course a book in itself. It's almost lamentable to have to cut Trumbull. In the third canto the Squire is very bold.

The Tory squire M'Fingal "swung . . . like a keg of ale." From a contemporary illustration to John Trumbull's epic poem. Courtesy of the New-York Historical Society, New York City.

M'Fingal, rising at the word,
Drew forth his old militia-sword;
Thrice cried "King George," as erst in distress,
Knights of romance invoked a mistress;
And, brandishing the blade in air,
Struck terror through th' opposing war.
The Whigs, unsafe within the wind
Of such commotion, shrunk behind.
With whirling steel around address'd,
Fierce through their thickest throng he press'd,
(Who roll'd on either side in arch,
Like Red Sea waves in Israel's march)
And, like a meteor rushing through,
Struck on their Pole a vengeful blow.
Around, the Whigs, of clubs and stones
Discharged whole volleys, in platoons,
That o'er in whistling fury fly;
But not a foe dares venture nigh.
And now perhaps with glory crown'd
Our 'Squire had fell'd the pole to ground,
Had not some Pow'r, a whig at heart,
Descended down and took their part;

. . . .

Who, at the nick of time alarming,
Assumed the solemn form of Chairman,
Address'd a Whig, in every scene
The stoutest wrestler on the green,
And pointed where the spade was found,
Late used to set their pole in ground,
And urged, with equal arms and might,
To dare our 'Squire to single fight.
The Whig thus arm'd, untaught to yield,
Advanced tremendous to the field:
Nor did M'Fingal shun the foe
But stood to brave the desp'rate blow;
While all the party gazed, suspended ,
To see the deadly combat ended;
And Jove in equal balance weigh'd
The sword against the brandish'd spade;
He weigh'd: but, lighter than a dream,
The sword flew up, and kick'd the beam.

But despite his bravado M'Fingal found himself alone with his enemies. His courageous Tory friends had failed him. Always a quick thinker, the Squire, after having participated in the melee, sought to placate his enemies. They, however, have other ideas.

At once the crew, at this dread crisis,
Fall on, and bind him, ere he rises,

And with loud shouts and joyful soul,
Conduct him prisoner to the pole
When now the mob in lucky hour
Had got their en'mies in their power,
They first proceed, by grave command,
To take the Constable in hand.
Then from the pole's sublimest top
The active crew let down the rope,
At once its other end in haste bind,
And make it fast upon his waistband;
Till like the earth, as stretch'd on tenter,
He hung self-balanced on his centre.
Then upwards, all hands hoisting sail,
They swung him, like a keg of ale,
Till to the pinnacle in height
He vaulted, like balloon or kite.

The beaten Squire sought to find an out. He wasn't very happy in his present position.

"Good Gentlemen and friends and kin,
For heaven's sake hear, if not for mine!
I here renounce the Pope, the Turks,
The King, the Devil, and all their works;
And will, set me but once at ease,
Turn Whig or Christian, what you please;
And always mind your rules so justly,
Should I live long as old Methus'lah,
I'll never join in British rage,
Nor help Lord North, nor Gen'ral Gage;
Nor lift my gun in future fights,
Nor take away your Charter-rights,
Nor overcome your new-raised levies,
Destroy your towns, nor burn your navies;
Nor cut your poles down while I've breath,
Though raised more thick than hatchel-teeth:
But leave King George and all his elves
To do their conq'ring work themselves."

This said, they lower'd him down in state,
Spread at all points, like falling cat;
But took a vote first on the question,
That they'd accept this full confession,
And to their fellowship and favor,
Restore him on his good behavior.

Not so our 'Squire submits to rule,
But stood, heroic as a mule.
"You'll find it all in vain, quoth he,
To play your rebel tricks on me.
All punishments, the world can render,
Serve only to provoke th' offender;

The will gains strength from treatment horrid
As hides grow harder when they're curried.
No man e'er felt the halter draw,
With good opinion of the law;
Or held in method orthodox
His love of justice, in the stocks;
Or fail'd to lose by sheriff's shears
At once his loyalty and ears. . . .
Did our mobb'd Ol'ver quit his station,
Or heed his vows of resignation?
Has Rivington, in dread of stripes,
Ceased lying since you stole his types?
And can you think my faith will alter,
By tarring, whipping or the halter?
I'll stand the worst; for recompense
I trust King George and Providence.
And when with conquest gain'd I come,
Array'd in law and terror home,
Ye'll rue this inauspicious morn,
And curse the day, when ye were born,
In Job's high style of imprecations,
With all his plagues, without his patience."

His threats, however, did not disturb or move the Patriots. While he spoke they found a Committee of Justice and sat on a bench near the pole to hold their Court. Soon they all agreed on a proper sentence for M'Fingal and the Clerk proclaimed the decree.

"That 'Squire M'Fingal having grown
The vilest Tory in the town,
And now in full examination
Convicted by his own confession,
Finding no tokens of repentance,
This Court proceeds to render sentence:
That first the Mob a slip-knot single
Tie round the neck of said M'Fingal,
And in due form do tar him next,
And feather, as the law directs;
Then through the town attendant ride him
In cart with Constable beside him,
And having held him up to shame,
Bring to the pole, from whence he came."
 Forthwith the crowd proceed to deck
With halter'd noose M'Fingal's neck,
While he in peril of his soul
Stood tied half-hanging to the pole;
Then lifting high the ponderous jar,
Pour'd o'er his head the smoking tar.

. . . .

186

Poor M'Fingal was then, after the tarring and feathering, put in a cart and displayed.

With like devotion all the choir
Paraded round our awful 'Squire;
In front the martial music comes
Of horns and fiddles, fifes and drums,
With jingling sound of carriage bells,
And treble creak of rusted wheels.
Behind, the crowd, in lengthen'd row
With proud procession, closed the show.
And at fit periods every throat
Combined in universal shout,
And hail'd great Liberty in chorus,
Or bawl'd "confusion to the Tories."
 And now the Mob, dispersed and gone,
Left 'Squire and Constable alone.
The constable with rueful face
Lean'd sad and solemn o'er a brace;
And fast beside him, check by jowl,
Stuck 'Squire M'Fingal 'gainst the pole,
Glued by the tar t' his rear applied,
Like barnacle on vessel's side.

But good old M'Fingal wasn't stilled. He began to have visions. He foresaw the events of the War.

As his prophetic soul grew stronger,
He found he could hold in no longer.
First from the pole, as fierce he shook,
His wig from pitchy durance broke,
His mouth unglued, his feathers flutter'd,
His tarr'd skirts crack'd, and thus he utter'd:
 "Ah, Mr. Constable, in vain
We strive 'gainst wind and tide and rain!
Behold my doom! this feathery omen
Portends what dismal times are coming.
Now future scenes, before my eyes,
And second-sighted forms arise.
I hear a voice, that calls away,
And cries 'The Whigs will win the day.'
My beck'ning Genius gives command,
And bids me fly the fatal land,
Where, changing name and constitution,
Rebellion turns to Revolution,
While Loyalty, oppress'd, in tears,
Stands trembling for its neck and ears.
 "Go, summon all our brethren, greeting,
To muster at our usual meeting;
There my prophetic voice shall warn 'em

M'Fingal's vision. Courtesy of the New-York Historical Society, New York City.

Of all things future that concern 'em,
And scenes disclose on which, my friend,
Their conduct and their lives depend.
There I—but first 'tis more of use,
From this vile pole to set me loose;
Then go with cautious steps and steady,
While I steer home and make all ready."

The best advice to give at this point is: go to the rare book room of a large public library or historical society and discover for yourself how the Squire made out.

Trumbull was one of the famous Hartford Wits.

[*A group of Connecticut reformers and satirists organized themselves into a "Friendly Club" at Hartford, Connecticut, and called themselves "The Hartford Wits."*

They wrote twelve satiric papers constituting The Anarchiad *which was first printed in the* New Haven Gazette *on October 26, 1786 and ran until September 13, 1787. The name, taken from the Miltonic "anarch," suggested the purpose, which was further explained in the subtitle "A Poem on the Restoration of Chaos and Substantial Night." The wits wanted to show in forceful satire the threats to the new nation by the promoters of local rebellion, paper money, and selfish greed. Government, finance, and commerce were unstable. These affairs were the subject of much discussion at the "Friendly Club." The twelve satiric papers were sent unsigned to the newspaper. They are believed to be the work of four men who had earlier revealed their patriotism either by serving in the army or by their writings—John Trumbull, leader of the group, David Humphreys, Joel Barlow, and Dr. Lemuel Hopkins.*

While serving abroad Colonel Humphreys was on the commission for treaties with foreign powers. He had shared in the popular curiosity over an anonymous English satire, The Rolliad. *On his return to America he was dismayed by the signs of insurrection in Shay's Rebellion. He suggested the use of satire in verse similar to the form of* The Rolliad *and Pope's* The Dunciad *to awaken public interest and also to teach lessons of patriotism. The lines selected are from* The Anarchiad.]

Faction

Behold those veterans worn with want and care,
Their sinews stiffened, silvered o'er their hair,
Weak in their steps of age, they move forlorn,
Their toils forgotten by the sons of scorn;
This hateful truth still aggravates the pain,
In vain they conquered, and they bled in vain.
Go then, ye remnants of inglorious wars,
Disown your marks of merit, hide your scars,
Of lust, of power, of titled pride accused,
Steal to your graves dishonored and abused.

For see, proud Faction waves her flaming brand,
And discord riots o'er the ungrateful land;
Lo, to the North a wild adventurous crew
In desperate mobs the savage state renew;
Each felon chief his maddening thousands draws,
And claims bold license from the bond of laws;
In other states the chosen sires of shame,
Stamp their vile knaveries with a legal name;
In honor's seat the sons of meanness swarm,
And senates base, the work of mobs perform,

To wealth, to power the sons of union rise,
While foes deride you and while friends despise.

Stand forth, ye traitors, at your country's bar,
Inglorious authors of intestine war,
What countless mischiefs from their labors rise!
Pens dipped in gall, and lips inspired with lies!
Ye sires of ruin, prime detested cause
Of bankrupt faith, annihilated laws,
Of selfish systems, jealous, local schemes,
And unioned empire lost in empty dreams;
Your names, expanding with your growing crime,
Shall float disgustful down the stream of time,
Each future age applaud the avenging song,
And outraged nature vindicate the wrong.

Yes, there are men, who, touched with heavenly fire,
Beyond the confines of these climes aspire,
Beyond the praises of a tyrant age,
To live immortal in the patriot page;
Who greatly dare, though warning worlds oppose,
To pour just vengeance on their country's foes.

. . . .

Yet what the hope? the dreams of congress fade,
The federal union sinks in endless shade,
Each feeble call, that warns the realms around,
Seems the faint echo of a dying sound,
Each requisition wafts in fleeting air,
And not one state regards the powerless prayer.

Ye wanton states, by heaven's best blessings cursed,
Long on the lap of fostering luxury nursed,
What fickle frenzy raves, what visions strange,
Inspire your bosoms with the lust of change?
And frames the wish to fly from fancied ill,
And yield your freedom to a monarch's will?

Go view the lands to lawless power a prey,
Where tyrants govern with unbounded sway;
See the long pomp in gorgeous state displayed,
The tinselled guards, the squadroned horse parade;
See heralds gay with emblems on their vest,
In tissued robes tall beauteous pages drest;
Where moves the pageant, throng unnumbered slaves,
Lords, dukes, and princes, titulary knaves
Confusedly shine, the purple gemmed with stars,
Sceptres, and globes, and crowns, and rubied cars,
On gilded orbs the thundering chariots rolled,
Steeds snorting fire, and champing bits of gold,
Prance to the trumpet's voice—while each assumes
A loftier gait, and lifts his neck of plumes.
High on the moving throne, and near the van,
The tyrant rides, the chosen scourge of man;

Clarions, and flutes, and drums his way prepare,
And shouting millions rend the conscious air;
Millions, whose ceaseless toils the pomp sustain,
Whose hour of stupid joy repays an age of pain.
   From years of darkness springs the regal line,
Hereditary kings by right divine:
'Tis theirs to riot on all nature's spoils,
For them with pangs unblest the peasant toils,
For them the earth prolific teems with grain,
Theirs, the dread labors of the devious main,
Annual for them the wasted land renews
The gifts oppressive, and extorted dues.

[The poem's ending might well have been put under Benjamin Franklin's first cartoon.]

                .   .   .   .
   Ere death invades, and night's deep curtain falls,
Through ruined realms the voice of Union calls,
Loud as the trump of heaven through darkness roars,
When gyral gusts entomb Caribbean towers,
When nature trembles through the deeps convulsed,
And ocean foams from craggy cliffs repulsed,
On you she calls! attend the warning cry,
"Ye live united, or divided die."

4

Spreading the News in Colonial
and Revolutionary War Days

1. The Broadside

The *broadside,* or *broadsheet,* as it was once known, is a large sheet of paper printed on one side only. It appeared soon after the invention of the printing press in 1450. According to colonial records, the broadside that came off the new printing press at Harvard College in 1638 was the first sheet of printed matter to have come off an American press.

After several decades this medium of circulation became popular in colonial America for the dissemination of news stories, marches, songs, parodies, romantic and satirical ballads, and other literary expressions of political and social satire. Announcements of town meetings, proclamations, playbills, and prayers for salvation all found their way onto the large sheets. Broadsides, usually anonymous and undated, could be written, published and peddled on the streets at a penny apiece within a few hours—although sometimes they were publicly posted.

In a report presented on April 15, 1872, Samuel F. Haven, then librarian of the American Antiquarian Society, called attention to broadsides and their value as "materials for history" which "imply a great deal more than they literally express and disclose visions of the interior condition of society such as cannot be found in formal narratives."

Over 60 broadsides were issued between 1772 and 1779, according to the list of 200 titles in the collection of broadsides belonging to the American Antiquarian Society for the period 1768–1800. One of the early American broadsides is a "Proclamation for Fast" issued

192

by the General Court of Massachusetts in 1680–81. Nearly 100 fast and thanksgiving proclamations were printed on broadsides before 1800.

From 1765 to 1775, when ballads served the cause of liberty, more verse is said to have been printed on broadsides than during any previous decade in American history. During the later years of the war, however, leading ballad writers preferred to reach the public through the columns of the newspapers which were appearing on a more regular and frequent basis, and broadsides began to take a back seat.

By the end of the eighteenth century, "every capital town on the Continent," according to a writer in the November 1796 edition of *Gentlemen's Magazine,* was printing a weekly paper. Several of them had one or more daily papers which brought the public humorous pieces as well as poems and news items, and thus the once popular printed sheet was crowded out by the press.

Subfcribers Names, who have agreed to pay Three Pounds yearly, for Five Years, commencing November the Ninth, 1766, ir the Encouragement of Learning, in King's-College, New-York. With the Subfcriptions received, and xpended by Dr. Cloffy.

His Excellency the Govnor, — £. 3— 4—0
    General Gage, — — 3— 0—0
Honourable Charles Ward Athorp, Efq; —
Mr. James M'Evers, — — 1—10—0
Mr. Charles M'Evers, — — 1—10—0
Major Moncrief, — — —
Mr. David Clarkfon, — — 1—10—0
Rev. Dr. Cooper, Prefident, — — 1—12—6
Rev. Dr. Auchmuty, — — 1—12-6
Rev. Charles Inglis, A. M. — — 1—12—6
Mr. John Livingfton, — — 1—10—0
Mr. George Harrifon, — —
Honourable Colonel Maitlan, — 3— 4—0
Rev. John Ogilvie, A. M. — — 1—12—6
Mr. Secretary French, — —
Honourable John Watts, Efq — — 1—12—0
Honourable William Walton, Efq; — 1—12—0
Honourable Jofeph Read, — — 3— 0—0
Leonard Lifpenard, Efq; — — 1—10—0
Samuel Verplank, A. M. — — 3— 0—0
Major James De Lancey, Efq — —
Robert Harpur, A. M. — —
Samuel Cloffy, M. D. — — 1—12—6
                                      33—14—6

Disburfements by Dr. CLOSSY.

1767. May 13, Cafh to Mr. Noel, for Mr. Benjamin
        Moore's Premium of Books, £. 5— 0—0
    17, To Mr. Galaudet, for four Silver Medals, 8— 0—0
    — To———Do. for a Copper-Plate, 0—15—0
    27, To———Do. for engraving a Stamp,
        with the College Arms, — 3—10—0
Nov. 3, To Mr. Galaudet, for four Silver Medals, 8— 0—0
    To Do. Remainder of a former Account, 0— 6—6

        Total expended, December 8, 1767, 25—11—6

        Balance in Cafh, in Dr. Cloffy's Hands, 8— 3—0

N. B. One Silver Medal was prefented to 33—14—6
Mr. Laight, for his Learning in Ethics.

A public announcement of the names of the subscribers to a fund to support King's College (later Columbia University) in New York. Courtesy of The New-York Historical Society, New York City.

To his Majesty GEORGE the *Second*, by the Grace of God of *Great Britain*, *France*, and *Ireland*, KING Defender of the Faith, and so forth.

The Humble Address of   Persons, Inhabitants of his Majesty's Plantations
in *North America*.

May it Please your Majesty.

WE the Subscribers being of the Number of your Majesty's most Dutiful and Loyal Subjects, Inhabiting the British Plantations in *North America*, beg Leave with the utmost Humility to approach your Majesty's Presence, by this Token of our Duty and Regard, which we are encouraged to lay at the Feet of our Sovereign, not only from the Ideas we entertain of its being at all Times agreeable to your Majesty to recieve Assurances of the Loyalty and Affection of your good Subjects, but also from an apprehension that such Proofs of sincere regard to the substantial Interests of your Crown and Kingdoms, from Thousands of your good People of *America*, as we have now to lay before your Majesty, will afford a more solid Satisfaction (at a Time when all your *American* Dominions are threatned either with present or future Ruin) than the most pompous Professions of Duty and Loyalty unaccompanied with corresponding Actions; Emboldened by this confidence, we beg leave to assure your Majesty, that we behold with Horror and Indignation, the Schemes which have long been secretly laid (and which our perfidious Neighbours at length are openly executing) for the Ruin and Destruction of all your Majesty's Dominions in *America*: We are affected with equal Horror and Detestation at the Prospect of that Slavery to an Arbitrary Prince and Popish Church, which the completion of those Schemes wou'd necessarily bring upon us, and our Posterity; with a proportionable Gratitude, we behold your Majesty's Paternal Care in sending Fleets and Armies for our Protection when we are unable to Protect ourselves, and when it is out of our Power without such aid to prevent that Misery that seems to be breaking in upon us like a Flood, and which if not seasonably prevented would deluge the whole Land in Ruin In such a situation as this, we should think ourselves inexcuseable if we were either insensible of your Majesty's Kindness, or unwilling to contribute our Mite towards repelling the common Danger-----Being Bound then by the double Ties of Duty and Gratitude to your Majesty, and by that regard to the Dignity of your Crown, to our Country, our Posterity, and our Holy Religion, that ought to fill the Breasts of every Friend to Liberty and the Protestant Cause, we are now come with the deepest Humility to offer our Service in such a way as we verily believe will (if your Majesty is pleased to accept thereof) Promote the Interests of your Crown and Kingdoms, and contribute to the safety of your *American Plantations* in the most effectual Manner within the Compass of our Power: The Service that we humbly offer, and of which we Pray your Majesty's Acceptance, is that of laying (as far as in us Lies) a Foundation for preventing the Encroachments of the *French*, and for extending your Dominions in *America*, by removing with our Family's, and Fortunes, to the New Colony beyond the *Allegheny Mountains*, which the Scheme that is now laid at your Majesty's Feet proposes, if it shall be found agreeable to your Royal Pleasure, to order such Settlement, and graciously to grant such Aid to the Design, as will be necessary for carrying it into Execution,---- And as the wise and seasonable Measures which your Majesty, at a vast expence, has been pleased to take, for the Security of your *American Dominions*, affords the most unquestionable Proofs, of your Majesty's Regard for their safety, so we doubt not your Royal Wisdom and Penetration, has discoverd the necessity and importance, of settling strong and numerous Colonies in the Neighbourhood of *Ohio*, and *Mississippi*, as well for the securing those important Parts, of your Dominions, as for doing it, in a manner the least Burthensome, and the most Advantageous, to your good Subjects of *Great Britain*, and *America*.

OUR most Humble Prayer therefore is, that your Majesty will graciously be pleased, to grant such Countenance and Assistance, to the present Scheme for settling a New Colony, as will be necessary, for the Encouragement of a People, on whose Fidelity, your Majesty may, with the utmost Confidence rely, and who at the same Time, esteem themselves bound by the most sacred and indissoluble Ties, to hand down the Blessings of civil and religious Liberty, inviolate, to their Posterity. And will our gracious Sovereign be pleased to permit us to hope, for that Favour, from his Royal Benignity, which our Zeal for his Service, and our Country's Cause, inclines us to wish.

HAVEING chearfully made a tender of our best Service. What now remains is, to offer up our Humble and Fervent Prayers to Almighty GOD the Sovereign Ruler of the Universe, by whom King's Reign, and Princes Decree Judgment, that he would be pleased to Crown your Majesty's Arms with Success, that your Enemy's may flee away and return no more, that your Majesty's Life, may long be continued a Blessing to your People, and full of Happiness to yourself, that when Death puts a Period to your Reign on Earth, your Majesty may receive a Crown of immortal Glory, and that there never may be wanting one of your illustrious Race, to sway the British Scepter in Righteousness. These then may it please your Majesty, are our Wishes, and these shall be our Prayers.

Dated at *Philadelphia*,
July 24th, 1755.

During the French and Indian War, British colonists ask the king's approval for a scheme to settle a new colony to the west of Pennsylvania. Courtesy of The New-York Historical Society, New York City.

A LIST of the SOCIETY for the Encouragement of ARTS, MANUFACTURES and COMMERCE. October the 1st, 1755.

The Right Hon. Jacob Lord Viscount FOLKESTONE, PRESIDENT.

The Right Hon. Robert Lord ROMNEY,
The Rev. Stephen HALES, D. D. F. R. S.
Charles Whitworth, Esq;
James Theobald, Esq; F. R. S.
} VICE-PRESIDENTS.

JOHN GOODCHILD, Esq; TREASURER.

Mr. WILLIAM SHIPLEY, SECRETARY.

Edward Ashe, Esq;
WILLIAM Lord Viscount BARRINGTON.
The Hon. Mr. Justice BATHURST.
Samuel Burroughs, Esq; *Master in Chancery.*
—— Baker, Esq;
Mr. Henry Baker, F. R. S.
Mr. Charles Gascoigne Bale.
Mr. Arthur Beardmore.
Francis Beauchamp, Esq;
Jeremiah Bentham, Esq;
Mr. —— Bird.
Mr. Frederick Brandenburgh.
Gustavus Brander, Esq; F. R. S.
Robert Bristow, Esq;
John Bucknal, Esq;

PHILIP Earl of CHESTERFIELD.
GEORGE Earl of CARDIGAN, F. R. S.
JAMES Marquis of CARNARVAN.
JOHN Lord CARYSFORT.
Sir Kenrick Clayton, Bart.
Mr. Charles Carlile.
Henry Cheere, Esq;
—— Chitil, Esq;
Bourchier Cleeve, Esq;
R Conyers, M. D.
George Cooke, Esq;
Richard Coombs, Esq;
Mr. Nicholas Crisp.

Mr. Richard Dalton.
Adam Dawson, Esq;
Mr. William Deards.
Peter Delme, Esq;
John Delme, Esq;
Triboudet Demainbray, L. L. D.
Mr. Robert Dodsley.

BROWNLOW Earl of EXETER.
Sir Charles Egleton.
Mr. John Ellis, F. R. S.

Francis Fane, Esq;
Thomas Frankland, Esq;
Thomas Edwards Freeman, Esq;

Right Hon. Lady BETTY GERMAIN.
Col. William Gansel.
Henry Gould, Esq;
Mr. Thomas Grignion.

Capel Hanbury, Esq;
Gabriel Hanger, Esq;
Mr. Pheasant Hartley.
Mr. Anthony Highmore.
Fraser Honywood, Esq;

STEPHEN THEODORE JANSSEN, Esq; *Lord Mayor of London.*
Israel Jalabert, Esq;
Mr. M. Jenour.

Sir William Lee, Bart.
Sir Charles Le Blon, Bart.
Stephen Law, Esq;
Mr. Robert Lambe;

Samuel Lloyd, Esq;
William Lock, Esq;
Mr. Charles Lowth.

GEORGE Earl of MACCLESFIELD, PRÆS. R. S.
Sir Richard Manningham, M. D. F. R. S.
Thomas Manningham, M. D.
Henry Manningham, Esq;
Benjamin Martyn, Esq;
Mr Husband Messiter.
Mr. John Moore.
William Morgan, Esq;

Robert Nettleton, Esq;

OTHER LEWIS HICKMAN Earl of PLIMOUTH.
JOHN Lord Bishop of PETERBOROUGH.
Charles Pinfold, L. L. D.
John Pitt, Esq;
Charles Powell, Esq;
George Putland, Esq;
Mr. Joseph Partridge.

Robert Quarme, Esq;

Sir Thomas Robinson, Bart.
James Ralph, Esq;
Mr. Samuel Richardson.

ANTHONY ASHLEY Earl of SHAFTESBURY, F. R. S.
Sir Thomas Samwell, Bart.
Mr. James Short, F. R. S.
Charles Stanhope, Esq; F. R. S.
Mr. George Stubbs.
Lawrence Sulivan, Esq;

Peter Theobald, Esq;
Mr. Henry Tolcher.
The Reverend Mr. Josiah Tucker.

ISAAC Lord Bishop of WORCESTER.
Edward Wade, Esq;
Mr. James Warner.
Thomas Watson, Esq;
Philip Carteret Webb, Esq; F. R. S.
Mr. Kemble Whatley.
James Whitchurch, Esq;
Taylor White, Esq; F. R. S.
Mr. William Willis.
Edward Wilmot, M. D.
Mr. George Woodfall.
Mr. John Wright.

Miss Elizabeth Vaughan.

Mr. Robert Young.

CORRESPONDING MEMBERS.

Joseph Bruni, M. D. *Prof. Anat. at Turin.*
Alexander Garden, M. D. *in South-Carolina.*
Rev. Richard Pococke, D. D. *Archdeacon of Dublin.*
James Mounsey, M. D. *Physician to the Army in Russia.*
David Maine, Esq; *in Scotland.*

This broadside is a public announcement of the membership of an arts, manufacturing, and commercial society. Courtesy of The New-York Historical Society, New York City.

A N

Evening THOUGHT.

SALVATION BY *CHRIST,*

WITH

PENETENTIAL CRIES:

Compofed by Jupiter Hammon, a Negro belonging to Mr Lloyd, of Queen's-
Village, on Long-Ifland, the 25th of December, 1760.

SALVATION comes by Jefus Chrift alone,
   The only Son of God ;
Redemption now to every one,
   That love his holy Word.
Dear Jefus we would fly to Thee,
   And leave off every Sin,
Thy tender Mercy well agree ;
   Salvation from our King.
Salvation comes now from the Lord,
   Our victorious King ;
His holy Name be well ador'd,
   Salvation furely briag.
Dear Jefus give thy Spirit now,
   Thy Grace to every Nation,
That han't the Lord to whom we bow,
   The Author of Salvation.
Dear Jefus unto Thee we cry,
   Give us thy Preparation ;
Turn not away thy tender Eye;
   We feek thy true Salvation.
Salvation comes from God we know,
   The true and only One ;
It's well agreed and certain true,
   He gave his only Son.
Lord hear our penetential Cry :
   Salvation from above ;
It is the Lord that doth fupply,
   With his Redeeming Love.
Dear Jefus by thy precious Blood,
   The World Redemption have :
Salvation comes now from the Lord,
   He being thy captive Slave.
Dear Jefus let the Nations cry,
   And all the People fay,
Salvation comes from Chrift on high,
   Hafte on Tribunal Day.
We cry as Sinners to the Lord,
   Salvation to obtain ;
It is firmly fixt his holy Word,
   Ye fhall not cry in vain.
Dear Jefus unto Thee we cry,
   And make our Lamentation :
O let our Prayers afcend on high ;
   We felt thy Salvation.

Lord turn our dark benighted Souls ;
   Give us a true Motion,
And let the Hearts of all the World,
   Make Chrift their Salvation.
Ten Thoufand Angels cry to Thee,
   Yea louder than the Ocean.
Thou art the Lord, we plainly fee ;
   Thou art the true Salvation.
Now is the Day, excepted Time ;
   The Day of Salvation ;
Increafe your Faith, do not repine :
   Awake ye every Nation.
Lord unto whom now fhall we go,
   Or feek a fafe Abode ;
Thou haft the Word Salvation too
   The only Son of God.
Ho ! every one that hunger hath,
   Or pineth after me,
Salvation be thy leading Staff,
   To fet the Sinner free.
Dear Jefus unto Thee we fly ;
   Depart, depart from Sin,
Salvation doth at length fupply,
   The Glory of our King.
Come ye Blefied of the Lord,
   Salvation gently given ;
O turn your Hearts, accept the Word,
   Your Souls are fit for Heaven.
Dear Jefus we now turn to Thee,
   Salvation to obtain ;
Our Hearts and Souls do meet again,
   To magnify thy Name.
Come holy Spirit, Heavenly Dove,
   The Object of our Care ;
Salvation doth increafe our Love ;
   Our Hearts hath felt thy fear.
Now Glory be to God on High,
   Salvation high and low ;
And thus the Soul on Chrift rely,
   To Heaven furely go.
Come Blefied Jefus, Heavenly Dove,
   Accept Repentance here ;
Salvation give, with tender Love ;
   Let us with Angels fhare.

F I N I S.

*This broadside is the earliest known published writing of an American Negro, of which only one copy has
survived. Courtesy of The New-York Historical Society, New York City.*

Joy to AMERICA !

At 3 this Day arrived here an Exprefs from *Bofton* with the following moft glorious News, on which *H. Gaine* congratulates the Friends of *America*.

Bofton, Friday 11 o'Clock, 16th May, 1766.

This Day arrived here the Brig *Harrifon*, belonging to *John Hancock*, Efq; Capt. *Shubael Coffin*, in 6 Weeks and 2 Days from *London*, with the following moft agreeable Intelligence, *viz.*

From the *LONDON GAZETTE*.

Weftminfter, March 18.

THIS day his Majefty came to the houfe of Peers, and being in his royal robes, feated on the throne, with the ufual folemnity, Sir *Francis Molineaux*, Gentleman ufher of the black rod was fent with a Meffage from his Majefty to the houfe of commons, commanding their attendance in the houfe of peers. The commons being come thither accordingly, his Majefty was pleafed to give his Royal Affent to

An ACT to *Repeal* an Act, made the laft Seffion of Parliament, entitled, An Act for granting and applying certain ftamp Duties, and other Duties in the *Britifh* Colonies and Plantations in *America*, towards further defraying the *Expences* of defending, protecting, and fecuring the fame ; and for mending fuch Parts of the feveral Acts of Parliament relating to the Trade and Revenues of the faid Colonies and Plantations, as direct the Manner of determining and recovering the Penalties and Forfeitures therein mentioned.

When his Majefty went to the Houfe he was accompanied by greater Numbers of People than ever was known on the like Occafion ; many Copies of the Repeal were fent to Falmouth, to be forwarded to America ; and all the Veffels in the River Thames bound to America, had Orders to fail.

5 o'Clock, *P. M.* Since compofing the Above an Exprefs arrived from Philadelphia with a Confirmation of the Repeal, and that a printed Copy of it by the King's Printer lay in the Coffee-Houfe for the Perufal of the Publick.

The joyous news of the repeal of the Stamp Act reaches America. Courtesy of The New-York Historical Society, New York City.

A T this alarming Crifis when we are threatened with a Deprivation of thofe invaluable Rights, which our Anceftors purchafed with their Blood----Rights, which as Men, we defire from Nature; as Englifhmen, have fecured to us by our excellent Conftitution; and which once torn from us, will in all Probability never be reftored. At this important Time, when we are exerting every legal Effort to preferve to Ourfelves and Pofterity the complete and undifturbed Enjoyment of them, it is of the laft Confequence to act with Vigilance and Unanimity. It muft appear obvious to every unprejudiced Mind, that Supinenefs would prove as fatal to us, as a Difunion; and therefore, the more effectually to guard againft both---A Number of the Inhabitants of this City, have determined to drop all Party Diftinction that may have originated from a Difference in Sentiments in other Matters---to form Ourfelves into a Society, under the general and honourable Appellation, of the U̶N̶I̶T̶E̶D̶ S O N S o f L I B E R T Y,---and ftrictly to adhere to the following *R E S O L U T I O N S,*

I. To hold a general Meeting on the firft Monday Evening in every Month, at the Houfe of Mr. De La Montagne.

II. To convene occafionally if Circumftances occur to render it neceffary.

III. That we will Support the conftitutional Meafures entered into by the Merchants, Traders, and other Inhabitants of this City.

IV. The grand Defign of this Affociation being to Support the Meafures entered into by the Merchants, Traders, and other Inhabitants of this City---That, we will not in any Manner whatever counteract the Defigns of either Committee, but contribute to the effectual Execution of them, by all legal Means in our Power.

V. That we will not knowingly purchafe from, nor fell, to any Perfon or Perfons who fhall violate the Non-importation Agreement.

VI. T̶h̶a̶t̶ ̶w̶e̶ ̶w̶i̶l̶l̶ ̶n̶e̶i̶t̶h̶e̶r̶ ̶l̶e̶t̶ ̶H̶o̶u̶f̶e̶s̶ ̶t̶o̶,̶ ̶n̶o̶r̶ ̶h̶i̶r̶e̶ ̶t̶h̶e̶m̶ ̶f̶r̶o̶m̶.̶ That we will not employ, nor be employed by, nor in anywife hold Connection in Trade with, thofe who violate the Agreement, or with fuch as fhall Countenance their bafe Conduct, by dealing with them.

VII. That we do fteadily and invariably purfue fuch Meafures, ̶a̶n̶d̶ ̶f̶u̶c̶h̶ ̶o̶n̶l̶y̶,̶ as fhall appear beft calculated to promote the general Good of the Colonies. That the fole End of the U̶N̶I̶T̶E̶D̶ S O N S o f LIBERTY, is to fecure their common Rights---That the Object we have principally in View, is a repeal of the Acts impofing Duties on Paper, Glafs, &c. and that we will not as a Society under the faid Appellation, engage in any other Matter whatever.

N. B. The U̶n̶i̶t̶e̶d̶ Sons of Liberty, are to hold a Meeting on Monday Evening next, precifely at Seven o'Clock, at the Houfe of Mr. De La Montagne; and do hereby publicly invite every Lover of conftitutional Freedom, to meet with them at the above-mentioned Time and Place.

This important broadside announces the formation of a new society, to be called the Sons of Liberty, whose objective will be the "repeal of the Acts imposing Duties on Paper, Glass, etc." Courtesy of The New-York Historical Society, New York City.

WILLIAM JACKSON,

an *IMPORTER*; at the

BRAZEN HEAD,

North Side of the TOWN-HOUSE,

and *Oppofite the Town-Pump, in*

Corn-hill, BOSTON.

It is defired that the Sons and Daughters of *LIBERTY,* would not buy any one thing of him, for in fo doing they will bring Difgrace upon *themfelves,* and their *Pofterity,* for *ever* and *ever,* AMEN.

Maffachufets-Bay.

By the Governor.

A PROCLAMATION
For a Publick Thankfgiving.

FORASMUCH as the frequent Religious Obfervance of Days of Publick Thankfgiving tends to excite and preferve in our Minds a due Senfe of our Obligations to GOD, our daily Benefactor, the Mercies of whofe common Providence are altogether unmerited by us. :

I HAVE therefore thought fit to appoint, and I do, with the Advice of His Majefty's Council, appoint Thurfday the Twenty-firft Day of *November* next, to be obferved as a Day of Publick Thankfgiving throughout the Province, recommending to Minifters and People to affemble on that Day in the feveral Churches or Places for Religious Worfhip, and to offer up their humble and hearty Thanks to Almighty GOD, for all the Inftances of his Goodnefs and Loving-kindnefs to us in the Courfe of the Year paft ; more efpecially for that He has been pleafed to continue the Life and Health of our Sovereign Lord the KING—to increafe His Illuftrious Family by the Birth of a Prince—to fucceed His Endeavours for preferving the Blefling of Peace to His Dominions, when threatned with the Judgment of War— to afford a good Meafure of Health to the People of this Province----to continue to them their civil and religious Privileges----to enlarge and increafe their Commerce----and to favour them with a remarkably plentiful Harveft.

AND I further recommend to the feveral Religious Affemblies aforefaid, to accompany their Thankfgivings with devout and fervent Prayers to the Giver of every good and perfect Gift, that we may be enabled to fhew forth his Praife not only with our Lips, but in our Lives, by giving up ourfelves to his Service, and by walking before Him in Holinefs and Righteoufnefs all our Days.

AND all fervile Labour is forbidden on the faid Day.

GIVEN *at the Council Chamber in* Bofton, *the Twenty-third Day of* October, 1771, *in the Eleventh Year of the Reign of our Sovereign Lord* GEORGE *the Third, by the Grace of* GOD, *of* Great-Britain, France, *and* Ireland, KING, *Defender of the Faith,* &c.

By His Excellency's Command,
THO's FLUCKER, Secr'y.

T. Hutchinfon.

GOD Save the KING.

BOSTON: Printed by RICHARD DRAPER, Printer to His Excellency the Governor, and the Honorable His Majefty's Council. 1771.

An Anecdote of a certain CANDIDATE,

for the enfuing ELECTION.

HAPPENING to be at *Newark*, when he firſt heard that Mr. J——y, was acquitted of the Crime laid to his Charge————he ſhrugged up his Shoulders, and ſaid, That from the Diſpoſition himſelf had obſerved in the H——e of A——y, (or Words to that Effect) the Event did not in the leaſt ſurpriſe him; on the contrary, it was no more then what he expected; but that at another Election, the diſſenting Congregations would put up four *Diſſenters*, againſt four *Churchmen*.

THIS is a Fact which can be prov'd if neceſſary, and ſhews how well the Practices of ſome Men, agree with their Profeſſions, and that the Offer of which they ſo much vaunt Themſelves of having made to two certain Candidates.————Of the Epiſcopalians nominating two Members, and the Non-Epiſcopalians the other two, was only a meer Pretext to cloak their other malicious, invidious Deſigns; which appears ſtill more manifeſt, by their refuſing afterwards to concur with the popular Cry of joining the late Member, with the other three; and that the Nomination of four *Diſſenters*, was not in Conſequence of the Rejection of any Propoſal made to the two certain Candidates; but of a ſettled, pre-concerted Plan, which the certain Candidate had been Privy to, ſome Weeks before any ſuch boaſted *generous* Offer was made; and that if the two Candidates could have acceded to it (which was impoſſible, and highly improper for them to do,) ſome other ſtumbling Block would have been found out, and thrown in the Way, to diſturb the Quiet and Peace of this City.————

————Nor do I believe, that a certain turbulent, reſtleſs, ambitious Candidate, would have been ſatisfied with the Nomination of four Members, out of his own Meeting Houſe; or even with four Angels from Heaven, (if that could poſſibly be) unleſs his own dear, important, all-ſufficient *SELF*, could have been *One* of them.———— Nor will I ever believe, that any Man, would make ſo many, vain, idle, deſperate Attempts, and that at a great Expence, to ſerve the Public—for *Nothing*; eſpecially one, who is of a Profeſſion, not apt to undervalue their Services.

HONESTUS.

An Account of a late Military Massacre at Boston, or the Consequences of Quartering Troops in a populous well-regulated Town, taken from the Bos-Gazette, of March 12, 1770.

BOSTON, March 12, 1770.

THE Town of Boston affords a recent and melancholy Demonstration of the destructive Consequences of quartering Troops among Citizens in a Time of Peace, under a Pretence of supporting the Laws, and aiding Civil Authority; every consideratie and unprejudic'd Person among us was deeply imprest with the Apprehension of these Consequences when it was known that a Number of Regiments were ordered to this Town under such a Pretext, but in Reality to inforce oppressive Measures; to awe and controul the legislative as well as executive Power of the Province, and to quell a Spirit of Liberty, which however it may have been basely oppos'd and even ridicul'd by some, would do Honor to any Age or Country...

The BLOODY MASSACRE perpetrated in King-Street BOSTON on March 5th 1770 by a party of the 29th REGT.

BUTCHER'S HALL

Engrav'd Printed & Sold by PAUL REVERE BOSTON.

Unhappy Boston! see thy Sons deplore,
Thy hallow'd Walks besmear'd with guiltless Gore.
While faithless P—n and his savage Bands,
With murd'rous Rancour stretch their bloody Hands;
Like fierce Barbarians grinning o'er their Prey,
Approve the Carnage and enjoy the Day.

If scalding drops from Rage from Anguish Wrung,
If speechless Sorrows lab'ring for a Tongue,
Or if a weeping World can ought appease
The plaintive Ghosts of Victims such as these;
The Patriot's copious Tears for each are shed,
A glorious Tribute which embalms the Dead.

But know, Fate summons to that awful Goal,
Where Justice strips the Murd'rer of his Soul:
Should venal C—ts the scandal of the Land,
Snatch the relentless Villain from her Hand,
Keen Execrations on this Plate inscrib'd,
Shall reach a Judge who never can be brib'd.

The unhappy Sufferers were Mess. Sam' Gray Sam' Maverick, Jam' Caldwell, Crispus Attucks & Pat' Carr
Killed. Six wounded; two of them (Christ' Monk & John Clark) Mortally

S G   S M   J C   C A

P C

BOSTON, March 19.

Last Wednesday Night died, Patrick Carr, an Inhabitant of this Town, of the Wound he received in King-Street on the bloody and execrable Night of the 5th Instant...

SIR,

THE efforts made by the legiflative of this province in their laft feffions to free themfelves from flavery, gave us, who are in that deplorable ftate, a high degree of fatisfacton. We expect great things from men who have made fuch a noble ftand againft the defigns of their *fellow-men* to enflave them. We cannot but wifh and hope Sir, that you will have the fame grand object, we mean civil and religious liberty, in view in your next feffion. The divine fpirit of *freedom*, feems to fire every humane breaft on this continent, except fuch as are bribed to affift in executing the execrable plan.

WE are very fenfible that it would be highly detrimental to our prefent mafters, if we were allowed to demand all that of *right* belongs to us for paft fervices ; this we difclaim. Even the *Spaniards*, who have not thofe fublime ideas of freedom that Englifh men have, are confcious that they have no right to all the fervices of their fellowmen, we mean the *Africans*, whom they have purchafed with their money ; therefore they allow them one day in a week to work for themfelve, to enable them to earn money to purchafe the refidue of their time, which they have a right to demand in fuch portions as they are able to pay for (a due appraizment of their fervices being firft made, which always ftands at the purchafe money.) We do not pretend to dictate to you Sir, or to the honorable Affembly, of which you are a member : We acknowledge our obligations to you for what you have already done, but as the people of this province feem to be actuated by the principles of equity and juftice, we cannot but expect your houfe will again take our deplorable cafe into ferious confideration, and give us that ample relief which, *as men*, we have a natural right to.

BUT fince the wife and righteous governor of the univerfe, has permitted our fellow men to make us flaves, we bow in fubmiffion to him, and determine to behave in fuch a manner, as that w may have reafon to expect the divine approbation of and affiftance in, our peaceable nd lawful attempts to gain our freedom.

WE are willing to fubmit to fuch regulations and laws, as may be made relative to us, until we leave the province, which we determine to do as foon as we can from our joynt labours procure money to tranfport ourfelves to fome part of the coaft of *Africa*, where we propofe a fettlement. We are very defirous that you fhould have inftructions relative to us, from your town, therefore we pray you to communicate this letter to them, and afk this favor for us.

In behalf of our fellow flaves in this province,
And by order of their Committee.

PETER BESTES,
SAMBO FREEMAN,
FELIX HOLBROOK,
CHESTER JOIE.

For the REPRESENTATIVE of the town of *Thompfon*

Less than two years later, four "slaves" from the town of Thompson, near Boston, complain to their representative that their "natural rights" are being ignored. Courtesy of The New-York Historical Society, New York City.

B O S T O N, DECEMBER 1, 1773.

At a meeting of the PEOPLE of Boſton, and the neighbouring towns, at Faneuil-Hall, in ſaid Boſton, on Monday the 29th of November, 1773. nine o'clock, A. M. and continued by adjournment to the next day; for the purpoſe of conſulting, adviſing, and determining upon the moſt proper and effectual method to prevent the unlading, receiving, or vending the deteſtable tea, ſent out by the Eaſt India company, part of which being juſt arrived in this harbour:

IN order to proceed with due regularity, it was moved that a moderator be choſen, and

JONATHAN WILLIAMS, Eſq;
Was then choſen moderator of the meeting.

A MOTION was made, that as the town of Boſton had determined at a late meeting, legally aſſembled, that they would, to the utmoſt of their power, prevent the landing of the tea, the queſtion be put, Whether this body are abſolutely determined, that the tea now arrived in Captain Hall, ſhall be returned to the place from whence it came, at all events. And the queſtion being accordingly put, it paſſed in the affirmative. Nem. con.

It appearing that the hall could not contain the people aſſembled, it was voted, that the meeting be immediately adjourned to the Old South Meeting-Houſe. Leave having been obtained for this purpoſe, the people met at the Old South, according to adjournment

A motion was made, and the queſtion put, viz. Whether it is the firm reſolution of this body, that the tea ſhall not only be ſent back, but that no duty ſhall be paid thereon; and paſſed in the affirmative. Nem. con.

It was moved, that in order to give time to the conſignees to conſider and deliberate, before they ſent in their propoſals to this body, as they had given reaſon to expect it would have been done at the opening of the meeting, there might be an adjournment to three o' clock, P. M. and the meeting was accordingly for that purpoſe adjourned.

Three o'clock, P. M. met according to adjournment.

A motion was made, Whether the tea now arrived in Captain Hall's ſhip, ſhall be ſent back in the ſame bottom—Paſſed in the affirmative. Nem. con.

Mr Rotch the owner of the veſſel being preſent, informed the body, that he ſhould enter his proteſt againſt their proceedings.

It was then moved and voted, nem. con. That Mr. Rotch be directed not to enter this tea; and that the doing of it would be at his peril.

Alſo voted, that Captain Hall, the maſter of the ſhip, be informed, that at his peril, he is not to ſuffer any of the tea, brought by him, to be landed.

A motion was made, that in order for the ſecurity of Captain Hall's ſhip and cargo, a watch may be appointed—and it was voted that a watch be accordingly appointed to conſiſt of twenty-five men.

Captain Edward Proctor was appointed by the body to be the captain of the watch for this night, and the names were given in to the moderator, of the townſmen, who were volunteers on the occaſion.

It having been obſerved to the body, that Governor Hutchinſon had required the juſtices of the peace in this town to meet and uſe their endeavours to ſuppreſs any routs or riots, &c. of the people, that might happen—It was moved, and the queſtion put—Whether it be not the ſenſe of this meeting, that the Governor's conduct herein carries a deſigned reflection upon the people here met; and is ſolely calculated to ſerve the views of adminiſtration—Paſſed in the affirmative, nem. con.

The people being informed by colonel Hancock, that Mr. Copley, ſon-in-law to Mr. Clarke, ſen. had acquainted him, that the tea conſignees did not receive their letters from London till laſt evening, and were ſo diſperſed, that they could not have a joint meeting early enough to make their propoſals at the time intended; and therefore were deſirous of a further ſpace for that purpoſe.

The meeting out of great tenderneſs to theſe perſons, and from a ſtrong deſire to bring this matter to a concluſion, notwithſtanding the time they had hitherto expended upon them to no purpoſe, were prevailed upon to adjourn to the next morning nine o'clock.

Tueſday morning, nine o'clock, met according to adjournment.

The long expected propoſals were at length brought into meeting, not directed to the moderator, but to John Scollay, Eſq; one of the ſelectmen—It was however voted that the ſame ſhould be read, and they are as follow, viz.

Monday, Nov. 29, 1773.

SIR,

WE are ſorry that we could not return to the town ſatisfactory anſwers to their two late meſſages to us, reſpecting the teas; we beg leave to acquaint the gentlemen ſelectmen, that we have ſince received our orders, from the Hon. Eaſt India company.

We ſtill retain a diſpoſition to do all in our power to give ſatisfaction to the town, but as we underſtood from you and the other gentlemen ſelectmen, at Meſſrs. Clarkes interview with you laſt Saturday, that this can be effected by nothing leſs than our ſending back the teas, we beg leave to ſay, that this is utterly out of our power to do, but we do now declare to you our readineſs to ſtore the teas, until we ſhall have opportunity of writing to our conſtituents, and ſhall receive their further orders reſpecting them; and we do moſt ſincerely wiſh, that the town, conſidering the unexpected difficulties devolved upon us, will be ſatisfied with what we now offer.

We are, SIR,
Your moſt humble ſervants.
Tho. and Eliſha Hutchinſon,
Benja. Faneuil jun. for ſelf, and
Joſhua Winſlow, Eſq;
Richard Clarke, and Sons.

John Scollay, Eſq;

Mr. Sheriff Greenleaf came into the meeting, and begged leave of the moderator that a letter he had received from the Governor requiring him to read a proclamation to the people here aſſembled, might be read; and it was accordingly read.

Whereupon it was moved, and the queſtion put, whether the Sheriff ſhould be permitted to read the proclamation—which paſſed in the affirmative, nem con.

The proclamation is as follows, viz,

Maſſachuſetts-Bay, By the Governor.
To *Jonathan Williams*, Eſq; acting as moderator of an aſſembly of people in the town of Boſton, and to the people ſo aſſembled.

WHereas printed notifications were on Monday the 29th inſtant poſted in divers places in the town of Boſton, and publiſhed in the news-papers, of that day, calling upon the people to aſſemble together for certain unlawful purpoſes, in ſuch notifications mentioned; and whereas great numbers of people belonging to the town of Boſton, and divers others belonging to ſeveral other towns in the province, did aſſemble, in the town of Boſton, on the ſaid day, and did then, and there, proceed to chooſe a moderator, and to conſult, debate, and reſolve upon ways and means, for carrying ſuch unlawful purpoſes into execution; openly violating, defying, and ſetting at nought the good and wholeſome laws of the province, and the conſtitution of government under which they live: And whereas the people thus aſſembled, did vote or agree to adjourn or continue their meeting to this the 30th inſtant, and great numbers of them are again met, or aſſembled together, for the like purpoſes, in the ſaid town of Boſton.

IN faithfulneſs to my truſt, and as his Majeſty's repreſentative, within the province, I am bound to bear teſtimony, againſt this violation of the laws, and I warn, exhort, and require you, and each of you, thus unlawfully aſſembled, forthwith to diſperſe, and to ſurceaſe all further unlawful proceedings, at your utmoſt peril.

Given under my Hand, at Milton, in the Province aforeſaid, the 30th Day of November, 1773, and in the fourteenth Year of his Majeſty's Reign. T. Hutchinſon.

By his Excellency's Command, } THO. FLUCKER, Sec.

And the ſame being read by the Sheriff, there was immediately after, a loud and very general hiſs.

A motion was then made, and the queſtion put, whether the aſſembly would diſperſe and ſurceaſe all further proceedings, according to the Governor's requirement. It paſſed in the negative, nem con.

A propoſal of Mr. Copley was made, that in caſe he could prevail with the Meſſieurs Clarkes to come into this meeting, the queſtion might now be put, whether they ſhould be treated with civility while in the meeting, tho' they might be of different ſentiments with this body; and their perſons be ſafe until their return to the place from whence they ſhould come. And the queſtion being accordingly put, paſſed in the affirmative, nem. con.

Another motion of Mr. Copley's was put, whether two hours ſhall be given him, which alſo paſſed in the affirmative.

Adjourned to two o'Clock, P. M.

TWO o'clock P. M. met according to adjournment.

A motion was made and paſſed that Mr. Rotch, and Captain Hall, be deſired to give their attendance.

Mr. Rotch appeared, and upon a motion made, the queſtion was put, whether it is the firm reſolution of this body, that the tea brought by Captain Hall, ſhall be returned by Mr. Rotch, to England, in the bottom in which it came; and whether they accordingly now require the ſame? which paſſed in the affirmative, nem. con.

Mr. Rotch, then informed the meeting, that he ſhould proteſt againſt the whole proceedings as he had done againſt the proceedings on yeſterday, but that, though the returning the tea is an involuntary act in him, he yet conſiders himſelf as under a neceſſity to it, and ſhall therefore comply with the requirement of this body.

Capt. Hall being preſent was forbid to aid, or aſſiſt in unloading the tea at his peril, and ordered, that if he continues maſter of the veſſel, he carry the ſame back to London; who replied he ſhould comply with theſe requirements.

Upon a motion, reſolved, that John Rowe, Eſq. owner of part of Capt. Bruce's ſhip, expected with tea; as alſo Mr. Timmins, factor for Captain Coffin's brig, be deſired to attend.

Mr. Ezekiel Cheever, was appointed Captain of the watch for this night, and a ſufficient number of volunteers gave in their names for that ſervice.

VOTED, that the Captain of this watch be deſired to make out a liſt of the watch, for the next night, and ſo each Captain of the watch for the following nights, until the veſſels leave the harbour.

Upon a motion made, voted, that in caſe it ſhould happen, that the watch ſhould be any ways moleſted in the night, while on duty, they give the alarm to the inhabitants, by the tolling of the bells, and that if any thing happens in the day time, the alarm be by ringing of the bells.

VOTED, that ſix perſons be appointed to be in readineſs to give due notice to the country towns, when they ſhall be required ſo to do upon any important occaſion. And ſix perſons were accordingly choſen for that purpoſe.

John Rowe, Eſq. attended, and was informed, that Mr. Rotch had engaged, that his veſſel ſhould carry back the tea, ſhe brought, in the ſame bottom; and that it was the expectation of this body, that he does the ſame, by the tea expected in Capt Bruce; whereupon he replied, that the ſhip was under the care of the ſaid maſter, but that he would uſe his utmoſt endeavours, that it ſhould go back as required by this body, and that he would give immediate advice of the arrival of ſaid ſhip.

It was then voted, that what Mr. Rowe and Mr. Timmins had offered, was ſatisfactory to the body.

VOTED, That it is the ſenſe of of this body, that Capt. Bruce ſhall, on his arrival, ſtrictly conform to the votes paſſed reſpecting Captain Hall's veſſel, as tho' they had been all paſſed in reference to Capt. Bruce's ſhip.

Mr. Timmins appeared, and informed, that Capt. Coffin's brig, expected with tea, was owned in Nantucket, he gave his word of honour that no tea ſhould be landed while ſhe was under his care, nor touched by any one until the owner's arrival.

Mr. Copley returned and acquainted the body, that as he had been obliged to go to the Caſtle, he hoped that if he had exceeded the time allowed him they would conſider the difficulty of a paſſage by water at this ſeaſon, as his apology: He then further acquainted the body, that he had ſeen all the conſignees, and though he had convinced them that they might attend this meeting with ſafety, and had uſed his utmoſt endeavours to prevail upon them to give ſatisfaction to the body; they acquainted him, that believing nothing would be ſatisfactory ſhort of re ſhipping the tea, which was out of their power, they thought it beſt not to appear, but would renew their propoſal of ſtoring the Tea, and ſubmitting the ſame to the inſpection of the committee, and that they could go no further, without incurring their own ruin; but as they had not been active in introducing the tea, they ſhould do nothing to obſtruct the people in their procedure with the ſame.

It was then moved, and the queſtion put, Whether the return made by Mr. Copley from the conſignees, be in the leaſt degree ſatisfactory to this body, and paſſed in the negative. Nem. Con.

Whereas a number of merchants in this province have inadvertently imported tea from Great Britain, while it is ſubject to the payment of a duty impoſed upon it by an act of the Britiſh Parliament, for the purpoſe of raiſing a Revenue in America, and appropriating the ſame without the conſent of theſe who are required to pay it:

RESOLVED, That in thus importing ſaid tea, they have juſtly incurred the diſpleaſure of our brethren in the other Colonies.

And Reſolved further, That if any perſon or perſons, ſhall hereafter import tea from Great-Britain, or if any maſter or maſters of any veſſel or veſſels, in Great-Britain, ſhall take the ſame on board, to be imported to this place, until the ſaid unrighteous act ſhall be repealed, he, or they, ſhall be deemed by this body, an enemy to his country; and we will prevent the landing and ſale of the ſame, and the payment of any duty thereon. And we will effect the return thereof to the place from whence it ſhall come.

RESOLVED, That the foregoing Vote be printed and ſent to England, and all the ſea ports in this province.

Upon a motion made, voted, that fair copies be taken of the whole proceedings of this meeting, and tranſmitted to New-York and Philadelphia, and that

Mr. SAMUEL ADAMS,
Hon. JOHN HANCOCK, Eſq;
WILLIAM PHILLIPS, Eſq;
JOHN ROWE, Eſq;
JONATHAN WILLIAMS, Eſq;
Be a Committee to tranſmit the ſame.

Voted, That it is the determination of this body, to carry their votes and reſolutions into execution, at the riſque of their lives and property.

Voted, That the committee of correſpondence for this town, be deſired to take care that every other veſſel with tea, that arrives in this harbour, have a proper watch appointed for her.—Alſo voted, that thoſe perſons who are deſirous of making a part of theſe nightly watches, be deſired to give in their names at Meſſrs. Edes and Gill's Printing office.

Voted, That our brethren in the country be deſired to afford their aſſiſtance upon the firſt notice given; eſpecially if ſuch notice be given upon the arrival of Capt. Loring, in Meſſrs. Clarkes' brigantine.

Voted, That thoſe of this body who belong to the town of Boſton, do return their thanks to their brethren who have come from the neighbouring towns, for their countenance and union with this body, in this exigence of our affairs.

VOTED, That the thanks of this meeting be given, to Jonathan Williams, Eſq; for his good ſervices as moderator.

VOTED, That this meeting be diſſolved, And it was accordingly diſſolved.

A citizens' committee of distinguished Bostonians resolves to enforce an embargo on British tea and other goods. Courtesy of The New-York Historical Society, New York City.

Colony of RHODE-ISLAND, &c.

At a Town-Meeting held at NEWPORT, the 12th Day of January, 1774, HENRY WARD, Esq; MODERATOR.

WHEREAS the East-India Company, notwithstanding the resolutions of the Americans not to import TEA while it remains subject to the payment of a DUTY, in America, have attempted to force large quantities thereof into some of our sister colonies, without their consent, in order to be sold, in this country, on their account, and risque : And whereas they may attempt to introduce it into this colony : We, the inhabitants of this town, legally convened, in town-meeting, do firmly resolve,

1st. That the disposal of their own property is the inherent right of freemen ; that there can be no property in that which another can, of right, take from us, without our consent ; that the claim of Parliament to tax America, in other words, a claim of right to levy contributions on us at pleasure.

2. That the duty imposed, by parliament, upon Tea, landed in America, is a tax on the Americans, or levying contributions on them without their consent.

3. That the express purpose for which the tax is levied on the Americans, namely, for the support of government, administration of justice, and defence of his Majesty's dominions, in America, has a direct tendency to render assemblies useless ; and to introduce arbitrary government and SLAVERY.

4. That a virtuous and steady opposition to this ministerial plan of governing America, is absolutely necessary to preserve even the shadow of Liberty ; and is a duty which every freeman in America owes to his country, to himself, and to his posterity.

5. That the resolutions lately entered into by the East-India Company, to send out their tea to America, subject to the payment of DUTIES, on its being landed here, is an open attempt to inforce this ministerial plan, and a violent attack upon the liberties of America.

6. That it is the duty of every American to oppose this attempt.

7. That whoever shall, directly or indirectly, countenance this attempt, or in any wife aid, or abet, in unloading, receiving, or vending the tea sent, or to be

sent out by the East-India Company, or by any other person, while it remains subject to the payment of a duty here, is an enemy to this country.

8. That Col. Joseph Wanton, jun. Henry Ward, John Mawdsley, John Collins, and William Ellery, Esquires, or the major part of them, be appointed a committee for this town, to correspond with all other committees, appointed by any other towns in this colony, or the towns in any of the other colonies ; which committee, or the major part of them, shall, upon information or suspicion of any tea being imported into this town, subject to a duty, immediately wait on the master of the vessel who shall bring the same, or the merchant to whom it shall belong, requesting that it may not be landed, and immediately call a town-meeting, to consider what steps to take ; and that said committee inquire into the late rise of tea, and use their utmost influence to bring it down to the usual price as it was at a short time past.

9. RESOLVED, That this meeting will heartily join with, and, to the utmost of our power, stand by and support our sister colonies, in all laudable measures, for the preservation of the general and particular rights and privileges of North America.

VOTED, That the foregoing RESOLVES be published in the NEWPORT MERCURY ; and that the committee of correspondence transmit copies of them to the several towns in this colony, with a request to them to come into similar resolutions, if they shall think proper.

    A true copy :

    Witness

        WM. CODDINGTON, Town Clerk.

It was also voted, at said meeting, that the printer of the Newport Mercury, should be requested to acquaint the public, in his next paper, that the paragraph inserted last Monday, containing an intimation, that some matter of importance to the liberties of America had been suppressed, was founded upon mistake, and that that matter hath been cleared up, entirely to the satisfaction of the town.

*** Every one of the above VOTES passed without a single dissentient, except that to inquire into the rise of TEA, against which there were but about 3 or 4 hands up. —— Notwithstanding the weather was extremely cold, there never was so full a town-meeting here, as the above, except sometimes in the highest struggle of parties, for representatives, &c.

Printed by SOLOMON SOUTHWICK

Resolutions of a Newport, Rhode Island town meeting, 1774, urging action against the tea duty. From the copy in the New York Public Library.

T H E

ALARMING BOSTON
PORT ACT,

Which prohibits the Entry and Clearance of all Veſſels whatſoever at that Port, from the enſuing 1ſt Day of June, 1774, and transfers the Seat of Government and of the Cuſtom-Houſe to the Town of S A L E M.

✕✕✕✕✕✕✕✕✕✕✕✕✕✕✕✕✕✕✕✕✕✕✕✕✕✕✕✕✕✕✕✕✕✕✕✕✕✕

An A C T to diſcontinue, in ſuch manner, and for ſuch time as are therein mentioned, the landing and diſcharging, lading or ſhipping, of goods, wares, and merchandiſe, at the town, and within the Harbour of Boſton, in the province of Maſſachuſetts Bay, in North America.

WHEREAS dangerous commotions and inſurrections have been fomented and raiſed in the town of Boſton, in the province of Maſſachuſetts Bay, in New England, by divers ill-affected perſons, to the ſubverſion of his Majeſty's government, and to the utter deſtruction of the publick peace, and good order of the ſaid town; in which commotions and inſurrections certain valuable cargoes of teas, being the property of the Eaſt India Company, and on board certain veſſels lying within the bay or harbour of Boſton, were ſeized and deſtroyed: And whereas, in the preſent condition of the

A broadside announcing and printing the text of the Boston Port Act. New-York Historical Society, New York City.

the said town and harbour, the commerce of his Majesty's subjects cannot be safely carried on there, nor the customs payable to his Majesty duly collected; and it is therefore expedient that the officers of his Majesty's customs should be forthwith removed from the said town: May it please your Majesty that it may be enacted; and be it enacted by the King's most excellent Majesty, by and with the advice and consent of the Lords Spiritual and Temporal, and Commons in this present Parliament assembled, and by the authority of the same, That from and after the first day of June, 1774, it shall not be lawful for any person or persons whatsoever to lade or put, or cause to procure to be laden or put, off or from any quay, wharf, or other place, within the said town of Boston, or in or upon any part of the shore of the Bay, commonly called The Harbour of Boston, between a certain other headland or point called Nahant Point, on the eastern side of the entrance into the said bay, and a certain headland or point called Alderton Point, on the western side of the entrance into the said bay, or in or upon any island, creek, landing-place, bank, or other place, within the said bay or headlands, into any ship, vessel, lighter, boat, or bottom, any goods, wares, or merchandise whatsoever, to be transported or carried into any other country, province, or place whatsoever, or into any other part of the said province of the Massachusetts Bay, in New England; or to take up, discharge, or lay on land, or cause or procure to be taken up, discharged, or laid on land, within the said town, or in or upon any of the places aforesaid, out of any boat, lighter, ship, vessel, or bottom, any goods, wares, or merchandise whatsoever, to be brought from any other country, province, or place, or any other part of the said province of the Massachusetts Bay, in New England, upon pain of the forfeiture of the said goods, wares, and merchandise, and of the said boat, lighter, ship, vessel, or other bottom into which the same shall be put, or out of which the same shall be taken, and of the guns, ammunition, tackle, furniture, and stores, in or belonging to the same: And if any such goods, wares, or merchandise, shall, within the said town, or in any the places aforesaid, be laden or taken in from the shore into any barge, hoy, lighter, wherry, or boat, to be carried on board any ship or vessel out-ward bound to any other country or province, or other part of the said province of the Massachusetts Bay, in New-England, or be laden or taken into such barge, hoy, lighter, wherry, or boat, from or out of any ship or vessel coming in and arriving from any other country or province, or other part of the said province of the Massachusetts Bay in New England, such barge, hoy, lighter, wherry, or boat, shall be forfeited and lost.

And be it further enacted by the authority aforesaid, That if any wharfinger, or keeper of any wharf, crane or quay, or their servants, or any of them, shall take up or land, or knowingly suffer to be taken up or landed, or shall ship off, or suffer to be waterborne, at or from any of their said wharfs, cranes or quays, any such goods, wares or merchandise; in every such case, all and every such wharfinger, and keeper of such wharf, crane or quay, and every person whatever who shall be assisting, or otherwise concerned in the shipping or in the loading or putting on board any boat or other vessel, for that purpose, or in the unshipping such goods, wares and merchandise, or to whose hands the same shall knowingly come after the loading, shipping, or unshipping thereof, shall forfeit and lose treble the value thereof, to be computed at the highest price which such sort of goods, wares and merchandise, shall bear at the place where such offence shall be committed, at the time when the same shall be so committed, together with the vessels and boats, and all the horses, cattle, and carriages, whatsoever made use of in the shipping, unshipping, landing, removing carriage, or conveyance of any of the foresaid goods, wares and merchandise.

And be it further enacted by the authority aforesaid, That if any ship or vessel shall be moored or lie at anchor, or be seen hovering within the said bay, described and bounded as aforesaid, or within one league from the said bay so described, or the said headlands, or any of the islands lying between or within the same, it shall and may be lawful for any Admiral, Chief Commander, or commissioned Officer of his Majesty's fleet or ships of war, or for any Officer of his Majesty's customs, to compel such ship or vessel to depart to some other port or harbour, or to such station as the said Officer shall appoint, and to use such force for that purpose as shall be found necessary: and

if

LORD NORTH'S SOLILOQUY.

A PLAGUE take that Boston port act, and all the Bostonians---those obstinate people will be my downfall--those puritannical rascals will be my ruin---the public at home now perceive the drift and consequences of that act, and think it endangers their own freedom and safety---the merchants already feel the bad effects of it, and murmur greatly- the cry is strong against me---I shall be hunted down---I was afraid of that d---n'd act at first--it was none of mine--I was not the father of it--I did not beget it--I only supported it according to the directions of the closet--It is confounded hard, that I must be responsible for obeying the Commands of the Thane--I should have been turned out if I had not.--But hold,--let me consider I shall be dismissed now if I complain--I must not recant--I must proceed let the consequences be what they will.--It those stubborn people cannot be cajoled, they must be forced -we must compel them to submit--more soldiers must be sent,--but how shall we prevent the desertion of them?--We must send the third regiment of guards--they are a tried corps-- we may surely depend upon them.--It will cost a great sum to send forces over sufficient to subdue the obstinacy of these rebellious Americans;--the people of England will grumble to pay new taxes for such a purpose -but I need not regard their grumbling--they have no spirit--I wish the people of New-England had no more.--I am sure of carrying what I please in the House, aye, and out of the House too --I have totally conquered all opposition at home; -I must do the same abroad.--That which gives me the most uneasiness, is the haughty menacing behaviour of the Spanish Court.--Should Spain prevail upon the French to join with her in breaking the peace, it would put a stop to all the fine projects of our Cabinet.--We must persuade France to keep the peace, let it cost what it will--a French war must, at all events, be prevented--for should that happen, we should never be able to compel the colonies to a proper obedience--and it shall be prevented, if gold hath the same influence in France as it hath in England.--We must force the Americans to submit by fire and sword, and for which we must select such officers for the conducting this affair, as will obey the private orders of the Cabinet.---We must also raise some regiments of Papists in Canada---they may also recruit our army there---they will be glad to cut the throats of those heretics, the Bostonians. ---A Popish army is by much the fittest for our purpose---they will obey the commands of the crown without any hesitation---they have been trained up in principles of passive obedience, and we may be assured they will not desert---This must be my way---it will answer my end---it will be relished by the Cabinet---and I shall keep my place.

New-York: Printed by JOHN ANDERSON, at Beekman's-Slip.

A Patriot's satirical attack on Lord North. Courtesy of The New-York Historical Society, New York City.

PHILADELPHIA.

In *CONGRESS*, *Thursday*, September 22, 1774.

RESOLVED, *nemine contradicente*

THAT the Congreſs requeſt the Merchants and Others, in the ſeveral Colonies, not to ſend to Great Britain any Orders for Goods, and to direct the execution of all Orders already ſent, to be delayed or ſuſpended, until the ſenſe of the Congreſs, on the means to be taken for the preſervation of the Liberties of *America*, is made public.

An Extract from the Minutes,
CHARLES THOMSON, *Sec.*

Printed by *W.* and *T. BRADFORD.*

The Philadelphia Congress resolves to cease all trade with Britain, 1774. Courtesy of The New-York Historical Society, New York City.

GENTLEMEN,

THE diftreffed and alarming fituation of our Country, occafioned by the fanguinary meafures adopted by the Britifh Miniftry, (to enforce which, the Sword has been actually drawn againft our brethren in the Maffachufetts,) threatening to involve this Continent in all the horrors of a civil War, obliges us to call for the united aid and council of the Colony, at this dangerous crifis.

Moft of the Deputies who compofed the late Provincial Congrefs, held in this City, were only vefted with powers, to choofe Delegates to reprefent the Province at the next Continental Congrefs, and the Convention having executed that truft, diffolved themfelves : It is therefore thought advifeable by this Committee, that a Provincial Congrefs be immediately fummoned to deliberate upon, and from time, to time to direct fuch meafures as may be expedient for our common fafety.

We perfuade ourfelves, that no arguments can now be wanting to evince the neceffity of a perfect union; and we know of no method in which the united fenfe of the people of the province can be collected, but the one now propofed.—We therefore entreat your County heartily to unite in the choice of proper perfons to reprefent them, at a Provincial Congrefs to be held in this City, on the 22d of May next.—Twenty Deputies are propofed for this City, and in order to give the greater weight and influence to the councils of the Congrefs, we could wifh the number of Deputies from the Counties, may be confiderable.

We can affure you, that the appointment of a Provincial Congrefs, approved of by the inhabitants of this city in general, is the moft proper and falutary meafure that can be adopted in the prefent melancholy ftate of this Continent ; and we fhall be happy to find, that our brethren in the different Counties concur with us in opinion.

By Order of the Committee,

ISAAC LOW, CHAIRMAN.

A call for the establishment of a Provincial Congress in New York, "to direct such measures as may be expedient for our common safety." Courtesy of The New-York Historical Society, New York City.

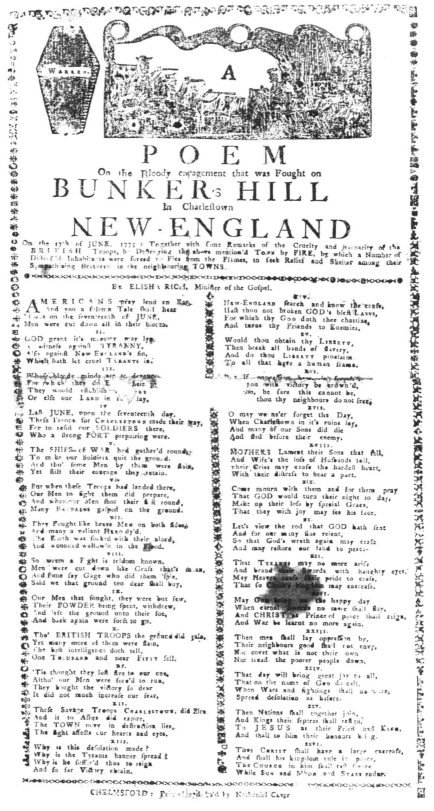

The engagement at Bunker's Hill gave rise to this poetic broadside. Courtesy of The New-York Historical Society, New York City.

A SONG,

Composed by the British Soldiers, after the fight at

Bunker Hill, June 17, 1775.

IT was on the seventeenth by brake of day,
 The Yankees did surprise us.
With their strong works they had thrown up,
 To burn the town and drive us;
But soon we had an order come,
 An order to defeat them:
Like rebels stout they stood it out,
 And thought we ne'er could beat them.

About the hour of twelve that day,
 An order came for marching,
With three good flints and sixty rounds,
 Each man hop'd to discharge them.
We marched down to the long wharf,
 Where boats were ready waiting;
With expedition we embark'd,
 Our ships kept cannonading.

And when our boats all filled were
 With officers and soldiers,
With as good troops as England had,
 To oppose who dare controul us;
And when our boats all filled were,
 We row'd in line of battle,
Where show'rs of balls like hail did fly,
 Our cannon loud did rattle.

There was Cop's hill battery near Charlestown,
 Our twenty-fours they played,
And the three frigates in the stream,
 That very well behaved;
The Glasgow frigate clear'd the shore,
 All at the time of landing,
With her grape shot and cannon balls,
 No Yankees e'er could stand them.

And when we landed on the shore,
 We drew up all together;
The Yankees they all man'd their works,
 And thought we'd ne'er come thither:
But soon they did perceive brave Howe,
 Brave Howe our bold commander,
With grenadiers, and infantry,
 We made them to surrender.

Brave William Howe, on our right wing,
 Cry'd boys fight on like thunder;
You soon will see the rebels flee,
 With great amaze and wonder.
Now some lay bleeding on the ground,
 And some full fast a running,
O'er hills and dales and mountains high,
 Crying, zounds! brave Howe's a coming.

They began to play on our left wing,
 Where Pegot he commanded;
But we return'd it back again,
 With courage most undaunted.
To our grape shot and musket balls,
 To which they were but strangers,
They thought to come in with sword in hand,
 But soon they found their danger.

And when the works we got into,
 And put them to the flight, sir,
Some of them did hide themselves,
 And others died with fright sir.
And then their works we got into,
 Without great fear or danger,
The work they'd made so firm and strong:
 The Yankees are great strangers.

But as for our artillery,
 They all behaved dinty;
For while their ammunition held,
 We gave it to them plenty.
But our conductor he got broke,
 For his misconduct, sure, sir;
The shot he sent for twelve pound guns
 Were made for twenty-four, sir.

There's some in Boston pleas'd to say,
 As we the field were taking,
We went to kill their countrymen,
 While they their hay were making;
For such stout Whigs I never saw;
 To hang them all I'd rather,
For making hay with musket-balls
 And buck-shot mixed together.

Brave Howe is so confiderate,
 As to prevent all danger;
He allows half a pint a day;
 To rum we are no strangers.
Long may he live by land and sea,
 For he's beloved by many;
The name of Howe the Yankees dread,
 We see it very plainly.

And now my song is at an end;
 And to conclude my ditty,
It is the poor and ignorant,
 And only them, I pity.
And as for their king John Hancock,
 And Adams, if they're taken,
Their heads for signs shall hang up high,
 Upon that hill call'd Bacon.

LOCKWOOD, BROOKS & CO., 381 WASHINGTON ST., BOSTON.

The British troops had their version of the affair also. Courtesy of The New-York Historical Society, New York City.

Proclamation!

For Suppreſſing REBELLION and SEDITION.

G E O R G E R.

WHEREAS many of our Subjects in divers parts of our Colonies and plantations in North-America, miſled by dangerous and ill deſigning men, and forgetting the allegiance which they owe to the power that has protected and ſuſtained them, after various diſorderly acts committed in diſturbance of the public peace, to the obſtruction of lawful commerce, and to the oppreſſion of our loyal ſubjects carrying on the ſame, have at length proceeded to open and avowed Rebellion, by arraying themſelves in a hoſtile manner to withſtand the execution of the law, and traiterouſly preparing, ordering, and levying war againſt us: And whereas there is reaſon to apprehend that ſuch Rebellion hath been much promoted and encouraged by the traiterous correſpondence, counſels, and comfort of divers wicked and deſperate perſons within this realm. To the end therefore, that none of our ſubjects may neglect or violate their duty through ignorance thereof or through any doubt of the protection which the law will afford to their loyalty and zeal, We have thought fit, by and with the advice of our Privy Council, to iſſue this our royal Proclamation, hereby declaring, that not only all our officers civil and military are obliged to exert their utmoſt endeavours to ſuppreſs ſuch Rebellion, and to bring the traitors to juſtice; but that all our ſubjects of this realm, and the dominions thereunto belonging, are bound by law to be aiding and aſſiſting in the ſuppreſſion of ſuch Rebellion, and to diſcloſe and make known all traiterous conſpiracies and attempts againſt us, our crown and dignity; and We do accordingly ſtrictly charge and command all our officers, as well civil as military, and all other our obedient and loyal ſubjects, to uſe their utmoſt endeavours to withſtand and ſuppreſs ſuch Rebellion, and to diſcloſe and make known all treaſons and traiterous conſpiracies which they ſhall know to be againſt us, our crown and dignity; and for that purpoſe, that they tranſmit to one of our principal Secretaries of State, or other proper officer, due and full information of all perſons who ſhall be found carrying on correſpondence with, or in any manner or degree aiding or abetting the perſons, now in open arms and rebellion, againſt our government, within any of our colonies and plantations in North-America, in order to bring to condign puniſhment, the authors, perpetrators, and abettors of ſuch traiterous deſigns.

GIVEN at our Court at St. James's, the twenty-third day of Auguſt, one thouſand, ſeven hundred, and ſeventy-five, in the fifteenth year of our reign.

GOD SAVE THE KING.

A distressed George III reacts to the news of rebellion in his American colonies. Courtesy of The New-York Historical Society, New York City.

JONATHAN TRUMBULL, Esq;

Governor of the English Colony of *Connecticut*, in *New-England*, in AMERICA :

A PROCLAMATION.

WHEREAS it is *Resolved by the General Assembly of the Colony of* Connecticut, *held at* New-Haven, *on the second* Thursday *of Instant* October, *that an Embargo be laid upon the Exportation out of this Colony by Water, the following Articles of Provision, viz.* Wheat, Rye, Indian Corn, Pork, Beef, Live Cattle, Peas, Beans, Butter, Cheese, Bread, Flour, *and every Kind of Meal (except necessary Stores for Vessels bound to Sea ;) and that such Embargo continue and remain until the first Day of* June *next.* Provided nevertheless, *That His Honor the Governor, he, and he is fully impowered to grant Permits for the Exportation out of this Colony by Water, Live Cattle and Provisions in such Cases, and to such Ports and Places as he shall judge necessary and expedient for the public Service.* Provided also, *That His Honor the Governor, by and with the Advice of the Council, may discontinue the Embargo in Whole or in Part, at any Time when it shall by them be judged expedient ; and that a Proclamation be issued accordingly.*

I DO therefore hereby strictly prohibit and forbid all Persons from Transporting and from Shipping on Board any Vessel for Transportation by Water, any of the aforesaid Articles, except as before excepted, from this Time to the first Day of *June* next, under the Penalties of the Law in that Case provided : And I do require and enjoin all Persons to exert themselves accordingly, that this Embargo be effectually carried into Execution.

Given under my Hand in the Council Chamber in *New-Haven*, this 19th Day of *October*, in the 15th Year of his Majesty's Reign. *Annoq; Dimini*, 1775.

JON^TH. TRUMBULL.

GOD save the KING.

The governor of Connecticut issues a directive to enforce the exportation embargo. Courtesy of The New-York Historical Society, New York City.

A
DOSE
FOR THE
TORIES.

COME hither brother tradesman,
    And hear what news I bring,
Its of a Tory ministry,
A Parliament, and King,
    A packing they must go, must go, must
    go, or a begging we shall go.

With places and with pensions,
Like Charles and James of old,
They rob us of our Liberty,
And sell us all for gold,
    And a packing, &c.

The Jacobites and Tories,
Dance round us hand in hand,
Like locusts they surround the throne,
And fatten on the land,
    And a packing, &c.

Our brethren in America,
With tyranny they grieve,
And they to make us praise their deeds,
With lies they us deceive.
    And a packing, &c.

Their ports and harbours they've block't up,
And all their trade they've stopt,
So all the poor are left to starve,
And we must shut up shop.
    And a packing, &c.

With Popery and Slavery
America they treat,
And swear they will dragoon them all
If they will not submit.
    And a packing, &c.

Our Soldiers and our Sailors,
Their purpose will not suit,
They'll never against the people fight,
For Mansfield, or for Bute,
    And a packing, &c.

Our merchants have petitioned,
And all the town besides,
And Chatham has upbraided them,
But nothing bends their pride,
    And a packing, &c.

Then let us to the Palace,
And Parliament repair,
And see who will deny us right,
Or tell us if they dare,
    And a packing, &c.

Should they our just demands refuse,
Genius of Liberty,
Conduct such Traitors to the Block,
A sacrifice to thee,
    Then a singing we will go, we'll go,
    we'll go, and a singing we will go to
    Tower-Hill.

IRELAND Printed: AMERICA Re-Printed, in the Year MDCCLXXV.

British imperialism rankled elsewhere as well. Here an Irish nationalist commiserates with his "brethren in America." American Antiquarian Society, Worcester, Massachusetts.

Song for *St. George's* Day.

Tune, *Hail England, Old England.*

FOR Ages the Nations beheld with furprize
   The Triumphs of Britain, whofe Fame fill'd the Skies!
With Ocean furrounded, enthron'd on her Ifle,
Where Virtue and Freedom rejoic'd in her Smile,
To the Summit of Glory unrivall'd She rofe,
The Boaft of her Friends, and the Dread of her Foes!

Huzza! O ye Britons! All Ages proclaim
Your Title to Crowns in the Temple of Fame!

Thus feated fublime, at her Feet fhe furvey'd
A *New* Scene of Triumph and Glory difplay'd.
To the Clouds, lo! the Winds tofs the Billows in vain,
And Neptune furrenders his Ample Domain!
From the Dawning of Day, as the Sun journeys round,
Britifh Banners are fpread, Britifh Thunders refound!

Huzza! O ye Britons! The Ocean is yours,
Your Empire extends and your Glory fecures!

[*Smile, Smile, Britannia Smile!*]

But lo! What Furies rife
  O'er this once happy Shore!
Thy Sons, O Britain, prize
  Thy wonted Love no more!
Rebellion proudly ftalks, and flings
Defiance at the beft of Kings!

Britons, ftrike home!
Let Vengeance, Vengeance arm your Hands!
Hafte, hafte to purfue, Hafte, hafte to purfue
  And quell the frantic Bands!
Now! feize and deftroy! Seize, feize and deftroy!
  Deftroy, deftroy the Frantic Bands!

[*Gramachree.*]

Ah no! the Royal George replies,
  While Juftice guards my Throne,
Let Pity melt in Britifh Eyes,
  Let Mercy ftill be fhown!
Difarm the rafh deluded Foe,
  But let not Havoc reign!
The Brave alone, in Triumph, know
  Soft Pity's tender Pain.

Though now, mifled by Folly's Dream,
  They Glory in their Shame,
Some loyal Hearts may yet redeem
  Their perjur'd Country's Fame.
Difarm the rafh deluded Foe
  But let not Havoc reign!
The Brave alone, in Triumph, know
  Soft Pity's tender Pain!

Then go, ye gallant How es! renown'd
  In Battle and in Peace,
Go heal defpairing Freedom's Wound,
  And bid Rebellion ceafe!
Difarm the rafh deluded Foe,
  But let not Havoc reign!
The Brave alone, in Triumph, know
  Soft Pity's tender Pain.

[*He comes! He comes! the Hero comes.*]

They come! They come! The Heroes come!
Soon fhall Rebellion's Voice be dumb!
The Dream of Pride and Folly o'er,
Frantic Bands fhall arm no more!

The Name of *Howe*, fo long rever'd,
Still more belov'd and more endear'd,
Shall now refound in loyal Strains,
Welcome to thefe Weftern Plains!

For now, *unaw'd*, the Mufe may fing
Long Life and Glory crown the King!
Be Faction dumb! Rebellion ceafe!
Welcome fweet returning Peace!

In the middle of the war, these songs in honor of the mother country appeared in New York, commemorating St. George's Day, 1777. Courtesy of The New-York Historical Society, New York City.

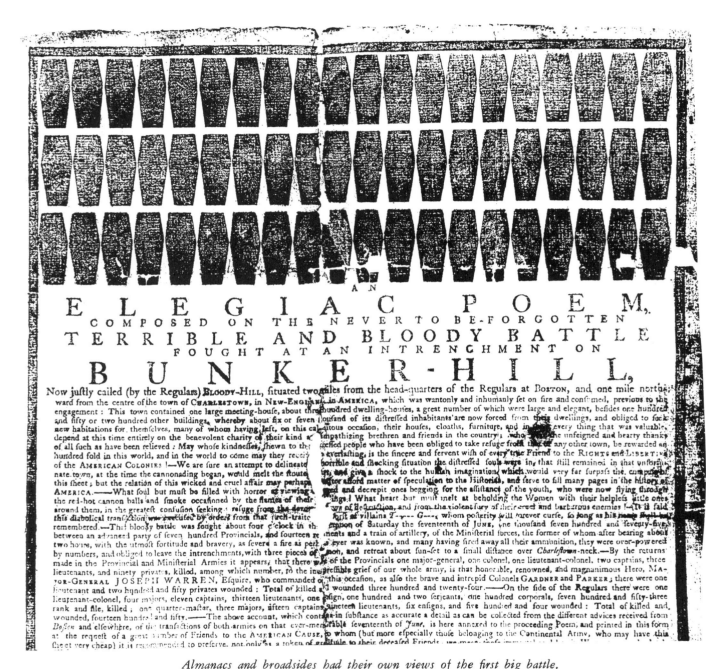

Almanacs and broadsides had their own views of the first big battle.

2. *The Almanac*

The first book produced by the Harvard College printing press was *An ALMANACK for New England for the Year 1639*, compiled by William Pierce, Mariner. This was not an unusual occurrence for the first production from presses in nearly all the English colonies were almanacs.

Produced by eminent men and scholars, the early almanacs served our forefathers as calendars of days, weeks, and months; as references to the coming eclipses; and as compendiums of astronomy, astrology, geology, meteorology, biography, history, tradition, and science. They carried the dates of notable births, marriages and deaths, of college commencements, election days, cattle shows and court sessions, as well as quaint sayings, enigmas, problems, tables of distances, practical information, and suggestions of various kinds. They frequently served as diaries and account books. Ship captains recorded in almanacs the important facts concerning their voyages, such as the dates of their arrival and departure and various occurrences at sea, and farmers made notes about their livestock and crops. Clergymen wrote minutes of their sermons.

Almanacs could be used for personal observations, too. An amusing anecdote is related about the Reverend Ezra Stiles, D.D. On February 13, 1789 he wrote in his almanac: "Gen. Ethan Allen of Vermont died and went to Hell this day."

Around the start of the eighteenth century censorship by the colonial governors, who had had the supervision of public prints, was removed. With the freedom of the press thus established, many new writers rushed into print and the almanac manufacturers increased in number. Over a period of time, astrological predictions (devoted primarily to the weather), humorous tales, jests, proverbs, medical essays, historical sketches, political tracts, and other information were gradually added, so that by the beginning of the nineteenth century the unpretentious eight-page calendar had grown to a forty-eight page pamphlet.

Authors with odd titles were numerous from the 1720s on. Among them were *Poor Joseph,* 1759; *Poor Will,* 1770, Philadelphia; *Poor Tom,* 1759, New York; *Poor Job,* 1750, Newport, Rhode Island; *Poor Roger,* 1762, New York; *Poor Thomas,* 1763, New York; and, of course, *Poor Richard's Almanack,* the brainchild of Benjamin Franklin, which appeared in Philadelphia in 1733 and continued until 1767.

In 1726 the most outstanding almanac ever published in America made its appearance. It was issued under the title "An Astronomical Diary and Almanack." The "Astronomical Diary" was compiled by Nathaniel Ames, a distinguished physician and mathematician who was also an innkeeper at Dedham, Massachusetts. Ames was a man of great originality and vigor and his publication was the most popular almanac in New England, with a circulation of 60,000 copies. Publications appeared annually until his death in July 1764.

In those pre-copyright law days, copies were surreptitiously obtained, and "quarrels and bickerings among printers, relative to the genuine Ames' Almanack, were frequent." Occasionally the Doctor himself certified, by card, a "correct edition."

Ames's almanac was regarded as better than Franklin's, and is probably the most pleasing representative we have of a form of literature that furnished so much entertainment to our ancestors, and that has preserved for us so many hints about the nature of their life and thought.

Through his almanac Nathaniel Ames brought his readers all sorts of knowledge and nonsense, in prose and verse, from literature, history, and "his own mind;" all were presented with "brevity, variety, and great tact." He made available to readers in the outposts of New England some of the best English literature. And, as the public expected the almanac-maker to be a prophet, the physician gratified their wishes by freely predicting future events with tongue in cheek. He is said to have laughed the loudest at his own failure to make accurate predictions, and mixed in delightful juxtaposition, absurd prognostications, jests, and aphorisms of profound wisdom, which were, and still are, extremely readable.

Poor Richard attained immediate success in a rather unusual fashion. Franklin cleverly elected to forecast the death of a man he considered his most formidable competitior. His announcement of this "sad fact" as well as the deceased's immediate denial were widely publicized, and for twenty-five years this almanac was a best seller in the colonies. Using the pseudonym Richard Saunders, Franklin borrowed proverbs and maxims from English as well as other literatures and converted them into plain prose.

In 1763 Benjamin West, noted astronomer and mathematician, became the author of the first almanac printed at Providence. He was also author of the *Bickerstaff Almanacks* which appeared at Boston and other New England cities in 1768 and for several years afterward.

The "Thomas" almanacs were likewise very popular in New England, particularly in Mas-

This is the title page of Bickerstaff's Almanack for 1770, with a facsimile of the engraving that adorns i The portrait of James Otis is supported on one side by Liberty and on the other by Hercules, or Perseve ance. At the feet of the latter, preparing to strike a lethal blow, is the venomous rattlesnake, an emble used on some of the colonial flags when the war began. This signified America's intention, under th guiding Spirit of Liberty, to persevere, and strike a deadly blow if necessary.

Bickerstaff's almanack was replete with political sentiments favorable to freedom. It contained the cel brated "Massachusetts Song of Liberty."

sachusetts. One, issued by Isaiah Thomas about 1774, was continued by his son, Isaiah, Jr., until early in the nineteenth century; the other Thomas almanac, issued first in 1793, was published by Robert B. Thomas and continued until his death, after which the almanac appeared under the title of *Thomas's Almanack.*

Today found primarily in rare collections of historical societies and libraries, their paper often crumbling and discolored, almanacs are difficult to read without a magnifying glass. It is even more difficult to have them reproduced. This is part of the challenge to those interested in pursuing the literary curiosities of our past. As Moses Coit Tyler, noted historian of American literature, wrote in 1897:

No one who would penetrate to the core of early American literature, and would read in it the secret history of the people in whose minds it took root, and from whose minds it grew, may by any means turn away in lofty literary scorn from the almanack—most despised, most prolific, most indispensable of books, which every man uses, and no man praises; the very quack, clown, pack-horse, and Pariah of modern literature; the supreme and only literary necessity even in households where the Bible and the newspaper are still undesired or unattainable luxuries.

B I C K E R S T A F F'S
BOSTON ALMANACK,
For the Year of our LORD 1770. Being the fecond Year after Leap Year.

The   Hon. JAMES OTIS, jun. Esq;

B O S T O N :
Printed by MEIN and FLEEMING, and to be SOLD by JOHN MEIN, at the
LONDON BOOK-STORE, North-fide of *KING-STREET.*
[Price feven Coppers fingle, and 25 *s.* Old Tenor, or 3 *s.* 4. Lawful the Dozen.]

Poor Richard, 1733.

A N

Almanack

For the Year of Chriſt

1 7 3 3,

Being the Firſt after LEAP YEAR:

And makes ſince the Creation	Years
By the Account of the Eastern *Greeks*	7241
By the Latin Church, when ☉ ent. ♈	6932
By the Computation of *W. W.*	5742
By the *Roman* Chronology	5682
By the *Jewish* Rabbies	5494

Wherein is contained

The Lunations, Eclipſes, Judgment of the Weather, Spring Tides, Planets Motions & mutual Aſpects, Sun and Moon's Riſing and Setting, Length of Days, Time of High Water, Fairs, Courts, and obſervable Days.

Fitted to the Latitude of Forty Degrees, and a Meridian of Five Hours Weſt from *London*, but may without ſenſible Error, ſerve all the adjacent Places, even from *Newfoundland* to *South-Carolina.*

By *RICHARD SAUNDERS,* Philom.

PHILADELPHIA:

Printed and ſold by *B. FRANKLIN*, at the New Printing-Office near the Market.

Title page of the most famous American almanac. Courtesy of the New-York Historical Society, New York City.

An ASTRONOMICAL-DIARY : Or,

ALMANACK

FOR THE YEAR OF OUR LORD CHRIST,

I 7 6 2.

Being the 2d Year after Biffextile or Leap-Year.
Calculated for the Meridian of BOSTON in NEW-
ENGLAND, Lat. 42 Deg. 25 Min. North.

CONTAINING

Eclipfes ; Afpects ; Courts
Feafts & Fafts of the Church ;
Spring Tides ; Lunations ;
Judgment of the Weather ;
Sun & Moon's Rifing & Setting.
Alfo, The Roads and beft
tages. —— A Table of the

Weight and Value of Coins.
—Table of Gold & Silver
by Weight, in old Tenor
from one Grain to an Ounce.
—An *Exact* Table to bring
Old Tenor into Lawful Money
from 7¼ d, to 500 £.

A Page for the Ladies.— On TEA.— On Nurfing Children.

By NATHANIEL AMES.

NOW we the long expected Year behold
Which Aftrologic Prophecies foretold,
And great Events fince 'Time began conceal'd
Rufh forth, and are to open View reveal'd :
Th'Objector fays, "What Things are come to pafs;
Does not each Scene continue as it was ?"
No : ——————————
The beft of Kings has laid his Scepter down,
And GEORGE the Third adorns the Britifh Crown,
New-conquered Realms join to his boundlefs Sway
And Savage Chiefs their willing Homage pay ;
He Reigns o'er Realms to former Kings unknown,
Whofe vanquifh'd Monarchs due Subjection own.

BOSTON : Printed & Sold by JOHN DRAPER, in Cornhill
RICHARD DRAPER in Newbury-Street ; GREEN & RUSSELL
and EDES & GILL in Queen-Street ; and THOMAS & JOHN
FLEET, at the Heart and Crown in Cornhill.
Sold alfo by the BOOKSELLERS

tobacco 6⅞

Title page of Ames's almanac. Courtesy of the New-York Historical Society, New York City.

Edge's and Giles's North American Almanack, *1770. "A Prospective View of the Town of Boston." Courtesy of The New-York Historical Society, New York City.*

The Maſſachuſetts CALENDAR;
OR AN
ALMANACK
FOR THE
Year of our Lord Chriſt 1774;
Being the ſecond after Biſſextile or Leap Year;
By EZRA GLEASON.

The wicked Stateſman, or the Traitor to his Country, at the Hour of DEATH.
BOSTON.: Printed by ISAIAH THOMAS: Sold at his Printing Office near the Market, and at his ſhop near the Mill-Bridge [Price 7 coppers ſingle, and 20 s. old tenor the dozen.]

Ezra Gleason's almanac for the year 1774. The cover shows hellish demons attacking "the Traitor to his Country" at the hour of his death. Courtesy of The New-York Historical Society, New York City.

223

A German engraving in which Washington is called the father of his country ("des Landes Vater") for the first time in print. It was printed in Lancaster, Pennsylvania by Francis Bailey in 1779. Lancaster County Historical Society.

DESCRIPTION of the FIGURES.

A STAGE raised on the body of a cart, on which was an effigy of General ARNOLD sitting; this was dressed in regimentals, had two faces, emblematical of his traiterous conduct, a mask in his left hand, and a letter in his right hand, telling him that he had done all the mischief he could do, and now he must hang himself.

At the back of the General was a figure of the Devil, dressed in black robes, shaking a purse of money at the general's left ear, and in his right hand a pitchfork, ready to drive him into hell as the reward due to the many crimes which the thirst of gold had made him commit.

In the front of the stage and before General Arnold, was placed a large lanthorn of transparent paper, with the consequences of his crimes thus delineated, i. e. on one part, General Arnold on his knees before the Devil, who is pulling him into the flames—a label from the General's mouth with these words, "My dear Sir, I have served you faithfully," to which the Devil replies, "And I'll reward you". On another side, two ropes from a gallows, inscribed, "The Traitor's reward." And on the front of the lanthorn was wrote the following: "MAJOR GENERAL BENEDICT ARNOLD, late COMMANDER of the FORT WEST-POINT. THE CRIME OF THIS MAN IS HIGH TREASON. "He has deserted the important post WEST-POINT, on Hudson's River, committed to his charge by His Excellency the Commander in Chief, and is gone off to the enemy at New-York,

"His design to have given up this fortress to our enemies, has been discovered by the goodness of the Omnificent Creator, who has not only prevented his carrying it into execution, but has thrown into our hands ANDRE, the Adjutant-General of their army, who was detected in the character of a spy.

"The treachery of this ungrateful General is held up to public view, for the exposition of infamy; and to proclaim with joyful acclamation, another instance of the interposition of bounteous Providence.

"The effigy of this ingrate is therefore hanged (for want of his body) as a Traitor to his native country, and a Betrayer of the laws of honour."

The procession began about four o'clock, in the following order:

Several Gentlemen mounted on horse-back.
A line of Continental Officers.
Sundry Gentlemen in a line.
A guard of the City Infantry.

Just before the cart, drums and fifes playing the Rogues March.
Guards on each side.

The procession was attended with a numerous concourse of people, who after expressing their abhorence of the Treason and the Traitor, committed him to the flames, and left both the effigy and the original to sink into ashes and oblivion,

'TWAS *Arnold's* roost, sir *Harry* fought,
   Arnold ne'er enter'd in his thought,
How ends the bargain? let us see,
The fort is safe, as safe can be,
His favourite *per force* must die,
His view's laid bare to ev'ry eye;
His money's gone—and lo! he gains
One scoundrel more for all his pains.
ANDRE was gen'rous, *true*, and *brave*,
And in his room, he buys a knave.
'Tis sure ordain'd, that *Arnold* cheats
All those, of course, with whom he treats.
Now let the Devil suspect a bite
Or *Arnold* cheats him of his right.

Mothers shall fill their children, and joy---Arnold!---
Arnold shall be the bug-bear of their years.
Arnold!---vile, treaiberous, and leagued with Satan,

A woodcut in the Continental Almanack *for 1780 depicted the traitor Benedict Arnold. American Antiquarian Society, Worcester, Massachusetts.*

The TIMES are **Dreadful, Difmal, Doleful, Dolorous,** and **DOLLAR-LESS.**

An Emblem of the Effects of the STAMP
O! the fatal Stamp.

Thurfday, *October* 31, 1765.

THE

NUMB. 1195.

PENNSYLVANIA JOURNAL;

AND

WEEKLY ADVERTISER.

EXPIRING: In Hopes of a Refurrection to LIFE again.

I AM forry to be obliged to acquaint my Readers, that as The STAMP-ACT, is fear'd to be obligatory upon us after the *Firft of November* enfuing, (the *fatal To morrow)* the Publifher of this Paper unable to bear the Burthen, has thought it expedient to ftop a while, in order to deliberate, whether any Methods can be found to elude the Chains forged for us, and efcape the infupportable Slavery, which it is hoped, from the laft Reprefentations now made againft that Act, may be effected. Mean while, I muft earneftly Requeft every Individual of my Subfcribers, many of whom have been long behind Hand, that they would immediately Difcharge their refpective Arrears that I may be able, not only to fupport myfelf during the Interval, but be better prepared to proceed again with this Paper, whenever an opening for that Purpofe appears, which I hope will be foon.

WILLIAM BRADFORD

Publisher William Bradford announces the demise of of his newspaper as a result of the Stamp Act, 1765. Courtesy of The New-York Historical Society, New York City.

3. Newspapers

The English term *newspaper* was used for the first time in 1670, when it appeared in a letter addressed to Charles Perret, second editor of *The Oxford Gazette.* The expression was found in the request, "I wanted your newes paper Monday last post."

The first American newspaper to appear in Colonial America was Benjamin Harris's *Publick Occurrences,* which came off the press on September 25, 1690, in Boston. It ceased to exist after four days when the Governor and council of Massachusetts "disallowed" its further publication because Harris had neglected to obtain permission for his venture.

The action taken by the Governor in suppressing *Publick Occurrences* and the continuing opposition of the clergy prevented any attempt to start another newspaper until the eighteenth century. News was disseminated through an occasional broadside, pulpit announcements, and publicly posted letters.

In 1704 John Campbell, the Scottish Boston postmaster, founded *The Boston News-Letter.* The first copy was printed on both sides of a half-sheet folio and dated "From Monday April 17 to Monday April 24, 1704."

The News-Letter lasted until the Revolution, and was followed in quick succession by *The Boston Gazette* and *The American Weekly Mercury,* which appeared in Philadelphia. When the Stamp Act took effect on November 1, 1765, Franklin's *Pennsylvania Gazette* came off the press. Before long newspapers appeared in other colonies, north and south, and our colonial journalism soon became an important literary force. The daily paper did not appear until the Republic was established.

During the Revolutionary War, whenever the British occupied a "strategic city" the Patriot printer took his newspaper elsewhere. Many newspapers were forced to suspend publication, and news of the battles had to be spread on printed handbills carried by post riders and hawked through the town.

RISING GLORY OF AMERICA.

NOW mighty ſcenes are op'ning to our view,
We leave the *Eaſtern* world, behold the *New*;
See fair COLUMBIA in dawning luſtre ſhine!
Her ports, her groves, her hills, her dales, her mines.
Her varied climes, her different ſoils produce
Whate'er man wants for ornament or uſe.
The blooming mountains and the fertile vales,
The flow'ry meadows and the ſpicy gales,
The fragrant fields the gardens ſtill more fair,
With rich perfumes tinge all the paſſing air.
Here Heaven bids FREEDOM rear her ſhining dome,
In theſe bright realms fix her eternal home;—
Virtue and Science lift her glory high,
Beneath her frown the tyrants fall and die.
Her ſons ſhall taſte the pureſt joys that flow,
All Freedom gives or Virtue can beſtow.
No hoſtile King dares bid them furl their ſails,
In every ocean ſhare the friendly gales.
By ev'ry human ear, by ev'ry tongue,
Her glory ſhall be heard, her praiſes ſung.
Now heaven born Peace in all her beauty ſhines,
And ev'ry joy the human breaſt entwines;—
Now god like patriots ſhare the public ſmile,
And reap the high reward of all their toil;
With tranſports riſing high, with joys divine,
See Freedom flouriſh, ſee their country ſhine,
Their glorious deeds, their glorious names go round,
And each bright circle echoes to the ſound;
While Heav'n and Conſcience ſhout the great applauſe,
Of him who fought for Liberty and Laws!
Hail happy times! the golden days are come,
And fair Creation ſmiles in all her bloom.
The tide of human glory riſes high,
And joys celeſtial ſparkle in each eye!
The humble cottage and the ſhining dome,
The ſplendid palace and the peaſant's home;
Equal their bliſs, their joys alike ſincere,
While heav'n born Freedom gilds the rolling year.
With genius fir'd, inſpir'd with rays divine,
Firſt Heirs of Freedom in her Council ſhine,
In this bright roll of Fame ſee WASHINGTON,
Whoſe deeds immortal travel with the ſun;
Heroes and Patriots cluſter in their train,
Rich heirs of glory bright'ning Virtue's reign;
While millions round the world their fame prolong,
In proſe, in verſe, in tragedy and ſong.
By beauteous virgins, muſick on each tongue,
In ſweeteſt ſymphony their praiſe is ſung;
This theme immortal wings its chearful round,
The ſons of honour triumph in the ſound!
Now human pleaſure feels its true ſublime,
To joy untailed in the realms of time.

A SOLDIER.

To the PRINTER.

If you will give the following SONGS *a place in your paper you will oblige your friend,* BOB JINGLE.

MAKE room O ye kingdoms in hiſt'ry renowned,
Whoſe arms have in battle with glory been crowned:
Make room, for *America*, another great nation,
Ariſes to claim in your councils a ſtation.

Her ſons fought for Freedom, and by their own bravery,
Have reſcu'd themſelves from the ſhackles of ſlavery:
America's free, and tho' Britain abhor'd it,
Yet Fame a new volume prepares to record it.

Fair Freedom in Britain her throne had erected,
But her ſons growing venal and ſhe diſreſpected,
The goddeſs offended forſook the baſe nation,
And fix'd on our mountains, a more honor'd ſtation.

With glory immortal, ſhe here ſits enthroned,
Nor fears the vain vengeance of Britain, diſowned;
Whilſt WASHINGTON guards her, with heroes ſurrounded,
Her foes ſhall with ſhameful defeat be confounded.

To arms, then, to arms, 'tis fair freedom invites us,
The trumpet ſhrill ſounding, to battle excites us;
The banners of Virtue, unfurl'd, ſhall wave o'er us,
Our Heroe lead on, and our foes fly before us.

On *Heav'n* and *Waſhington* placing reliance,
We'll meet the bold Britton and bid him defiance,
Our cauſe we'll ſupport, for 'tis juſt and 'tis glorious,
When men fight for *Freedom* they muſt be victorious.

The TOAST.

'Tis Waſhington's Health; fill a bumper all round,
For he is our glory and pride:
Our arms ſhall in battle with conqueſt be crown'd,
Whilſt Virtue and He's on our ſide.

'Tis Waſhington's Health; loud cannon ſhould roar,
And trumpets the truth ſhould proclaim;
There cannot be found, ſearch all the world o'er,
His equal in Virtue and Fame.

'Tis Waſhington's Health; our Heroe to bleſs,
May Heav'n look graciouſly down!
Oh, long may he live! our hearts to poſſeſs,
And Freedom ſtill call him her own!

Juſt publiſhed and now ſelling by JOHN DUNLAP, *in Lancaſter,*
[Price 2s. 6d. ſingle—2s. by the quantity]

THE
AMERICAN CRISIS.
NUMBER V.
Addreſſed to GENERAL SIR WILLIAM HOWE.
By the AUTHOR of COMMON SENSE.

To be SOLD *by Public Vendue,*

At Birdſborough Forge, in Union Townſhip, Berks County, for caſh, on Monday the 6th of April inſt.

A NUMBER of half blooded breeding Mares and Colts, of ſize and figure, very particular care having been taken in the choice of the mares and the covering horſes. Alſo a number of ſheep of good breed, a quantity of old iron, and ſeveral other articles. And on the next day will be ſold at Reading, five Teams; the horſes for draft peculiarly fine, the waggons and harneſs in good order and fit for any ſervice: Alſo a quantity of valuable Houſhold Furniture made of mahogany, walnut, &c. Attendance will be given at both places by

MARK BIRD.

TO be ſold, on Wedneſday the 8th day of April, (inſt.) at ten o'clock in the forenoon, a two ſtory log HOUSE, ſituate in Middletown, 30 feet by 26 on the main ſtreet, with a two ſtory kitchen, a large two ſtory ſhed, 65 feet long, with ſtables thereunto belonging, and a good pump in the yard. One other Lot, the corner of Pine and High-ſtreets, all in good repair. Alſo, a quantity of Houſehold Furniture too tedious to enumerate —Attendance will be given and the terms of ſale made known by

JACOB CREAMER.

To be SOLD by PUBLIC VENDUE,

On the ninth day of April inſt. on the premiſes,

THAT valuable Plantation and old accuſtomed Tavern lately belonging to Bartle Bartleſon, of Norriton Townſhip, Philadelphia County, deceaſed; containing one hundred and fifty one acres of extraordinary good land, ſituate on the great road leading from Philadelphia to Reading, about eighteen miles from the city of Philadelphia aforeſaid. There are on ſaid plantation a commodious ſtone dwelling-houſe, barn, ſheds and other out-houſes, about forty acres of good watered meadow which produceth hay of the beſt quality, about ten acres of good bearing orchard, one hundred acres thereof cleared, and the remainder good timber land. The whole is in good repair, and may be entered upon immediately. Attendance will be given and the terms made known on ſaid day, by

ELIZABETH BARTLESON, Executrix.

N. B. If ſaid plantation is not ſold on ſaid day, it will be rented to the higheſt bidder.

TO be ſold by way of public vendue, on Tueſday the 14th day of April inſt. a valuable PLANTATION, ſituate in Paxton townſhip, Lancaſter county, (with a clear deed) containing 160 acres. There are about 70 acres cleared, and 8 acres of very good meadow cleared, and more may be made, all very well watered, with a good bearing orchard, containing 160 trees. On the premiſes is a good ſquare log dwelling houſe, good barn, and a good ſhop for any tradeſman, all in good repair. It is as good a ſituation for mills as any in the country.—At the ſame time and place will be ſold, a good waggon with a valuable team of horſes and their geers, all juſt fit for the roads, and other horſes. The ſale to begin at ten o'clock in the morning, when due attendance will be given, and the condition of ſale be made known by

PETER SHIELDS.

Lancaſter, February 23, 1778.

THE Truſtees of the *General Loan-Office* of the Common-Wealth of Pennſylvania, hereby give notice to the Public, That the ſaid Office will be opened on Monday the 9th day of March next, at Lebanon, in the County of Lancaſter, where attendance will be given for four weeks ſucceſſively*, and on the firſt Monday and five following days in the months of April, June, Auguſt, October and December:—Therefore all perſons concerned are hereby notified to attend and diſcharge their annual payments now in arrear; and to thoſe who incline to pay off the remaining quotas of their reſpective mortgage monies and the intereſt thereof, on ſo doing their bonds and title deeds will be delivered up, and their mortgages will be diſcharged.

* *The inclemency of the weather, and the river Suſquehanna not being paſſable, prevented the Truſtees meeting and attending the month of February, as by law is appointed; therefore the four weeks above mentioned are in lieu thereof.* 8 w.

To be HIRED *or* SOLD,

AN excellent CLOTHIER, an Engliſh ſervant man, who has three years and four months to ſerve. Likewiſe a quantity of fullers preſs papers, and three thouſand tenter hooks. Any perſon wanting may apply to the ſubſcriber, at Wye Mill, Talbot County, Maryland. JOSHUA KINNARD.

WHEREAS Elizabeth Finley, alias Armſtrong, the wife of the ſubſcriber, ... Finley, living in Elizabeth Town, Waſhington ... ty, Maryland, eloped from her ſaid huſband ... 14th day of Auguſt laſt, and carried her child ... her: Theſe are therefore to charge and forewarn ... perſons whatſoever not to harbour or entertain ... Elizabeth Finley, alias Armſtrong, or her child ... credit her in any ſum or ſums of money, goods, or ... other neceſſaries, on my account, as I am determined not to pay any debts by her contracted ſince her elopement from my bed and board; and I diſown her ... my wife forever. Given under my hand this ... day of February, 1778. SAMUEL FINLEY.

Lancaſter, March 11, 1778.

TWENTY DOLLARS REWARD.

DESERTED laſt night from Lancaſter, a ſoldier named JOHN KILPATRICK, a ... well made fellow, about 5 feet 7 inches high, ... ſandy hair, ſandy complexion, ſquints a little, and a little freckled: Had on and took with him a blue regimental coat faced with white, and one brown ... faced with buff, a pair of light coloured cloth breeches, a lincey jacket, a pair of coarſe white woollen ſtockings, and an old wool hat. He has taken a paſs from a man in this town named Lawrence Huſten, dated Head quarters, Nov. 17, 1777. Whoever takes up ſaid deſerter and confines him in any of the goals of this State, or ſends him to the 13th Pennſylvania Regiment, ſhall receive the above reward, from

JOHN VANPELT, Lieut. 13th P. R.

TWENTY DOLLARS REWARD.

RAN AWAY on the 12th inſt. (March) from the ſubſcriber, living in Baltimore County, in the State of Maryland, near Fauble's Tavern, a convict ſervant man named JOHN LENDRICKIN, a native of Ireland, and ſpeaks in that dialect; about ... feet high, 25 years of age, well ſet, black hair cut ſhort, ſandy coloured beard; had on when he went away, two old lincey jackets of a yellow colour, a ... linen hunting ſhirt, white ditto ſhirt and trowſers, both old and broke, a pepper and ſalt coloured pair ſtockings, half worn ſhoes, and a felt hat. The ſaid ſervant has the letters of his name in the inſide of one of his wriſts, put in by a thread: He was taken up ... M'Caliſter's Town but made his eſcape; he had ... a paſs ſigned thus, *Ben. Rogers*, which was taken from him, but as he is a good clerk it is likely he will forge another. Whoever ſecures ſaid ſervant in any goal, ſo that his maſter may have him again, ſhall receive the above reward, and reaſonable charges if brought home, paid by

THOMAS DOWNEY.

WAS STOLEN in the night of Saturday, the 7th inſt. (March) from the ſtable of the ſubſcriber at Windſor Forge, a large cheſnut HORSE, fifteen and a half hands high, about eight years old, his face and hind feet white, has a grey mane which lays to the left ſide, and his tail has been nicked; he was one of the Britiſh horſe, and a remarkable fine figure. TWENTY POUNDS Reward will be given for the horſe, or THIRTY POUNDS if the thief can be ſecured and brought to juſtice.

JOHN LARDNER.

Hoſpital Head Quarters, Manheim, March 5, 1778.

ALL perſons who have any demands againſt the Military Hoſpitals of the Middle Diſtrict, are deſired to apply to JOSEPH SHIPPEN, Eſq; Secretary and Paymaſter, at Manheim, near Lancaſter, for payment. The Medical Gentlemen will be waited on at the Hoſpitals where they are doing duty. All officers of the Hoſpital abſent on furlough are hereby directed to repair immediately to this place.

WILLIAM SHIPPEN, Jun. Director General.

March 4, 1778.

DESERTED from the Hoſpital at Euphrata, a ſoldier belonging to Capt. Jones's company, in Col. Chriſtopher Febecker's 2d Virginia regiment, named JAMES GORDON, about ... feet high; had on when he deſerted, a blue coat with a blue velvet collar, grey waiſtcoat, buckſkin breeches, and round hat; he has black hair, fair ſkin, and is much pitted with the ſmall pox. Whoever takes up and ſecures ſaid deſerter ſo that he may be had again, ſhall have FOUR DOLLARS reward.

ALBERT CHAPMAN, Commander.

TEN POUNDS REWARD.

STOLEN laſt night, out of the ſtable of Joſeph Hart, Eſq; in Warminſter Townſhip Bucks County, a large well-made ſtrawberry roan HORSE, eleven or twelve years old, a natural pacer, but trots ſome and canters pretty well, has a blaze in his face, his hind feet white, and ſome white on one or both of his fore feet, (this not quite certain) alſo a conſiderable mixture of white on the top or upper part of his tail; he has been uſed to the collar, which has left a mark of ſome depth on the top of his neck, now grown up with hair ſo as not to be eaſily diſcerned by the eye: He is gentle, ſhod all round, and in tolerable good order. Any perſon ſecuring the thief and horſe, ſo that the former may be brought to juſtice and the owner get his horſe, ſhall have the above Reward, or for the horſe alone FIVE POUNDS, paid by

Feb. 4, 1778. JOHN HART.

LANCASTER:
PRINTED BY JOHN DUNLAP.

A page from the Pennsylvania Packet *(temporarily published at Lancaster), April 8, 1778. It includes "The Toast" by Francis Hopkinson and another poem on the "Rising Glory of America" by "A Soldier." Pennsylvania Historical and Museum Commission.*

4. Magazines

The eighteenth century was far from being the heyday of the magazine. The climate wasn't right. Americans were too preoccupied, from the 1760s on, with "the disordered state" of public affairs to concern themselves with literature. It is important, however, in this section on news media to mention a few magazines that made a valiant effort to survive, and blazed a literary trail for the magazines that were to burgeon in more literary soil in the nineteenth century.

The first plan for a magazine was Benjamin Franklin's. However, a rival, Andrew Bradford, jumped the gun by getting out *The American Magazine,* or *A Monthly View of the Political State of the British Colonies,* on February 13, 1741, three days before the publication of the eminent doctor's *General Magazine, and Historical Chronicle, for All the British Plantations in America.* Both periodicals were issued in Philadelphia and both dealt primarily with state papers. The *General Magazine* was larger and contained a greater variety of subject matter than the *American Magazine.* The two expired within a short time because of lack of support.

According to Frank Luther Mott, the first really important magazine was *The American Magazine and Historical Chronicle,* which appeared in Boston in September of 1743 and lasted for more than three years. Like the earlier magazines it dealt mainly with politics. Four magazines appeared briefly in New York in the decade following the demise of the Boston periodical. Then a Philadelphia publisher came out with the *American Magazine and Monthly Chronicle.* With emphasis on political matters as well as comments on manners and society, the *Monthly Chronicle* was considered the most brilliant magazine to have come off an American press. It was also sufficiently amusing to remain popular for thirteen months. The *New American Magazine,* not quite as entertaining, also appeared during this period, in New Jersey.

From 1760 to 1774 only three magazines were started. One lasted nine months. In January of 1774 Isaiah Thomas published the *Royal American Magazine,* which boasted a series of engravings by Paul Revere (one is reproduced in the cartoon section of this book) which censured British oppression of the colonies. The magazine was discontinued on the eve of the Battle of Lexington. Meanwhile the *Pennsylvania Magazine* had been started, with Thomas Paine as its editor. This magazine carried the wartime commentary on the war, and used a variety of material from both American and British sources as well as some original contributions. An illustration appeared in each issue.

Only one other magazine was published during the war, H. H. Brackenridge's *United States Magazine,* which is authoritatively regarded as the most brilliant performance of the period.

After the war magazines began to appear in greater number. The leading four—*The Columbian* (1786), Carey's *American Museum* (1787), *The Massachusetts Magazine* (1788), and *The New York Magazine* (1780)—while undistinguished, did occasionally publish essays, poetry and stories, all anonymously.

The debut of the first American periodical, Andrew Bradford's The American Magazine for February 1740–1. Rare Book Division, The New York Public Library, Astor, Lenox, and Tilden Foundations.

The PLAN of the Undertaking.

THE Success and Approbation which the MAGAZINES, published in *Great-Britain*, have met with for many Years past, among all Ranks and Degrees of People, *Encouraged* us to *Attempt* a Work of the like Nature in *America*. But the Plan, on which we intend to proceed, being very different from the *British* Models; it therefore becomes necessary in the first Place, to lay before the Reader, a *general Prospect* of the present Design.

It is proposed to publish Monthly, *An Account of the publick Affairs transacted in His Majesty's Colonies, as well on the Continent of* America *as in the* West-India *Islands* : Under thisHead will be comprehended, Abstracts of the Speeches of the several Governors, the Addresses and Answers of the Assemblies, their Votes, Resolutions and Debates. So that this Part of the Work will contain Journals of the *most important* Proceedings of each particular Assembly. Moreover, at the End of every Sessions, we shall give an Extract of any remarkable Laws therein passed, with the Reasons on which they were founded, the *Grievances* intended to be remedied by them, and the *Benefits* expected from them.

THAT the Reader may be the better enabled to form a Judgment of the various Transactions intended to be set in View; Succinct Accounts will be given, *in the Course of the Work*, of the Situation, Climate, Soil, Productions, Trade and Manufactures of all the *British* Plantations; the Constitutions of those several Colonies, with their respective Views and Interests, will be opened and explained; and the Nature and Extent of the various Jurisdictions exercised in each Government particularly described.

IN handling so great a variety of Matter, *Mistakes*, thro' Misinformation or otherwise, will probably be committed; but as the MAGAZINE will be Monthly distributed among the Persons residing on the Spot, which the Affairs therein treated of regard; the Errors that may intervene, will be quickly discovered, and, on the least Intimation, corrected in the succeeding Numbers. By this Means the Reader will be furnish'd with such Descriptions of the *British* Plantations as

Bradford's explanatory prospectus for his magazine. Rare Book Division, The New York Public Library, Astor, Lenox, and Tilden Foundations.

231

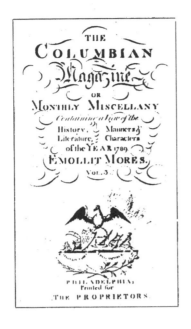

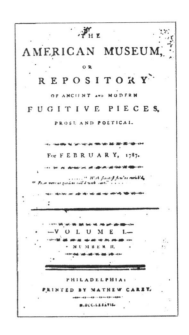

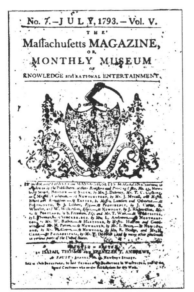

The four most important post-Revolutionary magazines, title pages and covers. Rare Book Division, The New York Public Library, Astor, Lenox, and Tilden Foundations. Found in Frank Luther Mott's History of American Magazines, *The Belknop Press of Harvard University, N. Y. 1930, opp. p. 114.*

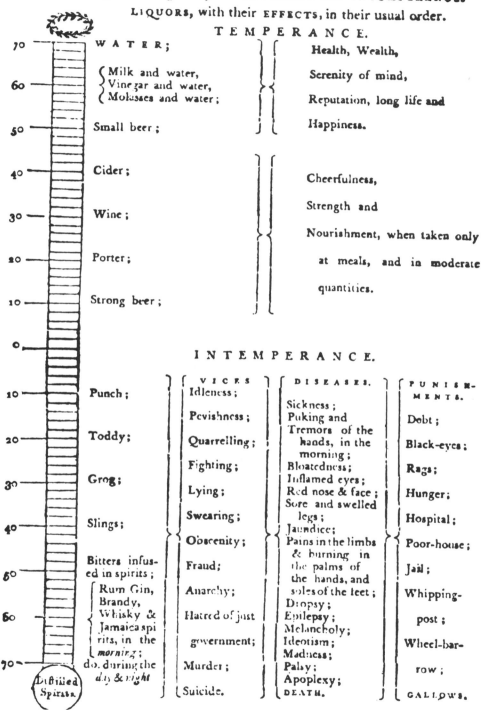

For the COLUMBIAN MAGAZINE.

A MORAL and PHYSICAL THERMOMETER:
Or;
A SCALE of the Progress of TEMPERANCE and INTEMPERANCE.
LIQUORS, with their EFFECTS, in their usual order.

TEMPERANCE.

70	WATER;	Health, Wealth,
60	Milk and water, Vinegar and water, Molasses and water;	Serenity of mind, Reputation, long life and
50	Small beer;	Happiness.
40	Cider;	Cheerfulness,
30	Wine;	Strength and
20	Porter;	Nourishment, when taken only at meals, and in moderate
10	Strong beer;	quantities.
0		

INTEMPERANCE.

		VICES	DISEASES.	PUNISHMENTS
10	Punch;	Idleness;	Sickness;	Debt;
20	Toddy;	Peevishness; Quarrelling;	Puking and Tremors of the hands, in the morning;	Black-eyes;
30	Grog;	Fighting; Lying;	Bloatedness; Inflamed eyes; Red nose & face; Sore and swelled	Rags; Hunger;
40	Slings;	Swearing; Obscenity;	legs; Jaundice; Pains in the limbs & burning in	Hospital; Poor-house;
50	Bitters infus- ed in spirits;	Fraud; Anarchy;	the palms of the hands, and soles of the feet; Dropsy;	Jail; Whipping-
60	Rum Gin, Brandy, Whisky & Jamaica spi- rits, in the morning;	Hatred of just government;	Epilepsy; Melancholy; Ideotism; Madness;	post; Wheel-bar-
70	do. during the day & night	Murder; Suicide.	Palsy; Apoplexy; DEATH.	row; GALLOWS.

Distilled Spirits

Doctor Benjamin Rush's "moral and physical thermometer" from the Columbia Magazine. Courtesy of The New-York Historical Society, New York City.

233

5

Swinging It in the Colonies

Although it has been accepted for over two centuries that the Puritans hated all forms of entertainment and recreation, and were opposed to social dancing, recent researchers have made the conclusive discovery that the situation was quite otherwise.

In his book *The Puritans and Music in England and New England,* Percy A. Scholes offers "overwhelming evidence" that the Puritans loved music and dancing. That they did not deem a dance floor "the symbol of eternal wickedness" is attested to by Beth Tolman and Ralph Page in *The Country Dance Book.* S. Foster Damon goes even further in *The History of Square Dancing* and informs us that Puritans "approved of dancing and enjoyed it thoroughly." In fact, they encouraged the practice with the justification that dancing "promotes grace and an erect carriage." They also believed that dancing taught manners, which was important, since "manners were a minor branch of morals." And the laws which are supposed to have been passed against music are untraceable.

None of this would have come as a surprise to Harriet Beecher Stowe. Over a century ago this wise little woman was wondering "how the idea ever got started that the New England clergy objected to dancing."

The Reverend John Cotton, we are now told, specifically approved of dancing—"yea, though mixt." Increase and Cotton Mather, on the other hand, preferred it "unmixt," but apparently not many people shared their views. In *Cloud of Witnesses,* Cotton Mather complains that he has heard "not so much as one word from my English Nonconformists" against the Boston balls where the dances were far from being "solos."

Dancing masters were another thorn in Cotton Mather's side, for they not only encouraged mixed dancing but, to make matters worse, they were not always simon-pure. After it became known that one scoffed at religion, he was ordered out of town in 1681. Cotton Mather whipped out *Arrows Against Profane and Promiscuous Dancing* (which he reissued in 1685) when Francis Stepney, another teacher of the terpischorean art, "chose Lecture Day for his classes" and defied the ministry in other ways.

In the 17th century dancing and dancing masters were acceptable in Charleston, South Carolina and in New Amsterdam, New York. Dutch Settlers tripped the light fantastic on special holidays, and dancing was encouraged at public fairs, "to improve agricultural practices."

By the 18th century, an increasing number of dancing masters began to appear in northern cities and on southern plantations, where a wealthy leisure class could afford to give lavish balls and assemblies.

A traveling Virginian gives this account of a Government Ball in the Council Room at Annapolis in 1744.

The Ladies of Note made a Splendant Appearance. In a Room Back from where they Danc'd was Several Sorts of Wines, Punch and Sweetmeats. In this Room those that was not engaged in any Dancing Match might better employ themselves at Cards, Dice, Backgammon, or with a cheerful Glass. The Ladies were so very agreeable and seem'd so intent on Dancing that one might have Imagin'd they had some Design on the Virginians, either Designing to make Tryal of their Strength and Vigour, or to convince them of their Activity and Sprightliness. After several smart engagements in which no advantage on either side was Observable, with a mutual Consent about 1 of the Clock in the Morning it was agreed to break up, every Gentleman waiting on his Partner home.

In some places and during certain periods in colonial America dancing was banned by the theological set and clergymen. It is quite a switch to learn that not all the clergy were as liberal as the Puritans!

In 1744, for example, all dance assemblies, as well as concert programs, were halted in Philadelphia, due to the hue and cry of the Quakers against such an "ungodly" form of recreation. This was not uncommon procedure in the Quaker city. At Boston, however, where dancing schools had appeared as early as the third quarter of the 17th century, "assemblies of the gayer sort" were frequent, "the gentlemen and ladys meeting almost every week at concerts of musick and balls."

Social dancing had not only become acceptable, but it was even regarded as an essential part of education. Thomas Jefferson insisted that his daughter dance from ten to one every day.

The way a ball was conducted in 18th-century Louisville is described by someone who visited that town when he was a young man.

After the managers had organized the Company by drawing numbers and appointing the opening with a Minuet, Uncle was called on and introduc'd to a Lady for the opening scene. The Managers who distributed the numbers called Gentⁿ No. 1, he takes his stand—Lady No. 1, she rises from her seat, the Manager leads her to the floor and introduces Gentⁿ No. 1, & so on till the floor is full. After all the Company have been thus call'd out then the Gentⁿ are free to seek his Partner but no monopoly. Lady at the head chooses the figure, but it is considered out of order for one Lady to head a figure twice unless all have been at the head. If there happen to be some ladies to whom from mistake or otherwise have been passed the Managers duty is to see to it. And another Custom was for a Gentⁿ to call on a Lady & inform her of an intended ball & ask permission to see her to the place & see her safe home again. If the Gentⁿ does not draw such Lady for the first Contra Dance he generally engages her for the first Volunteer.

From the lists of "modish dances" advertised by dancing masters in those days we learn that our forefathers became experts in the allemandes, cotillions, the galliard, rigadoon, courante and gavette, and the minuet. The colonists also performed the popular country dances or contra dances, such as jigs (also spelled jiggs), hops, and the Sir Roger de Coverley, forerunner of the Virginia reel. The minuet was really big. Everyone danced, even the minister, who is said to have been judged less by his pulpit oratory than "his skill in handling a different figure."

The officers in both armies were dance-mad. George Washington and Thomas Jefferson were enthusiastic about dancing long before the war. In his *Life of George Washington,* Washington Irving tells how the "young ladies of Maryland rode to the Assembly at Annapolis in scarlet riding-habits thrown over their satin ball dresses, kerchiefs drawn about the great masses of their puffed and pomaded hair, and after dancing through the night rode home again in the shadowy dawn." While frequently depicted dancing the minuet, George Washington favored the Sir Roger de Coverley.

Taverns vied with each other in attracting dancers, and some went so far as to provide carriages for the more distinguished guests. Michael Whidden's Inn in Portsmouth, New Hampshire was famous for its lavish assemblies where strict protocol was observed. Two floor managers in powdered wigs and gay attire, with hat under arm, met each lady at the door and swept her onto the dance floor. The dances generally lasted until dawn.

Not to be outdone by her sister cities, Philadelphia was the setting for a gay assembly in 1780. "A manager or Master of Ceremonies presided at these amusements," wrote the Marquis de Chastellux. "He presented to the gentlemen and lady dancers, billets folded up each containing a number; thus fate decided the male or female partner for the whole evening." All the dances were previously arranged and the dancers were called in their turn.

During the war years dances were frequently named after battles or military heroes. There was "Bourgoyne's Defeat," "Clinton's Retreat" and the "Brandywine Quickstep." "Stony Point," named after the site of Wayne's great victory, was a great favorite with the Continental Army. "A Successful Campaign" was the dance selected by diplomatic Peggy Champlin to open the Newport ball where she danced with George Washington to the piping of De Rochambeau and his fellow officers. Dancing was so important that managers for military affairs like this one were generally selected from among the most distinguished officers of the army.

Many of the wealthy class in America imitated English dances and balls. Dancing moved without any fanfare into the world of the new Republic and became an important feature at private and government affairs. There would of course be Cotton Mathers in the 19th century, and pious ladies in the White House who would shudder at the gyrations of the waltz and the abandonment of the polka, but no one would succeed in halting the progress of the dance. It had caught on in 18th century America and was here to stay.

Woodcut of a quadrille performed in a southern mansion in Washington's time. The Bettmann Archive.

4

Minuets composed for and performed at Lady Mary Cornwallis's Ball at Black-Land's House, 1780. a) Lord Cornwallis's martial minuet and Lady Mary Cornwallis's minuet. Courtesy of The New-York Historical Society, New York City.

Minuets for Lady Cornwallis's Ball. b) Miss Coghlan's minuet and Sir Henry Clinton's minuet. Courtesy of The New-York Historical Society, New York City.

Minuets for Lady Cornwallis's Ball. c) Colonel Tarleton's minuet and Miss Duberly's minuet. Courtesy of The New-York Historical Society, New York City.

FAVORITE COTILLIONS
INTRODUCED BY P.L.DUPORT FOR THE PIANO FORTE
HARP CLARINETT FLUTE AND FLAGELET
NEW YORK ENGRAVD AND PUBLISHD BY I AND M.PAFF

TWICE

ONCE

Nº I THE SIGNAL

2 COUPLE OPOSITE HALF RIGHT AND LEFT ANT SETT
TWO HANDS ROUND CORNER SIDE AND SETT
THE SAME FOR THE TWO OTHER COUPLE
4 COUPLES GRAND RIGHT AND LEFT TO THEIR PLACE
TWO HANDS ROUND TO THIR PARTNER AND SETT

COPY—RIGHT SECURED

Some favorite colonial cotillions, introduced by P. L. DuPort. a) The Signal. The Lincoln Center Library of the Performing Arts.

Nº II THE POLLE ～～

ONE COUPLE OPOSITE FORWARD AND SETT .
     CHASSEZ ON THE RIGHT HAND AND SETT
PIRROIT AND SETT TO THE OPOSITE PARTNER
     TWO HANDS ROUND AND SETT
THE SAME FOR THE 2D COUPLE
     TWO IST LADEIS CROSSOVR AND SETT
TWO GENTLMEN THE SAME AND SETT
     THE SAME 4 CHASSEZ CROSSWAYS AND SETT
BACK A GAIN THE SAME
     TO BE REPEATED FOR THE TWO OTHER COUPLE

Colonial cotillions. b) The Polle. Lincoln Center Library of the Performing Arts.

FAVORITE COTILLIONS
INTRODUCED BY P.L.DUPORT FOR PIANO FORTE
HARP CLARINETT FLUTE AND FLAGELET
NEW YORK ENGRAVD AND PUBLISHD BY I AND M PAFF

WALTZ

No VIIII THE WALTZ COTILLION

Colonial cotillions. c) The Waltz Cotillion. Lincoln Center Library of the Performing Arts.

Colonial cotillions. d) A "Menuit." Lincoln Center Library of the Performing Arts.

The Sir Roger de Coverley. Original drawing by Edward Tunis for his book Colonial Times. *World Publishing Company, 1957.*

Nº 3 Maſſachuſett's hop

Cast off between the 2ᵈ & 3ᵈ Cou. Sett. Cast off between the 3ᵈ & 4ᵗʰ Cou. Sett. Forward in a line with the 3ᵈ Cou. Sett. up to your place & cast off one Cou. Sett, corners Right hand to your place Sett & Two hands round

Nº 4 Rhode Iſland Jigg

Sett & Crofs hands 4, Dº back again. Down the Middle, up again. Right hand sideways, Turn round, Left hand sideways & turn round.

Oh, how they danced. Library of Congress.

19 Duport's Hornpipe.

Fine

Engraved by Wᵐ Pirſson Nº 41? Pearl Street. New York.

Dances were named after military heroes. Library of Congress.

Brandywine Quick Step. Library of Congress.

DURANG'S HORNPIPE

NEW YORK. Published at O.TORP'S Music Magazine, 465 Broadway.

Pennsylvania-born John Durang, the first native American performer of any reputation in the 1790s, popularized the hornpipe. Music from Paul Magriel (ed.), Chronicles of the American Dance, *Henry Holt & Co., N. Y., 1948. Courtesy The New York Public Library of the Performing Arts, Dance Division.*

6

Colonial Thespians and Theaters

The American theater was born in the colonial period and legitimized when the country became a nation. The pioneers of the American theater had to carve their stage out of a wilderness of bigotry and prejudice. While the French and English of Charleston, South Carolina hailed their coming as a revival of one of the "gentlemanly" pastimes of their old days in Europe, descendants of the Puritan settlers violently opposed the drama, and every other kind of exhibition, denouncing them as snares of the devil. Quakers and other religious and sectarian groups looked upon the early thespians as proponents of an immoral, illegitimate art which stimulated "immorality, impiety and contempt of religion," and anxiously sought to stamp out this evil. When the acted drama daringly penetrated into colonial towns, anti-theater literature with titles like "The Theatre, The High Road to Hell," was distributed. Providence, Rhode Island even passed "an Act to Prevent Stage Plays and other theatrical entertainments within this colony."

When the actors weren't bucking the clergy, they found themselves attacked by individuals like the witch-baiting judge, Samuel Sewall, and Increase Mather of Boston. Protesting against acting in his city, Sewall, in Cassandra-like fashion, warned his fellow citizens to refrain from letting "Christian Boston goe beyond Heathen Rome in the Practice of Shameful Vanities." Mather lamented, in a diatribe against sin published in 1687, that "there is much discourse of beginning Stage-Plays in New England." He associated this with the iniquity of "promiscuous dancing." In 1714 Samuel Sewall took definite steps to suppress the theatre. A riot was started in Boston in 1750 when two English actors attempted to put on a play and the commonwealth of Massachusetts seized the opportunity to pass a law forbidding playacting. Theatrical progress was retarded not only by moral prejudice, but by a lingering belief among the middle class that stage productions were frivolous and wasteful of precious time.

Despite this grim picture, by the first quarter of the century Puritanism's stranglehold on the New England colonists had weakened and gradually the early bans against the theater were relaxed. Throughout the colonies, a new leisure class had come into existence who could afford commercial forms of entertainment, and the theater came to life.

From 1700 on, English thespians frequently headed for the new world overseas to give preliminary performances in the West Indies and then make grand tours of the North American colonies.

It seems likely that the first professional performance in America of a play written in this country took place in 1703, when Anthony Aston, a strolling English player, noted in his journal: "We arrived in Charles-Town, full of Lice, Shame, Poverty, Nakedness and Hunger. I turned Player and Poet and wrote one Play on the Subject of the Country." The first performance of a play in Philadelphia was given in Plumstead's Store, the first in New York in Rip Van Dam's "convenient room;" in Charleston the courtroom was opened to the performance. The first building to be specifically constructed as a theater was in Williamsburg.

The first play written and printed in America, *Androboros* ("Maneater"), was by Governor Robert Hunter of New York. It was printed in 1714. During the next several decades the theatrical groups began to meet with less resistance. In 1750 the earliest known American playbill was printed for Otway's play, *The Orphan,* which was presented in New York on March 26, at the theater in Nassau Street. A fairly active season in New York was marked by the arrival of a theatrical company, "a company of comedians," headed by Thomas Kean and Walter Murray. This company had begun its career in a brick warehouse on Water Street in Philadelphia in August of 1749, with Addison's tragedy, *Cato,* and "probably other plays." When continued objections were raised against their performances, the company left for New York. With Governor Clinton's permission they opened their season on March 5 with Shakespeare's *King Richard III,* Thomas Kean playing the title role. Shakespearean plays were generally included in the repertories of the many itinerant companies.

Authorities on the history of the American theater regard the coming of Lewis Hallam's English company, in 1752, as the start of our theatrical history. Hallam's company opened in Williamsburg, Virginia, on September 15 of that year in *The Merchant of Venice.* The company remained in the Colony of Virginia for eleven months and then went to New York, where Hallam built a theater on the east side of Nassau Street, between Maiden Lane and John Street.

From then on the American theater began to grow. The colonists became enthusiastic theater-goers, and Royal Governors found the theater a useful way of entertaining visitors. The November 17, 1752 edition of the *Maryland Gazette* reports that on the ninth of that month the Royal Governor took the Emperor and Empress of the Cherokee nation and their son, the young Prince, as well as "several . . . warriors and Great Men and their Ladies, to see a performance of *Othello,* and a Pantomime Performance which gave them great surprise, as did the fighting with naked swords on the Stage, which occasioned the Empress to order some about her to go and prevent them from killing one another."

College thespians were active early in the century, putting on dramatic pieces in the form of oratorical exercises as well as plays. In 1736 college players produced the popular *Cato* and *The Drummer* in Williamsburg. While they were undergraduates at the College of New Jersey (later Princeton), Philip Freneau, the poet, and Hugh Henry Brackenridge, the poet-playwright, composed a poem called "The Rising Glory of America," which was read by Brackenridge at commencement in 1772. At the College of Philadelphia Francis Hopkinson wrote various dialogues, such as the "Exercise: Containing a Dialogue and Ode, sacred to the memory of his late gracious Majesty George II. Performed at the public commencement in the College of Philadelphia May 1761." This was written long before Hopkinson developed his strong anti-British feelings.

The theatrical season of 1773–1774 was the last before the Revolutionary War. Tension was mounting in the colonies and the final break with England was imminent. On October 20, 1774, the Continental Congress passed a resolution which brought an end to all types of extravagant and reckless expenditure of money:

We will, on our several stations, encourage frugality, economy and industry, and promote agriculture, arts, and the manufactures of this country, especially that of wool; and will discountenance and discourage every species of extravagance and dissipation, especially . . . exhibitions of shows, plays, and other expensive diversions and entertainments.

Professional actors left the country for the West Indies, not to return until after the war. Thus the first period in the history of the American theater drew to a close. However, the show did go on, now under the auspices of the amateurs. Military actors took the place of the professionals. Plays and dramatic satires were produced by ardent Loyalists and ardent Patriots. The much-lampooned General John Burgoyne was in charge of the theatricals given by the redcoats in Faneuil Hall, Boston. He wrote a farce for his players entitled *The Blockade of Boston.* The play was ready to be produced on the night of January 8, 1776 when the audience was "thrown into a panic" by an announced attack on Charlestown by the Americans. In the excitement the script was lost.

Redcoat thespians entertained their Tory audiences with performances of such plays as *The Busybody, Zara* and *Tamerlane,* in Boston, Philadelphia, and New York. Some British generals had their own thespian troupes. The "strolling company" of General Howe's army performed at the old Southwark Theatre in Philadelphia, which had been closed since 1754 because of Quaker opposition. Historians wax rhapsodic over the scenery painted by Major John André as well as over the costumes he designed for the performances. The "Gentleman Spy," as he is called by Adele Gutman Nathan, also wrote prologues and epilogues and excelled at charades, a popular pastime in New York during the war. During the winter and spring of 1777 the John Street Theatre, New York, was taken over by a company of British military actors who, "as a taunt to the Patriot sympathizers," renamed it The Theatre Royal. In January of 1778, General Henry Clinton took over the management of The Theatre Royal and his troupe became known as "Clinton's thespians."

On the American side, Hugh Henry Brackenridge, poet and playwright, wrote *The Battle of Bunkers-Hill* as an exercise for the students of Somerset Academy to perform. *The Fall of British Tyranny,* allegedly written by John Leacock and published in 1776, is said to have been the first literary piece in which George Washington appeared as a character.

Patriot officers also relieved the tedium of camp life by producing plays. In a letter written to his sister Rachel from Valley Forge on May 14, 1778, William Bradford, Jr. wrote, "The theatre is opened—Last Monday, *Cato* was performed . . . before a very numerous and splendid audience. His excellency [Washington] and Lady, Lord Stirling [an American officer] . . . were part of the assembly. The scenery was in Taste and the Performance admirable.—Col. George did his part to admiration. . . . If the Enemy does not retire from Philad soon, our Theatrical amusements will continue—*The Fair Penitent with the Padlock* will soon be acted. *The Recruiting Officer* is also on foot." These festivities were part of the celebration of the new French alliance.

In 1778, the Congress once again denounced theatrical entertainment as having a "fatal tendency to divert the minds of the people from a due attention to the means necessary for the defence of their country and the preservation of their liberties." A strong Congressional resolution determined that "any person holding an office under the United States who shall act, promote, encourage or attend such plays, shall be deemed unworthy to hold such office and shall be accordingly dismissed." This apparently did not apply to George Washington, who never would forego the opportunity to attend the theater, often prolonging his visit to a town in order that he might attend more than one performance—although he once was forced to refuse an invitation from Lafayette to attend the theater in Philadelphia.

The Congressional action did not always serve as a deterrent. The thespians of Portsmouth, New Hampshire, for example, gave a performance of *Cato* not long after the resolution. And in the last year of the war two plays were produced by American troops at Reading, Pennsylvania.

After the surrender of Cornwallis, the first French play in America, Beaumarchais's *Eugénie,* was presented by the pupils of a French professor in Philadelphia to an audience which included Washington, the French minister, and the French officers. The performance was at the Southwark Theatre in Philadelphia.

When the Revolutionary War ended, the American people's love of liberty prevailed against religious and lay opposition, and the theater in America was legitimized.

By a Company of COMEDIANS,
At the New-Theatre, in *Nassau-Street,*
This Evening being the 11th of *November,* will be presented,
(*By particular Desire*)
An Historical Play, call'd,

King RICHARD III.

CONTAINING

The Distress and Death of King *Henry* the VIth, the artful Acquisition of the Crown by *Crook-back'd Richard*; the Murder of the two young Princes in the Tower; and the memorable Battle of *Bosworth-Field,* being the last that was fought between the Houses of *York* and *Lancaster.*

Richard,	by	Mr. Ryan;
King Henry,	by	Mr. Hallam.
Prince Edward,	by	Master L. Hallam.
Duke of York,	by	Master A. Hallam.
Earl of Richmond,	by	Mr. Clarkson.
Duke of Buckingham,	by	Mr. Malone.
Duke of Norfolk,	by	Mr. Miller.
Lord Stanley,	by	Mr. Singleton.
Catesby,	by	Mr. Bell.
		Mr. Adcock.
Queen Elizabeth,	by	Mrs. Hallam.
Lady Anne,	by	Mrs. Adcock.
Duchess of York,	by	Mrs. Rigby.

To which will be added,
A Ballad FARCE call'd,

The DEVIL TO PAY.

Sir John Loverule,	by	Mr. Adcock.
Jobson,	by	Mr. Malone.
Butler,	by	Mr. Miller.
Footman,	by	Mr. Singleton.
Cook,	by	Mr. Bell.
Coachman,	by	Mr. Rigby.
Conjuror,	by	Mr. Clarkson.
Lady Loverule,	by	Mrs. Adcock.
Nell,	by	Mrs. Beccley.
Lucy,	by	Mrs. Clarkson.
Lucy,		Miss Lexe.

PRICES: BOX, 6s, PIT, 4s, GALLERY, 2s.
No Persons whatever to be admitted behind the Scenes.

N. B. *Gentlemen and Ladies that those Tickets, may have them at Mr. Parker's and Mr. Gaine's Printing-Offices.*
Money will be taken at the DOOR.
To begin at 6 o'Clock.

For the Benefit of Mrs. *Upton,*
(being the last Night of playing)

By his Excellency's Permission,

At the THEATRE in *Nassau-Street,*
On *Thursday* the 20th of *February,* will be acted, A TRAGEDY,
(never played here) called,

VENICE PRESERV'D,

OR,

A PLOT DISCOVER'D.

The Part of JAFFIER, to be perform'd by Mr. UPTON.

Priuli,		Mr. Leigh,
Pierre,		Mr. Petty,
Bedamar,	by	Mr. Fitzgerald,
Renault,		Mr. Tremain,
Eliot,		Mr. James,

The Part of BELVIDERA, to be perform'd by Mrs. UPTON.

Several select Pieces of Musick between the Acts; particularly, a SOLO on the *German Flute.*

A SONG by Mrs. *UPTON,* called *JOCKER.*

To which will be added,

MISS in her TEENS.

If thro' Ignorance, Mrs. *Upton,* as being a Stranger, shou'd neglect applying to any Gentlemen or Ladies, she hopes they'll excuse it.
To begin precisely at 6 o'Clock.

BOX, 5s. PIT, 4s. GALLERY, 2s.

Tickets to be had at the *Crown and Thistle,* and at Mr. *Exter's,* Hatter near the Dock.

N. B. *Those who please to favour her with their Company, may depend on seeing the Play decently perform'd, at last perfect, and that all or more than included in the Bill will be done.*

---

*British-born Robert Upton was the leading actor and manager of a company of comedians which appeared at the Nassau Street Theatre on December 30, 1751 in the first production of Othello in America. When his associates left for Virginia, he tried to carry on alone. Two weeks after he opened, he was doing so poorly that he placed a notice in the Post Boy which stated that "Mr. Upton (to his great disappointment) not meeting with encouragement enough to support the company for the season, intends to shorten by performing five or six plays only, for Benefits!" Attendance was small in New York in 1752 and Upton's repertory was said to be "meagre and inadequate." In less than two months the season ended. The final performance on March 4 was Venice Preserved, in which Mr. and Mrs. Upton played leading roles.
Courtesy the Bettmann Archive.*

---

*This notice of a performance of The Orphan, which appeared in the New York Gazette and Weekly Post Boy on April 2, 1750, is believed to be the first public announcement in America of an American play.
Courtesy of The New-York Historical Society, New York City.*

By his Excellency's Permission:
At the Theatre in *Nassau-Street,* This Evening will be presented,
A TRAGEDY, called,
The ORPHAN: Or, the Unhappy-Marriage.
To which will be added,
A FARCE, called, The
BEAU in the SUDDS.
Tickets to be had at the Theatre in *Nassau-Street,* and of the Printer hereof; PITT, 5s. Gallery 3s.
To begin precisely at half an Hour after 6 o'Clock.

The Vendue of the Sale of Mrs. *Alexer's* Goods, will begin again To-morrow Morning, at the *Meal-Market.*

To be sold, at Publick Vendue, on Tuesday the 3d of April next, in the Meal-Market.

A Parcel of *Ironmongery; such as Locks,* Hinges, Chizzels, Gimblets, &c. &c.

To be sold, at Publick Vendue on Tuesday the 3d April, at the Meal-Market:

A large Quantity of *Cordial Waters, viz.* Clove Water, Caraway Water, Orange Water, Geneva, Rosa Solis, &c. all in five Gallon Kegs; also a Negro Boy; the Sale to begin at Ten o'Clock, and continue till all is sold.

TO BE SOLD,
The *Dwelling-House, Store-House, and Lot of* Ground in Wall-Street, near the City-Hall, now in the Possession of Doctr. *Alexander Connoly.* Enquire of David Provoost, of Bergen County, in East-Jersey, or Catharine Beekman, Widow, and Abraham Lodge in New-York.

To be sold, a likely Negro Fellow, that understands all Sorts of Country Work, having been brought up to it: Also a Negro Wench that can do all sorts of Houshold Work: Enquire of the Printer.

Wanted, a good Negro Man, that understands Farming; either to hire or buy: Enquire of the Printer.

To be SOLD.

A very convenient Still-House situated in this City, so for the Distillations of the Cordial Waters, containing two Stills, one of about eighty Gallons; the other a rectifying Still of about six Gallons. Enquire of the Printer hereof.

Just published, and to be sold by the Printer hereof, Price stitch'd, 2s.
MEDITATIONS on Divine Subjects, by Mrs.
Mary Lloyd: To which is prefix'd, An Account of her Life and Character: By R. PEMBERTON.

Price Current in New-York

Wheat, per Bush. 4/ 4/3.	Molasses, 1s. 9d. per Gal.
Flour, per C. 12/.	West India Rum, 3s. 8d.
Milk Bread, 30s.	New-England Do. 2s. 4d.
White Do. 26s.	Bef, per Bar. 38s.
Middling. 24s.	Petit, 60s.
	India. 95.

For the Benefit of the Poor.

Thurſday, December 20, 1753.

At the New Theatre in Naſſau-Street.

This Evening, will be preſented,

(Being the laſt Time of performing till the Holidays,)

A COMEDY, called,

LOVE for LOVE:

Sir Sampſon Legend,	by Mr. Malone.
Valentine,	by Mr. Rigby.
Scandal,	by Mr. Bell,
Tattle,	by Mr. Singleton.
Ben (the Sailor,)	by Mr. Hallam.
Foreſight,	by Mr. Clarkſon.
Jeremy,	by Mr: Miller.
Buckram,	by Mr. Adcock.
Angelica,	by Mrs. Hallam.
Mrs. Foreſight,	by Mrs. Rigby.
Mrs. Frail,	by Mrs. Adcock.
Miſs Prue,	by Miſs Hallam.
Nurſe,	by Mrs. Clarkſon.

End of Act 1ſt, Singing by Mr. Adcock.

End of Act 2d, Singing by Mrs. Love.

In Act 3d, a Hornpipe by Mr. Hulett.

End of Act 4th, a Cantata by Mrs. Love.

To which will be added, a Ballad Farce, called,

FLORA, or, Hob in the Well.

Hob,	by Mr. Hallam,
Friendly,	by Mr. Adcock.
Sir Thomas Testy,	by Mr. Clarkſon.
Richard,	by Maſter L. Hallam:
Old Hob,	by Mr. Miller.
Flora,	by Mrs. Becceley,
Betty,	by Miſs Hallam.
Hob's Mother,	by Mrs. Clarkſon.

Prices : BOX, 6s. PIT, 4s. GALLERY, s.

No Perſons whatever to be admitted behind the Scenes.

N.B. Gentlemen and Ladies that chuſe Tickets, may have them at Mr. Parker
at Mr. Poin's Printing-Offices.

Money will be taken at the Door.

⁎⁎⁎ The Company having been ge Pence being impos'd on us, at the Door of the
houſe, we humbly nform'd, that we are now forc'd to refuſe taking
Pence at the Door. To begin at 6 o'

A playbill announcing a benefit for the poor, 1753.

This picture of the interior of the old John Street Theatre was copied from a woodcut dated December 7, 1767. A program of the theatre contains a notice of an odd kind of sit-in: "Ladies will please send their servants to keep their places at four o'clock." The performance started at six o'clock so that for two hours and longer the front seats of the boxes were occupied by black servants of every age, waiting for their masters and mistresses. Museum of the City of New York.

Pl. 1.

On Monday,

The SIXTEENTH Inftant, *February 1778.*

At the Theatre in Southwark,

For the Benefit of a PUBLIC CHARITY,

Will be reprefented a Comedy

CALLED THE

Conftant Couple.

TO WHICH WILL BE ADDED,

DUKE AND NO DUKE.

The CHARACTERS by the OFFICERS of the ARMY and NAVY.

TICKETS to be had at the Printer's: at the Coffee-houfe in Market-
    ftreet: and at the Pennfilvania Farmer, near the New-Market, and
    no where elfe.
BOXES and PIT, ONE DOLLAR.—GALLERY, HALF A DOLLAR.
Doors to open at Five o'Clock, and begin precifely at Seven.
No Money will, on any Account, be taken at the Door.
    Gentlemen are earneftly requefted not to attempt to bribe the
Door-keepers.
. N. B. Places for the Boxes to be taken at the Office of the
Theatre in Front-ftreet, between the Hours of Nine and Two o'clock:
After which Time, the Box-keeper will not attend.   Ladies or Gen-
tlemen, who would have Places kept for them, are defired to fend
their Servants to the Theatre at Four o'clock, otherwife their Places
will be given up.

****

PHILADELPHIA, PRINTED BY JAMES HUMPHREYS, JUNR.
Theaticals of the British Army in Philadelphia

The old Southwark Theatre was Philadelphia's first permanent theatre. A brick building, it was erected in 1766. After being closed by the Quakers, it was reopened by the British army of occupation in 1777. Many performances were put on there by military thespians. Courtesy of The New-York Historical Society, New York City.

For the BENEFIT of the WIDOWS and ORPHANS
of the ARMY.

On Monday

Next, the *Nineteenth* Inftant,

Will be Reprefented, at the THEATRE in Southwark,

A COMEDY, CALLED

NO ONE'S ENEMY
BUT HIS OWN,

AND

The Deuce is in Him.

The CHARACTERS by the OFFICERS of the ARMY and NAVY.

Admittance to the Boxes and Pit. A DOLLAR each:
Gallery, HALF A DOLLAR.

TICKETS to be had of the Printer; at the Coffee-houfe;
at the Pennfylvania Farmer, New-Market; of Mr. Smith,
at his Office in Front-ftreet, below the Drawbridge, and
a few Doors below Peter Suter, Hatter at Mr. John
Richmond's in Front-ftreet, between Chefnut and Wal-
nut-ftreets, and at the Turk's Head in Water-ftreet,
between Race and Vine ftreets.

As there is a fufficient Number of Tickets to be given
out, to admit as many as the Houfe will hold, no Money
can, on any Account, be taken at the Door.

The Doors to be open at Six o'Clock, and the Play to
begin precifely at Seven.

PHILADELPHIA, PRINTED BY JAMES HUMPHREYS, JUNR.
Theatricals of the British Army in Philadelphia

Another playbill announcing theatricals of the British army in Philadelphia. Courtesy of The New-York Historical Society, New York City.

THEATRE.

On ACCOUNT of the INDISPOSITION
of one of the ACTRESSES,

The Play,

Which was to have been
Performed

ON FRIDAY,

The Tenth Inftant,

Is obliged to be
POSTPONED.

APRIL 8th, 1778.

✻✤✻✤✻✤✻✤✻✤✻✤✻✤✻✤✻✤✻✤✻✤✻✤✻✤✻✤✻✤✻✤✻✤✻

PRINTED by JAMES HUMPHREYS, JUNR. in *Market-ftreet*, between *Front* and *Second-ftreets*.

MONDAY, *FEBRUARY* 16, 1778.	TUESDAY, MAY 19, 1778.
BOX, ONE DOLLAR.	BOX, *One Dollar.*
CONSTANT COUPLE.	DOUGLASS.
The Doors to be open at FIVE, and Play to begin at SEVEN o'Clock	The Doors to be open at FIVE, and Play to begin at SEVEN o'Clock
	6 60

Theatricals of the British Army in Philadelphia, with the box tickets used

A postponement notice, with copies of box tickets used in eighteenth-century theaters. Courtesy of The New-York Historical Society, New York City.

For the Benefit of Mr. SHAKESPEAR.

✱✱✱✱✱✱✱✱✱✱✱✱✱✱✱✱✱✱✱✱✱✱✱✱✱✱✱✱

(By Permiſſion.)

At the Theatre in Baltimore,

On FRIDAY EVENING, the 29th of *November*, 1782,
Will be preſented, the TRAGEDY of

OTHELLO,
The MOOR of VENICE.

Othello,   Mr.   H E A R D ;
Roderigo,   Mr. W A L L ;
Caſſio,   Mr. S H A K E S P E A R ;
Brabantio,   Mr. L E W I S ;
Duke, Mr. T W Y F O R D ; *Lodovico*, Mr. T I L Y A R D ;
Gratiano, Mr. S T R E E T ; *Montanio*, Mr. W I L L I S ;
Senators, Meſſrs. Atherton, Brown, Ford, &c. &c.
Iago,   Mr.   R Y A N.
Emilia,   Mrs. L Y N E ;
Deſdemona,   Mrs. R O B I N S O N.

Between the Play and Farce, a NEW PANTOMIME DANCE, called

HARLEQUIN LANDLORD.

Harlequin, Monſ. R O U S S E L ;
Columbine, Mrs. E L M ;
The other Characters, Meſſrs. Lewis, Lindſay, Atherton, &c. &c.

SINGING, by Mr. *FOSTER*.

To which will be added, a FARCE, called

THE CONTRACT;
Or, Better Late than Never.

Colonel Lovemore, (the old Batchelor) Mr. S H A K E S P E A R ;
Commodore Capſtern, (with Songs) Mr. L E W I S ;
Captain Sprightly, Mr. D A V I D S ;
Martin, Mr. W I L L I S.
Maria, Mrs. R O B I N S O N ;
Betty, Mrs. E L M ;
Miſs Eleanor, (the old Maid) Mrs. P A R S O N S.

Tickets to be had at Mr. *James Young's*, near the Fountain-Inn---at the *Exchange Coffee-Houſe*, Fell's-Point---and at the *Office* of the *Theatre*, where Places for the Boxes may be taken, from Ten to Twelve o'Clock every Day.

✼✿✼✿✼✿✼✿✼✿✼✿✼✿✼✿✼✿✼✿✼✿✼✿✼

BALTIMORE: Printed by M. K. GODDARD.

For the Benefit of Mrs. ELM.

✱✱✱✱✱✱✱✱✱✱✱✱✱✱✱✱✱✱✱✱✱✱✱✱✱✱✱✱

(By Permiſſion.)

At the Theatre in Baltimore,

On TUESDAY EVENING, the 26th of *November*, 1782,
Will be preſented, a COMEDY, called the

RECRUITING OFFICER.

Captain Plume,   Mr.   S T R E E T ;
Worthy,   Mr.   R Y A N ;
Serjeant Kite,   Mr.   L E W I S ;
Bullock,   Mr.   W I L L I S ;
Juſtice Scruple, Mr. Tilyard ; *Juſtice Balance*, Mr. Heard ; *Juſtice Scale*, Mr. Davids ; *Coſtar Pearmain*, Mr. Shakeſpear ; *Thomas Appletree*, Mr. Lindſay ;
Conſtable, Mr. Atherton ; *Collier*, Mr. Patterſon ;
Captain Brazen,   Mr.   W A L L.
Melinda,   Mrs.   R O B I N S O N ;
Roſe,   Miſs   W A L L ;
Lucy,   Mrs.   P A R S O N S ;
Sylvia,   Mrs.   E L M.

A *PROLOGUE*, by Mr. R Y A N.

An *EPILOGUE*, by Miſs WALL.

SINGING, by Mr. *FOSTER*.

To which will be added, a FARCE, called

THE APPRENTICE.

Dick, (the Apprentice)   Mr.   S T R E E T ;
Wingate,   Mr.   S H A K E S P E A R ;
Gargle,   Mr.   L E W I S ;
Catchpole, Mr. Tilyard ; *Bailiff's Follower*, Mr. Atherton ;
Watchmen, Meſſrs. Lindſay, Patterſon, &c.
Members of the Spouting Club, Meſſrs. Twyford, Davids, Wall, &c. &c.
Simon,   Mr.   W I L L I S.
Charlotte,   Mrs.   E L M.

After the Farce, a HORNPIPE, by Mr. PATTERSON.

Tickets to be had at Mr. *James Young's*, near the Fountain-Inn---at the *Exchange Coffee-Houſe*, Fell's-Point---at the *Office* of the *Theatre*, where Places for the Boxes may be taken, from Ten to Twelve o'Clock every Day---and of Mrs. *Elm*, at Mrs. Ruſſel's.

✼✿✼✿✼✿✼✿✼✿✼✿✼✿✼✿✼✿✼✿✼✿✼✿✼

BALTIMORE: Printed by M. K. GODDARD.

THEATRE.

By the Old American Company.

On *Wednesday Evening*, the 30th of *November*, will be performed,

A COMEDY, of *Shakespear's*,

CALLED, THE

Merchant of Venice.

Shylock,	Mr. HENRY,
Baſſanio,	Mr. HARPER,
Gratiano,	Mr. BIDDLE,
Lorenzo, *(with Songs)*	Mr. WOOLLS,
Launcellot,	Mr. MORRIS,
Salanio,	Mr. LAKE,
And, Anthonio,	Mr. WIGNELL.
Neriſſa,	Mrs. HARPER,
Jeſſica,	Miſs TUKE,
And, Portia,	Mrs. MORRIS.

End of Act 3d, a *Hornpipe.*

To which will be Added,

An ENTERTAINMENT, *Called,* The

Miller of Mansfield.

King Henry,	Mr. HENRY,
Dick,	Mr. HARPER,
Joe, *(with a Song)*	Mr. WOOLLS,
Lord Lurewell,	Mr. BIDDLE,
And, The Miller,	Mr. MORRIS.
Peggy,	Miſs TUKE,
Margery,	Miſs DURANG,
And, Kate,	Mrs. MORRIS.

The Doors will be open in future at *Five,* and the Curtain drawn up precisely at, *A Quarter after Six o'Clock.*

Places in the Boxes may be taken of Mr. *Delamater,* at the Box Lobby, every Day, from *Ten* to *Twelve* in the Forenoon, and from *Four* to *Five* in the Evening ; where alſo TICKETS may be had, and at Mr. GAINE's Book-Store, in *Hanover-Square.*

Ladies and Gentlemen are requeſted to deſire their Servants to take up and ſet down with their Horſes Heads towards the *East-River,* to avoid Confuſion ; alſo as ſoon as they are ſeated, to order their Servants out of the *Boxes.*

BOX 8s. PIT 6s. and GALLERY 4s.

⁂ No Perſon to be admitted behind the Scenes, on any Account whatever.

The Public are reſpectfully informed, the Days of Performance will be, *Mondays, Wednesdays* and *Fridays.*

Vivat Reſpublica.

Old American Company Theatre playbill for The Merchant of Venice *and* The Miller of Mansfield, *November 20, 1785. Courtesy of the Museum of the City of New York.*

The Contrast *by Royall Tyler was the first successful play by a native American. It was produced at the John Street Theatre April 16, 1787, by the best members of the Old American Company. Tyler wrote it in three weeks. A comedy with a happy ending, its theme, a reflection on the current joyous patriotism, is the contrast between the affectation and folly of the Europeanized American and the fine qualities of the true salt-of-the-earth citizen. The dialogue is lively even though there is little action. The humor focuses on the New England servant, Jonathan, considered by one writer "Tyler's distinctive contribution to drama." Harvard Theatre Collection.*

Royall Tyler, 1758–1826. From Arthur Hornblow, A History of the Theatre in America, *Vol. I, Philadelphia and London, J. B. Lippincott Co., 1919, p. 170.*

THEATRE.

By the Old AMERICAN COMPANY.

On *Monday Evening*, being the 26th of *March*, will be performed,

A COMEDY, called, The

Jealous Wife

Oakly,	Mr. HARPER,
Major Oakly,	Mr. MORRIS,
Sir Harry Beagle,	Mr. HENRY,
Ruffet,	Mr. BIDDLE,
Tom,	Mr. WOOLLS,
And, Charles Oakly.	Mr. WIGNELL.
Lady Freelove.	Mrs. MORRIS,
Harriet,	Miss TUKE,
Toilette,	Miss KENNA,
And, Mrs. Oakly,	Mrs. HARPER.

To which will be Added, *(Second Time,)*

A FARCE, called, The

Widow's Vow

Jerome,	Mr. WIGNELL,
Don Antonio,	Mr. MORRIS,
Carlos,	Mr. BIDDLE,
Servant,	Mr. McPHERSON,
And, Marquis,	Mr. HARPER.
Flora,	Mrs. HARPER,
Inis,	Miss TUKE,
Donna Isabella,	Miss KENNA,
And, Countefs,	Mrs. MORRIS.

The Doors will be opened at *Half after Five*, and the Curtain drawn up precisely at a *Quarter after Six* o'Clock.

PLACES in the BOXES may be taken at the Box Office, next the *Theatre*, of Mr. *Ryan*, from *Ten to One*, and *Three to Five*; where also TICKETS may be had, and at Mr. *Gaine's* Book-Store, and Printing-Office, in Hanover-Square.

BOX 8s. PIT 6s. GALLERY 4s.

No Person to be admitted behind the Scenes on any Account whatever.

The Days of Performance will be, as usual, *Mondays, Wednesdays,* and *Fridays.*

Vivat Refpublica.

The WIDOW'S VOW, as it is now acted at the *Theatre* in *New-York*, may be had of HUGH GAINE.

Old American Company Theatre playbill for The Jealous Wife *and* The Widow's Vow, *March 24, 1787. Courtesy of the Museum of the City of New York.*

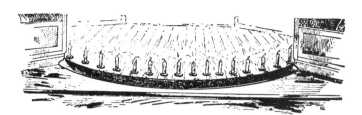

Candle footlights used in the early American theaters. From Arthur Hornblow, A History of the Theatre in America, *Vol. I, Philadelphia and London, J. B. Lippincott Co., 1919, p. 170*

Thomas Wignell, a theater manager, carrying a pair of silver candlesticks to light President Washington to his box. From Arthur Hornblow, A History of the Theatre in America, *Vol. I, Philadelphia and London, J. B. Lippincott Co., 1919, p. 128.*

7

Colonial Songs and Patriotic Marches
with Sheet Music

1. Songs

As the eighteenth century unfolded there were musical stirrings throughout the colonies. The well-to-do in the South, as well as those Bostonians who had acquired wealth and position, began importing musical instruments from England. Public concerts became popular and visiting celebrities from Europe appeared in urban centers. Ballad operas were presented by British companies, and chamber music was enjoyed in the homes of the affluent families in Philadelphia, Charleston, and Bethlehem.

However, the popular music among the colonists was largely vocal. Through the efforts of the composer William Billings, singing societies and church choirs were organized. Congregational singing became part of the church service. Numerous singing schools sprang up and singing masters traveled around the countryside conducting classes in churches, taverns, and schools. Secular music began broadening its horizons.

By the Revolutionary period Americans were emerging as a singing people. Ballads and songs appeared in overwhelming numbers on broadsides, in almanacs, and in newspapers, long before any collections were published. People sang from memory rather than notes, for little sheet music was printed.

During the war, songs were frequently made up on the march and many were adapted to familiar airs, even those of the enemy, including "Maggie Lawder," "Heart of Oak," and "Derry Down." At least a half dozen songs were adapted to the tune of "Yankee Doodle," the song that became the rallying cry of the Revolution:

> It suits for peace, it suits for fun,
> And just as well for fighting.

The Yankee became the symbol of the new American.

The popular drinking song, "To Anacreon in Heaven," which celebrates the delights of Bacchus and Amor, reached our shores after the War in time to provide the music for "Adams and Liberty." Later, Francis Scott Key was to write our national anthem to the same tune. Eighty-five American parodies were adapted to "To Anacreon in Heaven" between 1790 and 1818.

The trend in songs from 1765 on was the same as that in cartoons and ballads: to protest the various taxes such as the Stamp Act, to arouse the people to boycott English tea, and to ridicule British leaders in America and abroad. Finally, the war itself provided a popular theme.

"Those who cannot appreciate a priceless painting, a fine book, a treasured print, or a perfect poem," writes Harry Dichter, "can still find enjoyment in music. They may not be able to read or write, but—instinctively—they sing."*

Reproductions of several original songs with music may be found in this section. The time will soon be ripe for bicentennial sing-alongs and these lively airs are easily learned.

The World Turned Upside Down
or
The Old Woman Taught Wisdom
1767

[*In 1767 some still hoped that a crisis could be averted. The anonymous author of the song "The World Turned Upside Down, or The Old Woman Taught Wisdom" regarded the lyrics as "an humble attempt to reconcile the parent and her children, made by a peacemaker to Great Britain and her Colonies." It as sung to the tune of "Derry Down."*]

> Goody Bull and her daughter together fell out,
> Both squabbled, and wrangled, and made a——rout,
> But the cause of the quarrel remains to be told,
> Then lend both your ears, and a tale I'll unfold.

* Harry Dichter to Sylvia Dannett, February 6, 1972.

The old lady, it seems, took a freak in her head,
That her daughter, grown woman, might earn her own
     bread:
Self-applauding her scheme, she was ready to dance;
But we're often too sanguine in what we advance.

For mark the event; thus by fortune we're crossed,
Nor should people reckon without their good host;
The daughter was sulky, and wouldn't come to,
And pray, what in this case could the old woman do?

In vain did the matron hold forth in the cause,
That the young one was able; her duty, the laws;
In gratitude vile, disobedience far worse;
But she might e'en as well sung psalms to a horse.

Young, froward, and sullen, and vain of her beauty,
She tartly replied, that she knew well her duty,
That other folks' children were kept by their friends,
And that some folks loved people but for their own ends.

Zounds, neighbor! quoth Pitt, what the devil's the matter?
A man cannot rest in his house for your clatter;
Alas! cries the daughter, here's dainty fine work,
The old woman grown harder than . . .

She be——, says the farmer, and to her he goes,
First roars in her ears, then tweaks her old nose,
Hallo, Goody, what ails you? Wake! woman, I say;
I am come to make peace, in this desperate fray.

Adzooks, ope thine eyes, what a pother is here!
You've no right to compel her, you have not, I swear;
Be ruled by your friends, kneel down and ask pardon,
You'd be sorry, I'm sure, should she walk Covent Garden.

Alas! cries the old woman, and must I comply?
But I'd rather submit than the huzzy should die;
Pooh, prithee be quiet, be friends and agree,
You must surely be right, *if you're guided by me.*

Unwillingly awkward, the mother knelt down,
While the absolute farmer went on with a frown,
Come, kiss the poor child, there come, kiss and be friend
There, kiss your poor daughter, and make her amends.

No thanks to you, mother; the daughter replied:
But thanks to my friend here, I've humbled your pride
She be——, says the farmer, and to her he goes,
First roars in her ears, then tweaks her old nose,
Hallo, Goody, what ails you? Wake! woman, I say;
I am come to make peace, in this desperate fray.

Adzooks, ope thine eyes, what a pother is here!
You've no right to compel her, you have not, I swear;
Re ruled by your friends, kneel down and ask pardon,
You'd be sorry, I'm sure, should she walk Covent Garden.

Alas! cries the old woman, and must I comply?
But I'd rather submit than the huzzy should die;
Pooh, prithee be quiet, be friends and agree,
You must surely be right, *if you're guided by me.*

Unwillingly awkward, the mother knelt down,
While the absolute farmer went on with a frown,
Come, kiss the poor child, there come, kiss and be friends!
There, kiss your poor daughter, and make her amends.

No thanks to you mother; the daughter replied:
But thanks to my friend here, I've humbled your pride.

The Liberty Song
1768

[JOHN DICKINSON (1732–1808) *of Delaware was a member of the Pennsylvania Assembly in 1764, of the Provincial Congress of 1765, and also of the first Continental Congress. He wrote the principal part of the state papers of that Congress. He opposed the Declaration of Independence because he did not feel the Congress was strong enough. However he proved his loyalty to the patriotic cause a short time after the declaration by marching to Elizabethtown at the head of his regiment to repel the invading British. He became the author of the first patriotic song in America with his "Song for American Freedom" or, as it is better known, "The Liberty Song." Frank Moore narrates the story behind the song in his* Songs and Ballads of the American Revolution.

A short time after the refusal of the Massachusetts Legislature to rescind the Circular Letter of February 11, 1768, relating to the imposition of duties and taxes on the American colonies, John Dickinson of Delaware, the celebrated author of a series of essays entitled "The Farmer's Letters," wrote to James Otis of Massachusetts, as follows: "I enclose you a song for American freedom. I have long since renounced poetry, but as indifferent songs are very powerful on certain occasions, I venture to invoke the deserted muses. . . . My worthy friend, Dr. Arthur Lee, a gentleman of distinguished family, abilities, and patriotism in Virginia, composed eight lines of it. . . . "

"The Liberty Song" became the first separately printed sheet of music issued in the colonies. It was advertised for sale in the Boston Chronicle *from August 29 to September 5, 1768. No known copies of this edition are in existence. It became the official song of The Sons of Liberty. On August 14, 1769 John Adams attended the banquet celebrating the anniversary of the Stamp Act Riots and noted in his diary that 350 Sons of Liberty attended the affair and that "there was a large collection of good company. We had the Liberty Song (Dickinson's), and the whole company in the chorus."]*

Adapted to the tune of the English song "Heart of Oak," composed by Dr. William Boyce for a ballad opera in 1759, Dickinson's words were printed in the Boston Gazette, *July 18, 1768, from which it was reprinted, enjoying a widespread popularity throughout the colonies.*

Come join hand in hand, brave Americans all,
And rouse your bold hearts at fair Liberty's call;
No tyrannous acts, shall suppress your just claim,
Or stain with dishonor America's name.
    In freedom we're born, and in freedom we'll live;
        Our purses are ready,
        Steady, Friends, steady,
    Not as *slaves,* but as *freemen* our money we'll give.

Our worthy forefathers—let's give them a cheer—
To climates unknown did courageously steer;
Thro' oceans to deserts, for freedom they came,
And, dying, bequeath'd us their freedom and fame.

Their generous bosoms all dangers despis'd,
So highly, so wisely, their birthrights they priz'd;
We'll keep what they gave, we will piously keep,
Nor frustrate their toils on the land or the deep.

The Tree, their own hands had to Liberty rear'd,
They lived to behold growing strong and rever'd;
With transport then cried,—"Now our wishes we gain,
For our children shall gather the fruits of our pain."

How sweet are the labors that freemen endure,
That they shall enjoy all the profit, secure,—
No more such sweet labors Americans know,
If Britons shall reap what Americans sow.

Swarms of placemen and pensioners soon will appear,
Like locusts deforming the charms of the year:
Suns vainly will rise, showers vainly descend,
If we are to drudge for what others shall spend.

Then join hand in hand brave Americans all,
By uniting we stand, by dividing we fall;
In so righteous a cause let us hope to succeed,
For Heaven approves of each generous deed.

All ages shall speak with amaze and applause,
Of the courage we'll show in support of our laws;
To die we can bear,—but to serve we disdain,
For shame is to freemen more dreadful than pain.

This bumper I crown for our sovereign's health,
And this for Britannia's glory and wealth;
That wealth, and that glory immortal may be,
If she is but just, and we are but free.
    In freedom we're born, &c.

The Parody
1768

[*This parody upon the "Liberty Song" was first published in the* Boston Gazette *on September 26, 1768, with the subjoined brief notice: "Last Tuesday, the following song made its appearance from a garret at Castle William." The author is unknown.*]

Come shake your dull noddles, ye pumpkins, and bawl,
And own that you're mad at fair Liberty's call;
No scandalous conduct can add to your shame,
Condemn'd to dishonor, inherit the fame.
    In folly you're born, and in folly you'll live,
        To madness still ready,
        And stupidly steady,
    Not as men, but as monkeys, the tokens you give.

   · · · · · · · · · ·

The Tree, which the wisdom of justice hath rear'd,
Should be stout for their use, and by no means be spar'd:
When fuddled with rum the mad sots to restrain,
Sure Tyburn will sober the wretches again.

Your brats and your bunters by no means forget,
But feather your nests, for they're bare enough yet;

   · · · · · · · · · ·

For short is your harvest, nor long shall you know
The pleasure of reaping what other men sow.
Then plunder, my lads, for when red coats appear,
You'll melt like the locust when winter is near;
Gold vainly will glow, silver vainly will shine,
But, faith, you must skulk, you no more shall purloin.

All ages shall speak with contempt and amaze,
Of the vilest banditti that swarm'd in these days;
In defiance of halters, of whips and of chains,
The rogues would run riot.—fools for their pains.

Gulp down your last dram, for the gallows now groans,
And, over depress'd, her lost empire bemoans;
While we quite transported and happy shall be,
From mobs, knaves and villains, protected and free.

The Parody Parodied
or
The Massachusetts Liberty Song
1768

Historian Frank Moore, considered this loyal song "much the best of those composed during the earliest struggles of the Colonists." It was published in the St. James Chronicle *in London, November 8, 1768, as well as in America, and intended as an answer to the previous parody.*]

Come swallow your bumpers, ye tories, and roar,
That the sons of fair Freedom are hamper'd once more;
But know that no cut-throats our spirits can tame,
Nor a host of oppressors shall smother the flame.

In freedom we're born, and, like sons of the brave,
   We'll never surrender,
   But swear to defend her,
And scorn to survive, if unable to save.

Our grandsires, blest heroes! we'll give them a tear,
Nor sully their honors, by stooping to fear;
Thro' deaths and thro' dangers, their trophies they won,
We dare be their rivals, nor will be outdone.

Let tyrants and minions presume to despise,
Encroach on our rights, and make freedom their prize:
The fruits of their rapine they never shall keep;
Tho' vengeance may nod, yet how short is her sleep!

Our wives and our babes, still protected, shall know,
Those who dare to be free, shall for ever be so;
On these arms and these hearts they may safely rely,
For in freedom we'll live, or like heroes we'll die.

When oppress'd and reproach'd, our king we implore,
Still firmly persuaded our rights he'll restore;
When our hearts beat to arms, to defend a just right,
Our monarch rules there, and forbids us to fight.

Not the glitter of arms, nor the dread of a fray,
Could make us submit to their chains for a day;
Withheld by affection, on Britons we call,—
Prevent the fierce conflict which threatens your fall!

All ages shall speak, with amaze and applause,
Of the prudence we show in support of our cause;
Assur'd of our safety, a Brunswick still reigns,
Whose free loyal subjects are strangers to chains.

Then join hand in hand, brave Americans all!
To be free is to live, to be slaves is to fall;
Has the land such a dastard, as scorns not a lord,
Who dreads not a fetter much more than a sword.

In freedom we're born, and, like sons of the brave,
    We'll never surrender,
    But swear to defend her,
And scorn to survive, if unable to save.

"Heart of Oak"
by
Dr. William Boyce

The Scotch politicians have laid a deep scheme,
By invading America to bring Charlie in;
And if the Scotch mist's not remov'd from the throne,
The crown's not worth wearing, the kingdom's undone.

The placemen, and commoners, have taken a bribe
To betray their own country, and the empire beside;
And though the colonies stand condemned by some,
There are no rebels here, but are traitors at home.

The arbitrary minister, he acts as he please,
He wounds our constitution, and breaks through our laws;
His troops they are landed, his ships they are moor'd,
But boys all stand together, they will fall by the sword.

The great Magna Charta is wounded severe;
By accounts from the doctors, 'tis almost past cure.
Let's defend it with the sword, or die with the braves,
For we had better die in freedom, than live and be slaves.

They tax us contrary to reason and right,
Expecting that we are not able to fight;
But to draw their troop home, I do think would be best,
For Providence always defends the oppress'd.

The valiant Bostonians have enter'd the field,
And declare they will fall there before they will yield;
A noble example! In them we'll confide,
We'll march to their town, stand or fall by their side.

An union through the colonies will ever remain,
And ministerial taxation will be but in vain,
For we are all resolved to die or be free;
So they may repeal the acts, for repeal'd they must be.

Fish and Tea
1775

What a court, hath old England, of folly and sin,
Spite of Chatham and Camden, Barre, Burke, Wilkes
        and Glynn!
Not content with the game act, they tax fish and sea,
And America drench with hot water and tea.
        Derry down, down, hey derry down.

Lord Sandwich, he swears they are terrible cowards,
Who can't be made brave by the blood of the Howards;
And to prove there is truth in America's fears,
He conjures Sir Peter's ghost 'fore the peers.

Now, indeed, if these poor people's nerves are so weak,
How cruel it is their destruction to seek!
Dr. Johnson's a proof, in the highest degree,
His soul and his system were changèd by tea.

But if the wise council of England doth think,
They may be enslaved by the power of drink,
They're right to enforce it; but then, do you see?
The Colonies, too, may refuse and be free.

There's no knowing where this oppression will stop;
Some say—there's no cure but a capital chop;
And that I believe's each American's wish,
Since you've drench'd them with tea, and depriv'd 'em
        of fish.

        .   .   .   .

Three Generals[1] these mandates have borne 'cross the sea,
To deprive 'em of fish and to make 'em drink tea;
In turn, sure, these freemen will boldly agree,
To give 'em a dance upon Liberty Tree.

[1] *Three Generals.* According to Frank Moore "the subjoined impromptu was published at London, by some friend of
the colonies, on the departure of the British Generals for America:

        Behold! the Cerberus the Atlantic plough,
        Her precious cargo, Burgoyne, Clinton, Howe—
        Bow! wow! wow!

Then freedom's the word, both at home and abroad,
And ———, every scabbard that hides a good sword!
Our forefathers gave us this freedom in hand,
And we'll die in defence of the rights of the land.
        Derry down, down, hey derry down.

Chester
by
William Billings

[*Boston-bred* WILLIAM BILLINGS *was a tanner by trade and subsequently became a teacher. One of the earliest American composers, he became a prolific writer of songs and an enthusiastic singer himself.*

As Billings's reputation grew, his compositions appeared on Boston's concert programs, as well as those of other cities.

In 1770 he produced a volume of which he called The New England Psalm Singer, *the first sacred music collection entirely composed by an American. In this collection was a song called "Chester." After the War had been going on for two years, Billings added four additional timely verses, expressing his scorn for the British generals and their men, and this popular rousing tune expressed the burning patriotism of the Revolution. Battle-weary soldiers sang it night after night as they sat around their camp fires. In the opinion of one music critic, John Tasker Howard, Billings "was as much a force in America's democratic upheaval as were the instigators of the Boston Tea Party."*]

Let tyrants shake their iron rod,
    And slavery clank her galling chains;
We fear them not; we trust in God—
    New England's God for ever reigns.

Howe and Burgoyne, and Clinton, too,
    With Prescott and Cornwallis join'd;
Together plot our overthrow,
    In one infernal league combin'd.

When God inspir'd us for the fight,
    Their ranks were broke, their lines were forc'd;
Their ships were shatter'd in our sight,
    Or swiftly driven from our coast.

The foe comes on with haughty stride;
    Our troops advance with martial noise;
Their veterans flee before our youth,
    And generals yield to beardless boys.

What grateful offering shall we bring?
    What shall we render to the Lord?
Loud hallelujah let us sing,
    And praise his name on every chord.

Bunker Hill, or The American Hero
A "Sapphick Ode"
by
Nathaniel Niles

[NATHANIEL NILES *was born in Connecticut and educated at Harvard and the College of New Jersey. He tried his hand at many things, including peaching, law, medicine and politics. In the end he successfully combined invention and farming, first in Connecticut and then in Vermont.*

When Niles wrote this song he called it "The American Hero" but it became known in his time and since as "Bunker Hill." The battle of Bunker Hill brought the reality of war to the colonists. The green soldiers of a yet unformed nation were opposing one of the world's military powers. The song came to be considered the Yankee war-hymn of the Revolution and was sung at public meetings and in camps and churches. The music for the song was written by Andrew Law, who received his B.A. degree at Rhode Island College, now Brown University.]

Why should vain mortals tremble at the sight of
Death and destruction in the field of battle,
Where blood and carnage clothe the ground in crimson,
        Sounding with death-groans?

O, then, exult that God forever reigneth;
Clouds which, around him, hinder our perception,
Bind us the stronger to exalt his name, and
        Shout louder praises.

Then to the wisdom of my Lord and Master
I will commit all that I have or wish for,
Sweetly as babes' sleep will I give my life up,
        When called to yield it.

Now, Mars, I dare thee, clad in smoky pillars,
Bursting from bomb-shells, roaring from the cannon,
Rattling in grape-shot like a storm of hailstones,
        Torturing ether.

        .   .   .   .

From the dire caverns, made by ghostly miners,
Let the explosion, dreadful as volcanoes,
Heave the broad town, with all its wealth and people,
        Quick to destruction.

Still shall the banner of the King of Heaven
Never advance where I am afraid to follow:
While that precedes me, with an open bosom,
        War, I defy thee.

        .   .   .   .

Death will invade us by the means appointed,
And we must all bow to the king of terrors;
Nor am I anxious, if I am prepared,
    What shape he comes in.

Infinite Goodness teaches us submission,
Bids us be quiet, under all his dealings;
Never repining, but forever praising
    God, our Creator.

Well may we praise him: all his ways are perfect:
Though a resplendence, infinitely glowing,
Dazzles in glory on the sight of mortals,
    Struck blind by lustre.

Good is Jehovah in bestowing sunshine,
Nor less his goodness in the storm and thunder,
Mercies and judgment both proceed from kindness,
    Infinite kindness.

Columbia
by
Timothy Dwight

[*This war song was written by Dwight while he was acting as chaplain to the American army in the campaign against Burgoyne, 1777–1778. The song raised the spirits of the men, and seemed to give them a clear vision of the issue of all this havoc and horror: a new nation which would stand for the noble values of liberty and justice.*]

Columbia, Columbia, to glory arise,
The queen of the world, and the child of the skies!
Thy genius commands thee; with rapture behold,
While ages on ages thy splendors unfold.
Thy reign is the last, and the noblest of time,
Most fruitful thy soil, most inviting thy clime;
Let the crimes of the east ne'er encrimson thy name,
Be freedom, and science, and virtue thy fame.

To conquest and slaughter let Europe aspire;
Whelm nations in blood, and wrap cities in fire;
Thy heroes the rights of mankind shall defend,
And triumph pursue them, and glory attend.
A world is thy realm: for a world be thy laws,
Enlarged as thine empire, and just as thy cause;
On Freedom's broad basis, that empire shall rise,
Extend with the main, and dissolve with the skies.

Fair Science her gates to thy sons shall unbar,
And the east see thy morn hide the beams of her star.
New bards, and new sages, unrivalled shall soar
To fame unextinguished, when time is no more;
To thee, the last refuge of virtue designed,
Shall fly from all nations the best of mankind;
Here, grateful to heaven, with transport shall bring
Their incense, more fragrant than odors of spring.

Nor less shall thy fair ones to glory ascend,
And genius and beauty in harmony blend;
The graces of form shall awake pure desire,
And the charms of the soul ever cherish the fire;
Their sweetness unmingled, their manners refined,
And virtue's bright image, instamped on the mind,
With peace and soft rapture shall teach life to glow,
And light up a smile in the aspect of woe.

Thy fleets to all regions thy power shall display,
The nations admire, and the ocean obey;
Each shore to thy glory its tribute unfold,
And the east and the south yield their spices and gold.
As the day-spring unbounded, thy splendor shall flow,
And earth's little kingdoms before thee shall bow:
While the ensigns of union, in triumph unfurled,
Hush the tumult of war, and give peace to the world.

Thus, as down a lone valley, with cedars o'erspread,
From war's dread confusion I pensively strayed—
The gloom from the face of fair heaven retired;
The winds ceased to murmur; the thunders expired;
Perfumes, as of Eden, flowed sweetly along,
And a voice, as of angels, enchantingly sung:
"Columbia, Columbia, to glory arise,
The queen of the world, and the child of the skies."

The Epilogue

[*A good-humored Tory song to the tune of "Derry Down." It was printed on a broadside and posted in the streets of New York and Philadelphia, in October 1778.*]

Our farce is now finished, your sport's at an end!
But ere you depart, let the voice of a friend,
By way of a chorus, the evening crown
With a song to the tune of a hey derry down,
  Derry down, down, hey derry down.

Old Shakespeare, a poet who should not be spit on,
Although he was born in an island called Britain,
Hath said that mankind are all players at best—
A truth we'll admit of, for sake of the jest.

On this puny stage we've strutted our hour,
And have acted our parts to the best of our power;
That the farce hath concluded—not perfectly well—
Was surely the fault of the Devil in Hell!

This Devil you know, out of spleen to the Church,
Will oftentimes leave his best friends in the lurch,
And turn them adrift in the midst of their joy,—
'Tis a difficult matter to cheat the Old Boy.

Since this is the case, we must e'en make the best
Of a game that is lost: let us turn it to jest!
We'll smile, nay, we'll laugh, we'll carouse, and we'll
        sing,
And cheerfully drink life and health to the king.

Let Washington now from his mountains descend—
Who knows but in George he may still find a friend?
A Briton, although he loves bottle and wench,
Is an honester fellow than parléz-vous French.

Our great 'Independence' we give to the wind,
And pray that Great Britain may once more be kind:
In this jovial song all hostility ends,
And Britons and we will forever be friends.

Boys, fill me a bumper! now join in the chorus!
There is happiness still in the prospect before us,
In this sparkling glass, all hostility ends,
And Britons and we will for ever be friends!

The Battle of the Kegs
by
Francis Hopkinson

[FRANCIS HOPKINSON, *1737–1791, is credited with being America's first native composer.
He was also a political leader and writer and began publishing his political satires in 1774. This
song is based on an incident that took place in Philadelphia in 1777. David Bushnell, who in-
vented the American torpedo and other submarine machinery, dreamed up a unique way of an-
noying the royal fleet anchored off the shore of the Delaware River a few miles above Philadelphia. He got hold of a supply of kegs and had them charged with gunpowder, which was designed to explode as the kegs came in contact with enemy vessels. In the late autumn the kegs*

were set adrift in the river according to plan, but failed in their main objective. When they did explode in the vicinity of the vessels, however, the British troops and seamen became alarmed. For hours they kept up a continuous discharge of small arms and cannon, aiming at everything in the river during the ebbtide. Hopkinson's swinging, rollicking song to the tune of "Maggie Lawder" became popular with Washington's army, and Dr. Thacher wrote in his diary, "Our drums and fifes afforded us a favorite music till evening when we were delighted with the song composed by Mr. Hopkinson, 'The Battle of the Kegs,' sung in the best style by a number of gentlemen." Hopkinson wrote a mock-heroic narrative in prose for the New Jersey Gazette *January 27, 1778, as a preface to his verses, observing the effect of the kegs on the British soldiers.]*

Engraving for "The Battle of the Kegs." Prints Division, New York Public Library.

Some asserted that these kegs were filled with armed rebels, who were to issue forth, in the dead of night, as the Grecians did of old from the wooden horse at the siege of Troy and take the city by surprise; declaring that they had seen the points of bayonets sticking out of the bung-holes of the kegs. Other said that they were filled with inveterate combustibles which would set the whole Delaware in flames and consume all the shipping in the harbor. Whilst others conjectured that they were machines constructed by a magic, and expected to see them mount the wharves and roll, all flaming with infernal fire, through the streets of the city.

It is said His Excellency, Lord Howe, has despatched a swift-sailing packet, with an account of his signal victory to the court of London. In short, Monday the—day of January, 1778, will be ever memorable in history for the renowned Battle of the Kegs.

Gallants attend, and hear a friend,
    Trill forth harmonious ditty,
Strange things I'll tell, which late befell
    In Philadelphia city.

'Twas early day, as poets say,
    Just when the sun was rising,
A soldier stood, on a log of wood,
    And saw a thing surprising.

As in amaze he stood to gaze,
    The truth can't be denied, sir,
He spied a score of kegs or more,
    Come floating down the tide, sir.

A sailor, too, in jerkin blue,
    This strange appearance viewing,
First damn'd his eyes, in great surprise,
    Then said, "Some mischief's brewing."

From morn till night, these men of might
    Display'd amazing courage;
And when the sun was fairly down,
    Retir'd to sup their porridge.

An hundred men, with each a pen,
    Or more, upon my word, sir,
It is most true would be too few,
    Their valor to record, sir.

Such feats did they perform that day,
    Against those wicked kegs, sir,
That years to come, if they get home,
    They'll make their boasts and brags, sir.

A New Song
by
J. W. Hewlings
1775

[*The author of this ballad "on the present critical times" was a native of Nansemond, Virginia, where he died in the early part of the year 1793. The song is to the tune of "Heart of Oak."*]

Come rouse up my lads, and join this great cause,
In defence of your liberty, your property, and laws.
'Tis to honor we call you, stand up for your right,
And ne'er let our foes say, we are put to the flight.
For so just is our cause, and so valiant our men,
We always are ready, steady boys, steady;
We'll fight for our freedom again and again.

. . . .

Songs of victory in the South followed.

A New Song
1779

[*This ballad commemorates the attack upon Savannah. It appeared in Rivington's Tory Gazette as "A new song to an old tune, written by a Yankee, and sung to the tune of Doodle doo."*]

The Frenchmen came upon the coast,
Our great allies, and they did boast,
They soon would bang the British host,
Doodle doodle do, pa, pa, pa, pa, pa.

D'Estaing he wrote to General Lincoln,
And told him that he need not think on
Danger, but in quick step march down.
Doodle doodle do, pa, pa, pa, pa, pa.

So Lincoln came down to Savannah,
The French and we all sung hosanna,
We soon will take them every man-a.
Doodle doodle do, pa, pa, pa, pa, pa.

. . . .

But soon we found ourselves mistaken,
And were glad to save our bacon,
Rather than be killed or taken.
Doodle doodle do, pa, pa, pa, pa, pa.

. . . .

280

The French, it's true, behav'd quite civil,
Yet we wish'd them to the devil,
And hope that good may spring from evil.
    Doodle doodle do, pa, pa, pa, pa, pa.

And now that they on board are gone,
Have left poor us here all alone,
We've nought to do but sigh and moan.
    Doodle doodle do, pa, pa, pa, pa, pa.

The enemy must keep their post,
In spite of all the Gallic host,
And Georgia we've for ever lost.
    Doodle doodle do, pa, pa, pa, pa, pa.

A Song about Charleston
1780

[*The reduction of Charleston, South Carolina by the British in 1780 was well lyricized. This poem was written by an officer of the royal army and first published in a ballad-sheet, set to the tune of the "Watery God."*]

King Hancock sat in regal state,
And big with pride and vainly great,
    Address'd his rebel crew,
These haughty Britons soon shall yield
The boasted honors of the field,
    While our brave sons pursue.

Six thousand fighting men or more,
Protect the Carolina shore,
    And Freedom will defend;
And stubborn Britons soon shall feel,
'Gainst Charleston, and hearts of steel,
    How vainly they contend.

But ere he spake in dread array,
To rebel foes, ill-fated day,
    The British boys appear;
Their mien with martial ardor fir'd,
And by their country's wrongs inspir'd,
    Shook Lincoln's heart with fear.

See Clinton brave, serene, and great,
For mighty deeds rever'd by fate,
    Direct the thund'ring fight,
While Mars, propitious God of war,
Looks down from his triumphal car,
    With wonder and delight.

281

"Clinton," he cries, "the palm is thine,
'Midst heroes thou wert born to shine,
    A great immortal name,
And Cornwallis' mighty deeds appear,
Conspicuous each revolving year,
    The pledge of future fame."

Our tars, their share of glories won,
For they among the bravest shone,
    Undaunted, firm and bold.
Whene'er engag'd, their ardor show'd
Hearts which with native valor glow'd,
    Hearts of true British mould.

Cornwallis Burgoyned
1781

[*Several songs were composed to commemorate the surrender of the royal army at York-town. This one was published a short time after the event. It was adapted to the air "Maggie Lawder," which was at that time a great favorite in both armies.*]

When British troops first landed here,
    With Howe commander o'er them,
They thought they'd make us quake for fear,
    And carry all before them;
With thirty thousand men or more,
    And she without assistance,
America must needs give o'er,
    And make no more resistance.

But Washington, her glorious son,
    Of British hosts the terror,
Soon, by repeated overthrows,
    Convinc'd them of their error;
Let Princeton, and let Trenton tell,
    What gallant deeds he's done, sir,
And Monmouth's plains where hundreds fell,
    And thousands more have run, sir.

Cornwallis, too, when he approach'd
    Virginia's old dominion,
Thought he would soon her conqu'ror be;
    And so was North's opinion.
From State to State with rapid stride,
    His troops had march'd before, sir,
Till quite elate with martial pride,
    He thought all dangers o'er, sir.

But our allies, to his surprise,
   The Chesapeake had enter'd;
And now too late, he curs'd his fate,
   And wish'd he ne'er had ventur'd,
For Washington no sooner knew
   The visit he had paid her,
Than to his parent State he flew,
   To crush the bold invader.

When he sat down before the town,
   His Lordship soon surrender'd;
His martial pride he laid aside,
   And cas'd the British standard;
Gods! how this stroke will North provoke,
   And all his thoughts confuse, sir!
And how the Peers will hang their ears,
   When first they hear the news, sir.

. . . .

A TOAST — Written and Composed by Fraˢ. Hopkinson Esqʳ.

'Tis WASHINGTONS Health fill a bumper all round for he is our glory and pride our arms shall in battle with conquest be crownd whilst virtue and he's on our side our arms shall in battle with conquest be crownd whilst virtue and he's on our side and he's on our side

2
'Tis WASHINGTONS Health loud cannons should
And trumpets the truth should proclaim
There cannot be found search all the world o'er
His equal in virtue and fame

roar

3
'Tis WASHINGTONS Health our Hero to bless
May heaven look graciously down
Oh long may he live our hearts to possess
And freedom still call him her own

Hopkinson's "The Toast." Library of Congress.

"The Hill Tops," a new hunting song. Courtesy of the New-York Historical Society, New York City.

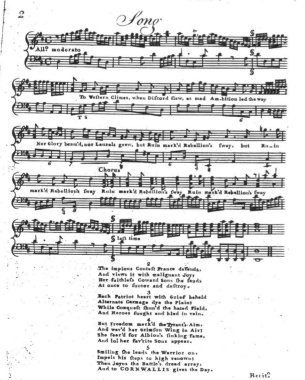

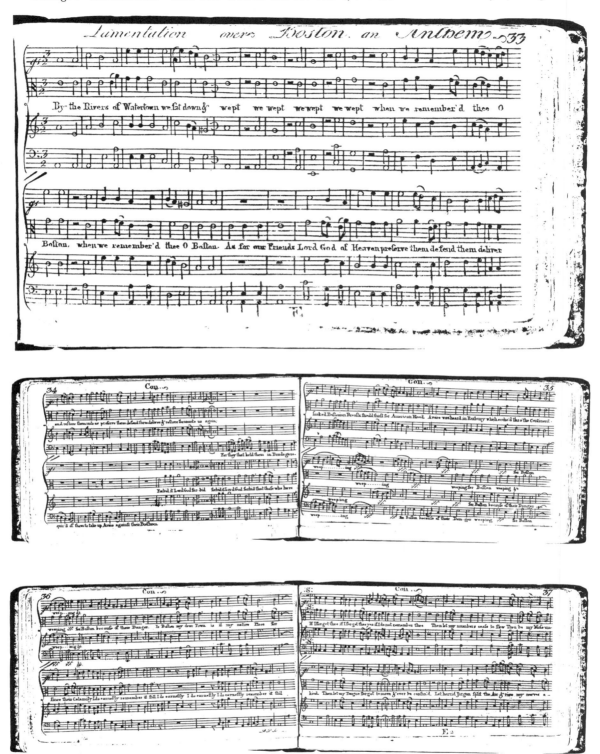

sunder Let hateful discord greet my ear as terrible as Thunder, Let harmony be banish'd hence and

Consonance depart; Let dissonance erect her throne and reign within my Heart.

287

Love of Home literally put Vermont on the Map—
"We owe no allegiance; we bow to no throne,
Our ruler is law, and the law is our own."
From the "Song of Vermonters." 1779.

"Song of Vermonters," 1779. Prints Division, New York Public Library.

MAGGIE LAWDER

A Favorite Scotch Song.

"Maggie Lawder," with variations for the piano forte. Library of Congress.

Derry Down

Der - ry down, down, hey, der - ry down.

"Derry Down." Library of Congress.

8

Hearts of Oak
with the words of the Liberty Song

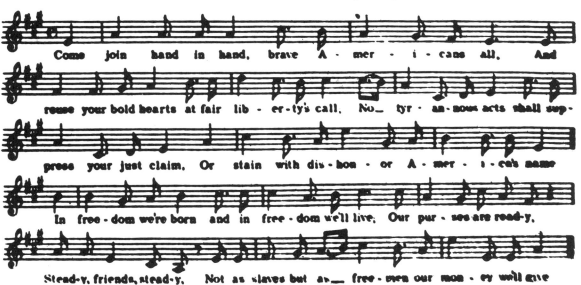

Come join hand in hand, brave A - mer - i - cans all, And

rouse your bold hearts at fair lib - er - ty's call. No tyr - an - nous acts shall sup -

press your just claim, Or stain with dis - hon - or A - mer - i - ca's name

In free - dom we're born and in free - dom we'll live; Our pur - ses are read - y,

Stead - y, friends, stead - y, Not as slaves but as free - men our mon - ey will give

"Heart of Oak." Library of Congress.

"The Anacreontic Song" as sung at the Crown and Anchor Tavern in the Strand, the words by Ralph Tomlinson Esq., late president of the Society. Library of Congress.

Chorus.

And be___fides I'll in_ftruct you like me to en_twine, The

And be___fides I'll in_ftruct you like me to en_twine, The

And be___fides I'll in_ftruct you like me to en_twine, The

And be___fides I'll in_ftruct' you like me to en_twine, The

Myr_tle of VE_NUS with BAC_CHUS'_s Vine.

Myr_tle of VE_NUS with BAC_CHUS'_s Vine.

Myr_tle of VE_NUS with BAC_CHUS'_s Vine.

Myr_tle of VE_NUS with BAC_CHUS'_s Vine.

2

The news through OLYMPUS immediately flew;
"When OLD THUNDER pretended to give himfelf Airs_
"If thefe Mortals are fuffer'd their Scheme to perfue,
"The Devil a Goddefs will ftay above Stairs.
 "Hark! already they cry,
 "In Tranfports of Joy,
"Away to the Sons of ANACREON we'll fly,
"And there, with good Fellows, we'll learn to intwine
"The Myrtle of VENUS with BACCHUS'S Vine.

3

"The YELLOW-HAIR'D GOD and his nine fufty Maids,
" From HELICON'S Banks will incontinent flee,
"IDALIA will boaft but of tenantlefs Shades,
"And the bi_forked Hill a mere Defart will be
 "My Thunder, no fear on't,
 "Shall foon do it's Errand,
"And, dam'me! I'll fwinge the Ringleaders, I warrant.
"I'll trim the young Dogs, for thus daring to twine
"The Myrtle of VENUS with BACCHUS'S Vine.

4

APOLLO rofe up; and faid, "Pr'ythee ne'er quarrel,
"Good King of the Gods, with my Vot'ries below:
"Your Thunder is ufelefs_then, fhewing his Laurel,
Cry'd, "Sic evitalile fulmen, you know!
 "Then over each Head
 "My Laurels I'll fpread;
"So my Sons from your Crackers no Mifchief fhall dread,
"Whilft fnug in their Club-Room, they jovially twine
"The Myrtle of VENUS with BACCHUS'S Vine.

5

Next MOMUS got up, with his rifible Phiz,
And fwore with APOLLO he'd chearfully join_
"The full Tide of Harmony ftill fhall be his,
"But the Song, and the Catch, & the Laugh fhall be mine,
 "Then, JOVE, be not jealous
 "Of thefe honeft Fellows.
Cry'd JOVE, "We relent, fince the Truth you now tell us;
"And fwear, by OLD STYX, that they long fhall intwine
"The Myrtle of VENUS with BACCHUS'S Vine.

6

Ye fons of ANACREON, then, join Hand in Hand;
Preferve Unanimity, Friendfhip, and Love!
'Tis your's to fupport what's fo happily plann'd;
You've the Sanction of Gods, and the FIAT of JOVE.
 While thus we agree,
 Our Toaft let it be.
May our Club flourifh happy, united, and free!
And long may the Sons of ANACREON intwine
The Myrtle of VENUS with BACCHUS'S Vine.

The **LIBERTY SONG.** *In Freedom we're born, &c.*

Come join hand in hand brave A-me-ri-cans all, And rouse your bold hearts at fair Li-ber-ty's call; No ty-rannous acts shall sup

press your just claim, Or stain with dishonour A-me-ri-ca's name, In Free-dom we're born and in Free-dom we'll

live, Our pur-ses are rea-dy, Steady, Friends, Steady. Not as Slaves, but as Freemen our mo-ney we'll give

Our worthy Forefathers--Let's give them a cheer
To Climates unknown did courageously steer;
Thro' Oceans, to deserts, for freedom they came,
And dying bequeath'd us their freedom and Fame.
 In Freedom we're born &c.
Their generous bosoms all dangers despis'd,
So highly, so wisely, their *Birthrights* they priz'd,
We'll keep what they gave, we will piously keep,
Nor frustrate their toils on the land and the deep.
 In Freedom we're born, &c.
The Tree their own hands had to liberty rear'd;
They liv'd to behold growing strong and rever'd;

With transport they cry'd, "now our wishes we gain,
for our children shall gather the fruits of our pain."
 In Freedom we're born &c.
 [pain
Swarms of placemen and pensioners soon will ap-
Like locusts deforming the charms of the year;
Suns vainly will rise, Showers vainly descend,
If we are to drudge for what others shall spend.
 In Freedom we're born &c.
Then join hand in hand brave Americans all,
By uniting we stand, by dividing we fall;
In so Righteous a cause let us hope to succeed,

For Heaven approves of each generous deed.
 In Freedom we're born, &c.
All ages shall speak with amaze and applause,
Of the courage we'll shew in support of our laws;
To die we can bear---but to serve we disdain,
For shame is to Freedom more dreadful than pain.
 In Freedom we're born, &c.
This bumper I crown for our Sovereign's health,
And this for Britannia's glory and wealth;
That wealth and that glory immortal may be,
If she is but just--- and if we are but Free
 In Freedom we're born &c.

Dickinson's "Liberty Song," 1768. Courtesy John Carter Brown Library, Brown University.

43. CHESTER

1770

The Singing-Master's Assistant
William Billings
(Boston, 1778)

William Billings
(1746–1800)

Let ty-rants shake their i-ron rod, And Slav'ry clank her gall-ing chains, We fear them not, we trust in God, New-eng-land's God for ev-er reigns.

"Chester." Library of Congress.

2
Howe and Burgoyne and Clinton too,
With Prescot and Cornwallis join'd,
Together plot our Overthrow
In one Infernal league combin'd.

3
When God inspir'd us for the fight,
Their ranks were broke, their lines were forc'd,
Their Ships were Shelter'd in our sight,
Or swiftly driven from our Coast.

4
The Foe comes on with haughty Stride,
Our troops advance with martial noise,
Their Vet'runs flee before our Youth,
And Gen'rals yield to beardless Boys.

5
What grateful Off'ring shall we bring,
What shall we render to the Lord?
Loud Hallelujahs let us Sing,
And praise his name on ev'ry Chord.
 William Billings

2. Marches

Marches, ever popular, appeal to everyone, particularly in a time of war. Lively and spirited military tunes have stirred people throughout the ages, evoking patriotic thoughts and emotions. Military music on the march helps lighten the soldier's burden and, for the moment, fatigue. During the Revolutionary War drummers and fifers helped the muster captains enlist recruits for their companies by playing martial music outside the recruiting center.

What were these marches that stirred our forefathers during the War of Independence? What airs did the fifers and drummers play to keep up the spirit of the Continental Army? Even those who are authorities on the history of American music do not seem to know the answer.

The sheet music of Revolutionary War marches is difficult to come by, for separate publications of music were practically unknown in America before 1789.

In 1889, when John Philip Sousa was bandmaster of the United States Marine Band, he was asked to compile a collection to be called *Airs of All Lands.* Sousa concluded after his research that the field music of the Revolutionary War, which was played by fifers and drummers, consisted mainly of "Dog and Gun," "On the Road to Boston," "Rural Felicity," "Washington's March" by Francis Hopkinson and "Yankee Doodle."

There is said to be no confirmation that any of the many compositions known as "Washington's March" was actually used until 1784, or that Francis Hopkinson was the composer of such a march. This information came to me from various music reference libraries.

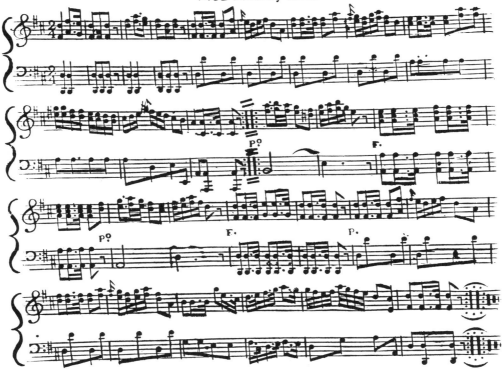

"Presidents March," 1798–99. Library of Congress.

What is known is that "Washington's March" was the first of many marches to be published in honor of George Washington. It was played and performed at a public celebration in Philadelphia in 1794.

By 1795 more sheet music was being printed. Reproductions of these and earlier marches are included in this section.

General Burgoyne's March

"General Burgoyne's March." Library of Congress.

"Federal March," 1788. Courtesy of Harry Dichter.

Dog and Gun.

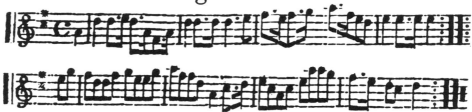

On the Road to Boston.
(March to Boston)

Rural Felicity.

Three popular airs of the Revolution. Courtesy of Harry Dichter.

PRESIDENTS MARCH AND CA IRA

Price 12 Cents

"Presidents March," 1789, and "Ca Ira," 1790. Joseph Hopkinson wrote the national song "Hail Columbia" to the music of the former in 1798. New York Public Library.

112. WASHINGTON'S MARCH
1794/95

G[eorge] Willig's *Musical Magazine*
(*Philadelphia*, 1794/95)

Pomposo

'The trills (tr) and the sign (∼) may be played ⎯ or ⎯
²The original has the sign (tr) over the G.

"Washington's March," 1794–95.

3. The Saga of Yankee Doodle

There is a legend that when Lord Cornwallis surrendered his sword and army to George Washington at Yorktown on October 19, 1781, the British band played "The World Turned Upside Down," and the Continental Army band broke into "Yankee Doodle." Probably such a dramatic incident never took place, but it is certainly likely that the Patriot bands played *Yankee Doodle* after this great victory, for it had been the rallying cry of the Revolution.

Much of the information about the origin of "Yankee Doodle" may be equally apocryphal, for the tune has been claimed in many lands. In Holland it was a reaper's song. After the laborers received "as much buttermilk as they could drink, and a tenth of the grain," for their wages, they sang the following words, while reaping, to the tune of "Yankee Doodle":

> Yanker, didel, doodle down,
>   Diddle, dudel, lanther,
> Yanke viver, voover vown,
>   Bothermilk and tanther.

The more you delve into its history, the more international the tune becomes. In southern Spain "Yankee Doodle" was said to bear a strong resemblance to the popular airs of Biscay, and, in the north, it was recognized as similar to the music for ancient sword-dance performed on solemn occasions by the people of San Sebastian. France found the tune to be that of an old vintage song. Even Italy claimed the tune for her own.

Somewhere along the way it reached England, possibly via Holland, before the reign of Charles I. At first it appeared as a nursery rhyme to Oliver Cromwell, but a derisive song about the "Lord Protector" of England was soon written and adapted to the tune by a loyal English poet:

> Nanky Doodle came to town
>   A riding on a pony,
> Stuck a feather in his hat
>   And called it macaroni.

This stanza is, of course, similar to the one later sung in America, which does not appear in any of the so-called accepted versions of "Yankee Doodle" in works by Edmund Stedman, Benson Lossing, or the Rev. Louis Albert Banks, D.D.

> Yankee Doodle went to town
>   A riding on a pony,
> Stuck a feather in his hat
>   And called it macaroni.

A *doodle* is defined in early English dictionaries as "a sorry trifling fellow," and the term is applied to Cromwell in that sense. A "macaroni" was a knot on which the feather was fastened.

Long before the Revolution there was a popular ditty in America known as "Lydia Fisher's Jig." Among the verses was the following:

"Lucy Locket lost her pocket
Lydia Fisher found it;
Not a bit of money in it.
Only binding round it."

A satirical poem accompanying a 1766 caricature of William Pitt, in which he appears on stilts, has this verse:

Stamp Act! le diable! dat is de job, sir;
Dat is in the Stiltman's rob, sir,
To be America's nabob, sir,
Doodle, noodle do.

At the time that Ferenc Kossuth, a leader of the Independence Party in Hungary, was in the United States making a plea for his country's liberty, he passed on to the editor of the *Boston Post* his claim to the lively tune. The Hungarians who had accompanied him heard the tune on a Mississippi River steamer and recognized it at once as one of their old national dance airs. According to the Reverend Louis Albert Banks, who recorded this incident, "They immediately began to caper and dance as they had been accustomed to do in Hungary."

"Yankee Doodle" is also attributed to Dr. Richard Schuckburg, a surgeon in the British army who is said to have combined medical skill with the talents of a musician. In June of 1755 New England troops were to join General Braddock's forces for an attack on the French and Indians at Niagara. The colonists came into Braddock's camp near Albany wearing ragged attire that ranged from the buckskins and furs of the American Indian to "some quaint old-fashioned military heirloom of a century past." Schuckburg, recalling the old air that had been sung in ridicule of Cromwell, wrote new words to it, deriding the uncouth appearance of the New England troops assembled there. He substituted "Yankey" for "Nankey" Doodle. (The change in the spelling of Yankey was not made until after the Revolution.)

The Americans liked the song and adopted it as their own, adding a few stanzas. Words and tune caught on. In a few days nothing was heard in provincial camps but the air of "Yankee Doodle." The music and verses are lively enough to overcome their awkward rhyme and uneven rhythm. This song became the best known and most famous of all songs written during the war. Soldiers whistled it with such mocking vim that Cornwallis is said to have exclaimed, "I hope to God I shall never hear that damned tune again."

It wasn't Cornwallis alone who felt that way. In his diary on July 24, 1775, Patriot Christopher Marshall noted: "General Gage's Troops are much dispirited . . . and are heartily disposed to leave off dancing any more to the tune of Yankee Doodle. . . ."

The tune was available to anyone who chose to write new words to it, and many did. In *The Contrast*, playwright Royall Tyler has his Yankee character Jonathan boast that while he knows only 190 of the verses of "Yankee Doodle," his sister Tabitha can sing them all.

The song was sufficiently well known to be mentioned in *The Disappointment*, or *The Force of Credulity*, a comic opera by Thomas Forrest, later a colonel in the Continental Army, that was published under the pseudonym Andrew Barton. This comedy, with songs interspersed, was written in two acts, and was scheduled to be given on April 20, 1767, by the American Company. It was based on a trick played by Forrest on an old Dutchman in Philadelphia who suffered from the then current mania of searching for the buried treasures of Blackbeard the Pirate. The play was withdrawn on April 16, according to an announcement in *The Pennsylvania Gazette,* because of "personal reflections that made it unfit for the stage." It was published in New York that year. The libretto contains eighteen songs with the names of the airs to which the words are to be sung. No music is included, but the fourth air is "Yankee Doodle":

> O! How joyful shall I be,
>> When I get de money.
> I will bring it all to dee;
>> O! my diddling honey.

In 1784 the comic opera *Two To One* was performed "with universal Applause" at the Theatre Royal in the Haymarket, London. It was composed by Dr. Arnold, "Organist and Composer to his Majejsty" for the Voice, Harpsichord, and Violin. One of the opera's airs, the Dicky Ditto, was sung to the tune of "Yankee Doodle":

> Adzooks, old Crusty.
>> Why so rusty,
>>> stupid, queer and mumpy!
> E-gad, if you don't mend your manners,
>> Somebody will bump you.
> Lumpy, thumpy, thwack and bump,
>> Pummel you, and bump-O!
> Humpy, stumpy, make you mump,
>> Kick a-bout your rump-O!

"Yankee Doodle" proved to be good martial music. In 1768, when British troops arrived in Boston Harbor, "the Yankee Doodle tune," noted a contemporary writer, "was the capital piece in the band of music at Castle William."

The earliest known edition in separate song form is "Yankee Doodle, or (as now Christened by the Saints of New England) The Lexington March, The Words to be Sung thro' the Nose, & in the West Country drawl & dialect." The first two lines of this version read, "Brother Ephraim sold his Cow/ and bought him a Commission."

"Yanky Doodle" appeared in print, without words, in James Aird's "Selection of Scotch, English, Irish and Foreign Airs," published in Glasgow in 1782.

One of the best known versions of the song is that given in his book* in 1898 by Louis Albert Banks, which follows here.

> Father and I went down to camp
>> Along with Captain Gooding,
> And there we saw the men and boys,
>> As thick as hasty pudding.

---

* Immortal Songs in Camp or Field.

Yankee Doodle, keep it up,
Yankee Doodle Dandy!
Mind the music and the step,
And with the gals be handy!

And there we see a thousand men
As rich as Squire David,
And what they wasted every day,—
I wish it had been savèd.

The 'lasses they eat up every day
Would keep our house all winter,—
They have so much that I'll be bound
They eat whene'er they've a mind to.

And there we see a whopping gun,
As big as a log of maple,
Mounted on a little cart,—
A load for father's cattle.

And every time they fired it off
It took a horn of powder,
And made a noise like father's gun,
Only a nation louder.

I went as near to it
As 'Siah's underpinning;
Father went as nigh agin,—
I thought the devil was in him.

Cousin Simon grew so bold,
I thought he meant to cock it;
He scared me so, I streaked it off,
And hung to father's pocket.

And Captain Davis had a gun
He kind o' clapped his hand on,
And stuck a crooked stabbing-iron
Upon the little end on 't.

And there I saw a pumpkin shell
As big as mother's basin;
And every time they sent one off,
They scampered like tarnation.

I saw a little bar'el, too,
  Its heads were made of leather;
They knocked on it with little plugs,
  To call the folks together.

And there was Captain Washington,
  With grand folks all about him;
They say he's grown so tarnal proud,
  He cannot ride without them.

He had on his meeting-clothes,
  And rode a slapping stallion,
And gave his orders to the men,—
  I guess there was a million.

And then the feathers in his hat,
  They were so tarnal fine-ah,
I wanted peskily to get
  To hand to my Jemima.

And then they'd fife away like fun
  And play on cornstalk fiddles;
And some had ribbons red as blood
  All wound about their middles.

The troopers, too, would gallop up,
  And fire right in our faces;
It scared me a'most to death
  To see them run such races.

And then I saw a snarl of men
  A-digging graves, they told me,
So tarnal long, so tarnal deep,—
  They allowed they were to hold me.

It scared me so I hooked it off,
  Nor stopped as I remember,
Nor turned about, till I got home,
  Locked up in mother's chamber.

The verses of "Yankee Doodle" which appear on *The New Yankee Doodle* song sheet printed and sold at J. Hewitt's Musical Repository are less commonly known. They show how a popular song was adapted to a political purpose in the time of patriotic fervor. The last four stanzas are printed here:

> The only way to keep off war,
>   And gaard 'gainst persecution,
> Is always to be well prepar'd,
>   With hearts of resolution.
> Yankee Doodle, let's Unite,
>   Yankee Doodle Dandy,
> As patriots, still maintain our right,
>   Yankee Doodle Dandy.
>
> Great WASHINGTON, who led us on,
>   And Liberty effected,
> Shall see we'll die or else be free—
>   We will not be subjected.
> Yankee Doodle, guard your coast,
>   Yankee Doodle Dandy—
> Fear not then or threat or boast,
>   Yankee Doodle Dandy.
>
> A Band of Brothers let us be,
>   While ADAMS guides the nation;
> And still our dear bought Freedom guard,
>   In ev'ry situation.
> Yankee Doodle, guard your coast,
>   Yankee Doodle Dandy—
> Fear not then or threat or boast,
>   Yankee Doodle Dandy.
>
> May soon the wish'd for hour arrive,
>   When PEACE shall rule the nations—
> And Commerce, free from fetters prove
>   Mankind are all relations.
> Then Yankee Doodle, be divine,
>   Yankee Doodle Dandy—
> Beneath the Fig tree and the Vine,
>   Sing Yankee Doodle Dandy.

Many popular songs were adapted to this rollicking tune. Some of the important adaptations are printed here.

Adam's Fall:
The Trip to Cambridge
1775

[*Despite the prominent position General Washington held at the head of an undisciplined army, and the effect which that position produced upon the minds of the well-regulated and disdainful royal troops, he was the subject of very few satirical ballads. Tory writers generally burlesqued the common interests of the people, or understood the whole breed of patriots as one rebel collection.*

The British were still in Boston after the arrival of Washington at Cambridge in 1775. One of their poets wrote a ballad at that time deriding the people of New England, to be sung to the tune of "Yankee Doodle." Some say this is the original "Yankee Doodle" song of the Revolution.]

When Congress sent great Washington
    All clothed in power and breeches,
To meet old Britain's warlike sons
    And make some rebel speeches;

'Twas then he took his gloomy way
    Astride his dapple donkeys,
And travelled well, both night and day,
    Until he reach'd the Yankees

Away from camp, 'bout three miles off,
    From Lily he dismounted,
His sergeant brush'd his sun-burnt wig
    While he the specie counted.

All prinked up in *full* bag-wig;
    The shaking notwithstanding,
In leathers tight, oh! glorious sight!
    He reach'd the Yankee landing.

The women ran, the darkeys too;
    And all the bells, they tollèd;
For Britain's sons, by Doodle doo,
    We're sure to be—consolèd.

Old mother Hancock with a pan
    All crowded full of butter,
Unto the lovely Georgius ran,
    And added to the splutter.

Says she, "Our brindle has just calved,
    And John is wondrous happy.
He sent this present to you, dear,
    As you're the 'country's papa.'"—

305

"You'll butter bread and bread butter,
    But do not butt your speeches.
"You'll butter bread and bread butter,
    But do not grease your breeches."

Full many a child went into camp,
    All dressed in homespun kersey,
To see the greatest rebel scamp
    That ever crossed o'er Jersey.

The rebel clowns, oh! what a sight!
    Too awkward was their figure.
'Twas yonder stood a pious wight,
    And here and there a nigger.

Upon a stump, he placed (himself,)
    Great Washington did he,
And through the nose of lawyer Close
    Proclaimed great Liberty.

The patriot brave, the patriot fair,
    From fervor had grown thinner,
So off they march'd, with patriot zeal,
    And took a patriot dinner.

Yankee Doodle's Expedition
to Rhode Island
1778

[*This is a Tory's humorous account of the unsuccessful attack on the British in Newport, Rhode Island, July, 1778 by the combined forces of Count D'Estaing, with the French fleet, and General Sullivan, later in command of the American forces. The ballad as printed in the Tory paper,* Rivington's Gazette, October 3, 1778.]

From Lewis, Monsieur Gerard came,
    To Congress in this town, sir,
They bow'd to him, and he to them,
    And then they all sat down, sir.

Begar, said Monsieur, one grand coup,
    You shall bientot behold, sir;
This was believ'd as gospel true,
    And Jonathan felt bold, sir.

So Yankee Doodle did forget
    The sound of British drum, sir,
How oft it made him quake and sweat,
    In spite of Yankee rum, sir.

He took his wallet on his back,
    His rifle on his shoulder,
And veow'd Rhode Island to attack,
    Before he was much older.

In dread array their tatter'd crew,
    Advanc'd with colors spread, sir,
Their fifes played Yankee doodle, doo,
    King Hancock at their head, sir.

What numbers bravely cross'd the seas,
    I cannot well determine,
A swarm of rebels and of fleas,
    And every other vermin.

Their mighty hearts might shrink they tho't,
    For all flesh only grass is,
A plenteous store they therefore brought,
    Of whiskey and molasses.

They swore they'd make bold Pigot squeak,
    So did their good ally, sir,
And take him pris'ner in a week,
    But that was all my eye, sir.

As Jonathan so much desir'd
    To shine in martial story,
D'Estaing with politesse retir'd,
    To leave him all the glory.

The Recess
1779

[*This satire first appeared in London, where it was written by "a true friend of the King and the Colonies." It was reproduced in America, in 1779, on a music sheet, adapted to the tune "Yankee Doodle."*]

And now our Senators are gone
    To take their leave of London,
To mourn how little they have done,
    How much they have left undone!

Heaven bless 'em in their summer seats,
    And grant their neighbors stare at
The long recounting of their feats,
    Though wond'ring much what they're at!

Bless'd be the times when men may do,
    What no one comprehendeth;
May boast of deeds that all must rue,
    Nor judge where nonsense endeth!

One year, with half ten thousand men,
    We swallow all our foes up;
The next, the times are turn'd, and then
    Old England's scale light goes up.

But still with courage and with glee,
    New laws we must be framing;
With paper and with parchment, we
    The savages are taming.

We swear the transatlantic folks
    Shall all obey our orders;
While they turn all we do to jokes,
    And cry out, "guard your borders."

Well, then, we'll go to war with France—
    Yes—no—we must—we mustn't;
John Bull shall teach Monsieur to dance—
    But can't—and there's the curse on't.

What's to be done?—we'll end the jar—
    But how?—Ah! there's the devil—
'Tis easier to provoke a war
    By far, than cure the evil.

We trust you'll nearer hit the point
    When you shall meet next winter;
And if you cannot set the joint,
    Be sure reduce the splinter.

The Dance
1781

[*This song commemorates Cornwallis's campaign, which had spread such desolation and ruin throughout the country over which they passed on their march from the South. The defeat and capture of this army brought great joy to the colonists. It appeared soon after his surrender. To the tune of "Yankee Doodle."*]

Cornwallis led a country dance,
    The like was never seen, sir,
Much retrograde and much advance,
    And all with General Greene, sir.

They rambled up and rambled down,
    Join'd hands, then off they run, sir,
Our General Greene to Charlestown,
    The earl to Wilmington, sir.

Greene, in the South, then danc'd a set,
    And got a mighty name, sir,
Cornwallis jigg'd with young Fayette,
    But suffer'd in his fame, sir.

Then down he figur'd to the shore,
    Most like a lordly dancer,
And on his courtly honor swore,
    He would no more advance, sir.

Quoth he, my guards are weary grown
    With footing country dances,
They never at St. James's shone,
    At capers, kicks or prances.

Yet are red heels and long-lac'd skirts,
    For stumps and briars meet, sir?
Or stand they chance with hunting-shirts,
    Or hardy veteran feet, sir?

He left him what was better yet,
    At least it was more use, sir,
He left him for a quick retreat,
    A very good excuse, sir.

To stay, unless he rul'd the sea,
    He thought would not be right, sir,
And Continental troops, said he,
    On islands should not fight, sir.

Another cause with these combin'd,
    To throw him in the dumps, sir,
For Clinton's name alarmed his mind,
    And made him stir his stumps, sir.

Now hous'd in York he challeng'd all,
    At minuet or all 'amande,
And lessons for a courtly ball,
    His guards by day and night conn'd.

This challenge known, full soon there came,
    A set who had the bon ton,
De Grasse and Rochambeau, whose fame
    Fut brilliant pour un long tems.

And Washington, Columbia's son,
    Whom easy nature taught, sir,
That grace which can't by pains be won,
    Or Plutus' gold be bought, sir.

Now hand in hand they circle round,
    This ever-dancing peer, sir;
Their gentle movements, soon confound
    The earl, as they draw near, sir.

His music soon forgets to play—
    His feet can no more move, sir,
And all his bands now curse the day,
    They jiggèd to our shore, sir.

Now Tories all, what can ye say?
    Come—is not this a griper,
That while your hopes are danc'd away,
    'Tis you must pay the piper.

YANKEE DOODLE, or
(as now Christened by the SAINTS of New England)
THE LEXINGTON MARCH

NB. The Words to be Sung thro' the Nose, & in the West Country drawl & dialect.

Brother Ephraim fold his Cow and bought him a Com‗miſion, and then he went to Canada to Fight for the Nation; But when Ephraim he came home he prov'd an arrant Coward, He woud'nt fight the Frenchmen there for fear of being devour'd.

2
Sheep's Head and Vinegar
  Butter Milk and Tanſy,
Boſton is a Yankee town
  Sing Hey Doodle Dandy:
Firſt we'll take a Pinch of Snuff
  And then a drink of Water,
And then we'll ſay How do you do
  And that's a Yanky's Supper

3
Aminadab is juſt come Home
  His Eyes all greaſd with Bacon,
And all the news that he cou'd tell
  Is Cape Breton is taken:
Stand up Jonathan
  Figure in by Neighbour,
Nathen ſtand a little off
  And make the Room ſome wider

4
Chriſtmas is a coming Boys
  We'll go to Mother Chaſes,
And there we'll get a Sugar Dram,
  Sweeten'd with Melaſſes:
Heigh ho for our Cape Cod,
  Heigh ho Nantaſket,
Do not let the Boſton wags,
  Feel your Oyſter Baſket.

5
Punk in Pye is very good
  And ſo is Apple Lantern,
Had you been whipp'd as oft as I
  You'd not have been ſo wanton:
Uncle is a Yankee Man
  'Ifaith he pays us all off,
And he has got a Fiddle
  As big as Daddy's Hogs Trough.

6
Seth's Mother went to Lynn
  To buy a pair of Breeches,
The firſt time Vathen put them on
  He tore out all the Stitches;
Dolly Buſhel let a Fart,
  Jenny Jones ſhe found it,
Ambroſe carried it to Mill
  Where Doctor Warren ground it.

7
Our Jemima's loſt her Mare
  And can't tell where to find her,
But ſhe'll come trotting by and by
  And bring her Tail behind her
Two and two may go to Bed;
  Two and two together,
And if there is not room enough,
  Lie one a top o'to'ther.

THE LEXINGTON MARCH

Sk:

"The Lexington March." Library of Congress.

"The New Yankee Doodle." Library of Congress.

AIR IV.   MR. EDWIN.

YANKEE DOODLE.
DICKY DITTO.

VIVACE.

Adzooks, old Crufty.

why fo rufty,   ftupid, queer, and mumpy! E _ gad, if you don't mend your manners, Somebody will lump you.

Lumpy, thumpy, thwack and bump, Pummel you, and bump—O!   Humpy, ftumpy, make you mump, Kick a—bout your rump—O!

2.	3.
Did little Dicky	A receipt I'll give,
Ever trick ye?	But as I live,
No — I'm always civil;	'I'd rather give him blows, Sir.
Then why fhould you, for my politenefs,	At St. Giles's he was bred,
Wifh me at the devil?	Altho' he wears good cloaths, Sir,
Crufty, rufty, flout and pout,	Noodle, doodle, ugly muns.
Did I ever trick ye?	Here's a pretty rig, Sir.
Fufty, mufty, turn me out?	Daggers, piftols, fwords, and guns,
Oh, poor, civil Dicky!	Oh! I'll hop the twig, Sir.

(31)

"Dicky Ditto," sung to the tune of "Yankee Doodle." Courtesy of Lester S. Levy.

Bibliography

Books and Periodicals

Alden, John Richard. *The American Revolution, 1775–1783.* New York: Harper and Brothers Publishers, 1954.

American Jest Book. Harrisburgh: printed for Mathew Carey, 1796.

American Manners & Morals. The Editors of American Heritage. New York: American Heritage Publishing Co., 1969.

America Vindicated From the High Charge of Ingratitude and Rebellion: with a Plan of Legislation, proposed to the consideration of both houses, for establishing a permanent and solid foundation, for a just constitutional union, between Great Britain and her Colonies, by a friend to both countries. Devizes, England: printed and sold by T. Burrough, 1774.

Banks, Rev. Louis Albert, D.D. *Immortal Songs of Camp and Field.* Cleveland: The Burrows Brothers Company, 1898.

Beard, Charles A. and Mary R. *A Basic History of the United States.* Philadelphia: The New Home Library, The Blakiston Company. 1944.

Becker, Stephen D. *Comic Art in America.* New York: Simon and Schuster, 1959.

Berger, Carl. *Broadsides and Bayonets.* Philadelphia: University of Pennsylvania Press, 1961.

Boatner, Mark Mayo III. *Encyclopedia of the American Revolution.* New York: David McKay Co., Inc., 1966.

Bowen, Catherine Drinker. *John Adams and The American Revolution.* An Atlantic Monthly Press Book. Boston: Little Brown and Company, 1950.

————. *Miracle at Philadelphia.* An Atlantic Monthly Press Book. Boston and Toronto: Little Brown and Company, 1966.

Brackenridge, Hugh. *Bunkers-Hill.* In Moses, Montrose Jonas, *Representative Plays by American Dramatists, 1765–1819.* New York: B. Blom, 1964.

Brigham, Clarence Saunders. *Paul Revere's Engravings.* Worcester, Mass.: American Antiquarian Society, 1954.

————. *History and Bibliography of American Newspapers 1690–1820* (Vol. I) Worcester, Mass.: American Antiquarian Society, 1947.

Briggs, Sam. "The Origin and Development of the Almanac." Tract #69 of *Western Reserve Historical Society Tracts* (Vol. II): Cleveland, Ohio, 1888.

Brown, Colonel T. Allston. "The Theatre in America." Written for *The New York Clipper,* 1888.

Burchnell, Elizabeth. *American Country Dances.* New York: G. Schirmer, 1918.

Burton, W. E. *Cyclopedia of Wit and Humor.* New York: Appleton and Company, 1858.

"Caricatures." In *American Heritage,* Vol. XXII, Number 4, June 1971.

Chapin, Howard M. "Colonial Humor." *American Collector,* Vol. 5, #6, March 1928.

Chinard, Gilbert. *Franklin-Brillon Letters.* Philadelphia: American Philosophical Society, 1933.

Chitwood, Oliver Perry. *A History of Colonial America.* New York: Harper and Brothers, 1948.

Coad, Oral Sumner, and Mims, Edwin Jr. *The American Stage.* In *Pageant of America* series, Vol. XIV. New Haven: Yale University Press. Toronto: Glasgow, Brook & Co. London: Humphrey Milford, Oxford University Press, 1929.

A Collection of Contra Dances. Hanover: printed by Dunham and True, 1796.

Commager, Henry Steele, and Morris, Richard B. *The Spirit of 'Seventy-Six,* Vol. 2. Indianapolis and New York: The Bobbs-Merrill Company Inc., 1958.

Crawford, Mary Caroline. "Old Boston Days and Ways." *Old-Time New England* Magazine, Vol. 46, April–June 1956.

Damon, S. Foster. *The History of Square Dancing.* Barre, Mass.: *Barre Gazette,* 1957.

Dance Clipping File, Dance Collection of the New York Public Library, New York, New York.

Dannett, Sylvia G. L., and Rachel, Frank. *Down Memory Lane, A Pictorial History of Ballroom Dancing.* New York: Greenberg, 1954.

Dannett, Sylvia G. L. *A Treasury of Civil War Humor.* New York and London: A. S. Barnes, 1963.

Davidson, Marshall B. *Life in America.* Boston: Houghton Mifflin Co., 1951.

DeMille, Agnes. *The Book of the Dance.* London: P. Hamlyn, 1963.

Dichter, Harry, and Shapiro, Elliott. *Early American Sheet Music, 1768–1889.* New York: R. R. Bowker Co., 1941.

Dickinson, John. *Letters From A Farmer in Pennsylvania to the Inhabitants of the British Colonies.* Philadelphia: 1774.

Dickinson, John. *The Miscellaneous Productions in Poetry and Prose of the late Samuel Field.* Greenfield, Massachusetts: Clark and Hunt, 1818.

Doyle, Mildred Davis. *Sentimentalism in American Periodicals.* New York: New York University Press, 1944.

Drepperd, Carl W. "Drawing Cards." *American Collector,* Vol. 13, No. 10, November 1944.

Dulles, Rhea Foster. *America Learns to Play, 1607–1940.* New York and London: D. Appleton-Century Co., 1940.

Earle, Alice Morse. *Colonial Dames and Good Wives.* Boston and New York: Houghton, Mifflin and Co., 1895.

Faugeres, Margaretta. *The Posthumous Works of Ann Eliza Bleecker in Prose and Verse.* New York: T. and J. Swords, 1793.

Forgotten Theatres of New York City. Scrapbook of Clippings, Theatre Research Library, The Library of the Performing Arts, Lincoln Center, New York City.

Franklin, Benjamin. *Satires and Bagatelles.* Detroit: Fine Book Circle, 1937.

Freneau, Philip. *Miscellaneous Works.* Philadelphia: Printed by Francis Bailey at Yorick's head in Market Street, 1788.

George, Mary Dorothy. *English Political Caricatures to 1792,* Vol. 1. Oxford: Clarendon Press, 1959.

Green, Joseph. *Entertainment for a Winter's Evening.* Boston: Printed and sold by G. Rogers, 1759.

Halsey, R. T. Haines. "Impolitical Prints. An Exhibition of Contemporary English Cartoons Relating to the American Revolution." *Bulletin* of the New York Public Library, New York, November 1939.

———. "English Sympathy With Boston During the American Revolution." *Old-Time New England,* Vol. XLVI, No. 3, Serial No. 64, June 1956.

Harris Collection of American Poetry and Plays. Series of Old American Songs, No. 4, Providence: Brown University, 1936.

Holliday, Carl. *The Wit and Humor of Colonial Days (1607–1800)*. Philadelphia and London: J. B. Lippincott, 1912.

Hopkins, Livingston. *A Comic History of the United States*. New York: The American Book Exchange, 1880.

Hornblow, Arthur. *A History of The Theatre in America*, Vol. 1. Philadelphia and London: J. B. Lippincott Co., 1919.

Howard, John Tasker and Bellows, George Kent. *A Short History of Music in America*. New York: Thomas Y. Crowell, 1967.

Howard, John Tasker. *Our American Music*. New York: Thomas Y. Crowell, 1965.

Hudson, Frederic. *Journalism in The U. S., 1690–1872*. New York: Harper & Brothers, 1873.

Hughes, Geun. *A History of the American Theatre, 1700–1950*. London and Toronto: Samuel French, 1951.

Hubbell, Jay Broadus. *The South in American Literature, 1607–1900*. Durham, N. C.: Duke University Press, 1954.

Johnson, Una E. *American Woodcuts*. Brooklyn: The Brooklyn Museum Press, The Brooklyn Institute of Arts and Sciences, 1950.

Kraus, Richard. *History of the Dance in Arts and Education*. Englewood Cliffs, N. J.: Prentice Hall Inc., 1969.

Liberty Songs. (n.p. 178?) 8 pp. Library of Congress, Washington, D. C.

Lee, James Melvin. *History of American Journalism*. Boston and New York: Houghton Mifflin and Company, 1917.

Literary History of the United States. Editors: Robert E. Spiller, Willard Thorp, Thomas H. Johnson, Henry Seidel Canby; Associates: Howard Mumford Jones, Dixon Wecter, Stanley T. Williams. Revised Edition in one volume. New York: The Macmillan Company, 1960.

Lewisohn, Ludwig. *Expression in America*. New York and London: Harper and Brothers, 1932.

Lossing, Benson J. *The Pictorial Field-Book of the Revolution*. New York: Harper and Brothers, 1859.

Lynch, John Gilbert Bohun. *A History of Caricature*. Boston: Little, Brown and Co., 1927.

Magriel, Paul, ed. *Chronicles of the American Dance*. New York: Henry Holt and Co., 1948.

Marble, Annie Russell. *Heralds of American Literature*. Chicago: The University of Chicago Press; London: T. Fisher Unwin, 1907.

Marks, Joseph E. *America Learns To Dance*. New York: Exposition Press, 1957.

Marshall, Christopher. *The Diary of Christopher Marshall*, Vol. I, 1774–1777. Philadelphia: Hazard and Mitchell, 1839–40.

Martin, Joseph. *A Narrative of Some of the Adventures, Dangers and Sufferings of A Revolutionary Soldier*. Hallowell, Maine: Glazier Masters & Co., 1830.

Matthews, Milford, M., ed. *A Dictionary of Americanisms*. Chicago: University of Chicago Press, 1951.

Miller, John C. *Origins of The American Revolution*. An Atlantic Monthly Press Book. Boston: Little, Brown and Company, 1943.

Moody, Richard, ed. *Dramas from the American Theatre, 1762–1909*. Cleveland and New York: The World Publishing Company, 1966.

Moore, Frank, ed. *Diary of the American Revolution*. New York: Charles Scribner, 1860 .

Moore, Frank. *Songs and Ballads of the American Revolution*. With notes and illustrations. New York: D. Appleton and Co., 1855.

Morris, Richard. *The American Revolution Reconsidered*. New York, Evanston, and London: Harper and Row, 1967.

Moses, Montrose J., ed. *Representative Plays by American Dramatists*, Vol. I, 1765–1819. New York: Benjamin Blom, Inc., 1918, 1948.

————. "His Excellency George Washington." *Theatre Arts Monthly*, Vol. XVI, No. 2, February 1932.

Mott, Frank Luther. *A History of American Magazines, 1741–1850*, Vol. I. New York and London: D. Appleton and Company, 1930.

Music in America. An anthology from the Landing of the Pilgrims to the close of the Civil War, 1620–1865. Compiled and edited by W. Thomas Marrocco and Harold Gleason. New York: W. W. Norton Inc., 1964.

Music from the Days of George Washington. Collected and Provided with an Introduction by Carl Engel. Washington, D. C.: U. S. George Washington Bicentennial Commission, 1931.

Murrell, William. *A History of American Graphic Humor.* New York: The Whitney Museum of American Art, 1938.

Nathan, Adele Gutman. *Major André, Gentleman Spy.* New York: Franklin Watts, 1972.

Niles, Hezekiah. *Weekly Register, (National Register* from September 1837), 1811–1849. Baltimore, 1811–1837, 1839–1848, Washington, 1837–1839, Philadelphia, 1848, 1849.

————. *Principles and Acts of the Revolution in America.* Baltimore: W. O. Niles, 1822.

Oxberry's Anecdotes of the Stage. London: G. Virtue, Ivy Lane, Paternoster Row, 1827.

Palmer, David Richard, *The River and the Rock.* New York: Greenwood Publishing Corporation, 1969.

Parton, James. *Caricature and Other Comic Art in All Times and in Many Lands.* New York: Harper and Brothers, 1877.

Prime, A. C. *Arts and Crafts in Philadelphia, 1721–1785.* Topsfield, Mass.: Walpole Society, 1929.

Proceedings of the American Antiquarian Society, New Series, Vol. XI, April 1896–April 1897. Published by the Society, Worcester, Mass., 1898.

Quinn, Arthur Hobson. *A History of the American Drama, from the beginning to the Civil War.* New York: Appleton-Century-Crofts, Inc., 1951.

————. *The Literature of the American People.* New York: Appleton-Century-Crofts, Inc., 1951.

Rourke, Constance, *American Humor.* New York: Harcourt, Brace and Company, 1931.

Sears, Robert. *Pictorial History of the American Revolution.* New York: R. Sears, 1845.

Sonneck, O. G. T. *Francis Hopkinson and James Lyon.* New York: Da Capo Press, 1967.

————. *Early Concert-Life In America.* New York: Masurgia Publishers, 1949.

————. *Early Opera in America.* New York: Benjamin Blom, Inc., 1915, 1943, 1963.

Stedman, Edmund C. and Hutchinson, E. M. *Library of American Literature,* Vols. 2 and 3. New York: Webster, 1891.

Stoudt, John Joseph. "The Poetry of the American Revolution." In *Bulletin of the Historical Society of Montgomery County, Pennsylvania,* Vol. XI, Number 2, Spring 1958. Published by the Society, Norristown, Pa.

Thatcher, James, M. D. *Military Journal of the American Revolution.* Hartford, Conn.: Hurlbut, Williams and Company, American Subscription Publishing House, 1862.

Theatre Clipping File, Theatre Collection of the New York Public Library, New York City.

Thompson, James Henry. *The First American Humorist. Reading and collecting,* Vol. #2 and #3. Chicago: Edited and Published by Ben Abramson, 1938.

Tolman, Beth, and Page, Ralph. *The Country Dance Book.* New York: A. S. Barnes and Co., 1937.

Townsend, Walsh Collection, Theatre Room, Library of the Performing Arts, Lincoln Center, New York City.

Trumbull, John. *M'Fingal, An Epic Poem.* New York: John Buel, 1795.

Tunis, Edward. *Colonial Living.* Cleveland and New York: World Publishing Co., 1957.

Tyler, Moses. *The Literary History of the American Revolution.* New York: G. P. Putnam's and Sons, 1897.

————. *History of American Literature During Colonial Times.* New York: G. P. Putnam's and Sons, 1897.

Vail, R. W. G. "Our Friendly Enemies, the pro-American Caricature of a London Woman Printseller of 1776–1778," *New-York Historical Society Quarterly,* Vol. XLII. New York: January 1958.

Ward, Christopher. *The War of the Revolution,* Vol. I. New York: The Macmillan Company, 1952.

Warren, Mrs. Mercy. "The Group." In Montrose Moses's *Representative Plays by American Dramatists.*

Wegelin, Oscar. "The Beginning of the Drama in America." In *The Literary Collector,* New York: George D. Smith, 1905.

Weiss, Henry. "A Brief History of American Jest Books." In *Bulletin of New York Public Library,* Vol. 47, #4, April 1843.

Weitenkampf, Frank. *American Graphic Art.* New York: Henry Holt and Co., 1912.

————. "F. O. C. Darley." In *American Illustrator,* New-York Historical Society, New York City.

———. *The United States in Separately Published Cartoons.* With an annotated list by the New York Public Library, 1953.

———. "Political Caricature in the U. S." In *Bulletins of the New York Public Library,* Vol. 56, No. 3, March 1952.

Weitenkampf, Frank, and Nevins, Allan. *A Century of Political Cartoons: Caricatures in the U. S., 1800–1900.* New York: Chas. Scribner's Sons, 1944.

Willis, Eola. *The Charleston Stage in the XVIII Century.* Columbia, S. C.: The Stole Co., 1924.

Winslow, Ola Elizabeth, comp. and ed. *American Broadside Verses.* From imprints of the 17th and 18th centuries. New Haven, Connecticut: Yale University Press, 1930.

Newspapers, Magazines, Pamphlets

Ames's Almanack. Published in Boston by Nathaniel Ames, 1762, 1764.

Bickerstaff's Almanack. Published by Isaac Bickerstaff, Boston, 1779.

Essex Almanack, The. Published by Philo Freeman. Salem, Mass., 1773.

Gleason's Almanack. Published by Ezra Gleason. Boston, 1774.

New England Almanack. Published by Isaiah Thomas. Massachusetts Bay, 1775.

New York *Journal,* July 30, 1767. Published by John Holt. New York, 1766–1776.

New York Gazette, The, January 19, 1730. Established by William Weyman, New York.

New York Gazette and Weekly Mercury, The, October 11, 1779. Printed by Hugh Gaine, New York.

North-American Almanack. Edes, Benjamin E. and Giles, John. Boston, 1768.

Royal American Magazine, January, 1774. Isaiah Thomas, founder and editor, engravings by Paul Revere. Boston, 1774–1775.

Microfilm and Microprint

Billings, William. *The Singing Master.* Boston: Draper, Folsom, 1778.

Bristol, Roger Pattrell. *The American Bibliography of Charles Evans,* Vol. 13. American Antiquarian Society. Worcester, Mass., 1959; Gloucester, Mass., 1967.

Weitenkampf, Frank. *The Social History of the United States in Caricature.* Filmed by the New York Public Library. New York: 1953.

Index

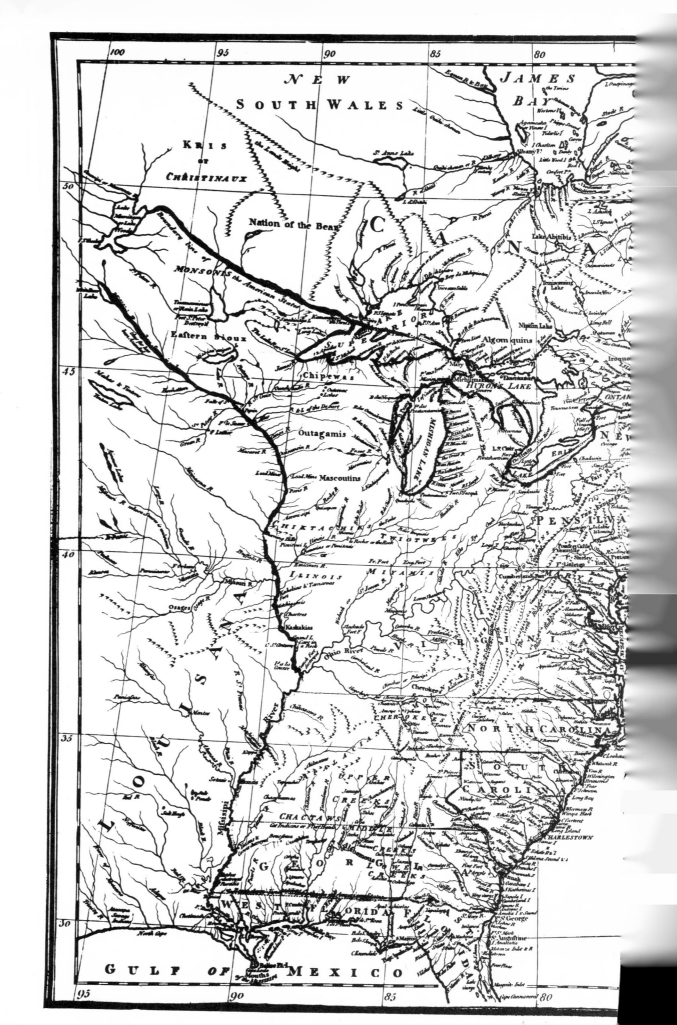